Anne Bradstreet and Her Time

Helen Campbell

INTRODUCTION.

Grave doubts at times arise in the critical mind as to whether
America has had any famous women. We are reproached with the fact,
that in spite of some two hundred years of existence, we have, as
yet, developed no genius in any degree comparable to that of
George Eliot and George Sand in the present, or a dozen other as
familiar names of the past. One at least of our prominent literary
journals has formulated this reproach, and is even sceptical as to
the probability of any future of this nature for American women.

What the conditions have been which hindered and hampered such
development, will find full place in the story of the one woman
who, in the midst of obstacles that might easily have daunted a
far stouter soul, spoke such words as her limitations allowed.
Anne Bradstreet, as a name standing alone, and represented only by a
volume of moral reflections and the often stilted and unnatural
verse of the period, would perhaps, hardly claim a place in formal
biography. But Anne Bradstreet, the first woman whose work has
come down to us from that troublous Colonial time, and who, if
not the mother, is at least the grandmother of American literature,
in
that her direct descendants number some of our most distinguished
men of letters calls for some memorial more honorable than a page
in an Encyclopedia, or even an octavo edition of her works for the
benefit of stray antiquaries here and there. The direct ancestress
of the Danas, of Dr. Oliver Wendell Holmes, Wendell Phillips,
the Channings, the Buckminsters and other lesser names, would
naturally inspire some interest if only in an inquiry as to just
what inheritance she handed down, and the story of what she failed
to do because of the time into which she was born, holds equal
meaning with that of what she did do.

I am indebted to Mr. John Harvard Ellis's sumptuous edition of
Anne Bradstreet's works, published in 1867, and containing all her
extant works, for all extracts of either prose or verse, as well
as for many of the facts incorporated in Mr. Ellis's careful
introduction. Miss Bailey's "History of Andover," has proved a
valuable aid, but not more so than "The History of New
England,"
by Dr. John Gorham Palfrey, which affords in many points, the most
careful and faithful picture on record of the time, personal

facts, unfortunately, being of the most meager nature. They have been sought for chiefly, however, in the old records themselves; musty with age and appallingly diffuse as well as numerous, but the only source from which the true flavor of a forgotten time can be extracted. Barren of personal detail as they too often are, the writer of the present imperfect sketch has found Anne Bradstreet, in spite of all such deficiencies, a very real and vital person, and ends her task with the belief which it is hoped that the reader may share, that among the honorable women not a few whose lives are to-day our dearest possession, not one claims tenderer memory than she who died in New England two hundred years ago.

NEW YORK, 1890.

CONTENTS.

CHAPTER I.

THE OLD HOME.

The birthday of the baby, Anne Dudley, has no record; her
birthplace even is not absolutely certain, although there is
little doubt that it was at Northhampton in England, the home of
her father's family. She opened her eyes upon a time so filled
with crowding and conflicting interests that there need be no
wonder that the individual was more or less ignored, and personal
history lost in the general. To what branch of the Dudley family
she belonged is also uncertain. Moore, in his "Lives of the
Governors of New Plymouth and Massachusetts Bay," writes: "There
is a tradition among the descendants of Governor Dudley in the
eldest branch of the family, that he was descended from John
Dudley, Duke of Northumberland, who was beheaded 22 February,
1553." Such belief was held for a time, but was afterward
disallowed by Anne Bradstreet. In her "Elegy upon Sir Philip
Sidney," whose mother, the Lady Mary, was the eldest daughter of
that Duke of Northumberland, she wrote:

"Let, then, none disallow of these my straines,
Which have the self-same blood yet in my veines."

With the second edition of her poems, however, her faith had
changed. This may have been due to a growing indifference to
worldly distinctions, or, perhaps, to some knowledge of the
dispute as to the ancestry of Robert Dudley, son of the Duke, who
was described by one side as a nobleman, by another as a
carpenter, and by a third as "a noble timber merchant"; while a
wicked wit wrote that "he was the son of a duke, the brother of a
king, the grandson of an esquire, and the great-grandson of a
carpenter; that the carpenter was the only honest man in the family
and the only one who died in his bed." Whatever the cause may
have been she renounced all claim to relationship, and the lines
were made to read as they at present stand:

"Then let none disallow of these my straines
Whilst English blood yet runs within my veines."

In any case, her father, Thomas Dudley, was of gentle blood and
training, being the only son of Captain Roger Dudley, who was
killed in battle about the year 1577, when the child was hardly
nine years old. Of his mother there is little record, as also of
the sister from whom he was soon separated, though we know that
Mrs. Dudley died shortly after her husband. Her maiden name is
unknown; she was a relative of Sir Augustine Nicolls, of Paxton,
Kent, one of His Majesty's Justices of his Court of Common Pleas,
and keeper of the Great Seal to Prince Charles.

The special friend who took charge of Thomas Dudley through
childhood is said to have been "a Miss Purefoy," and if so, she
was the sister of Judge Nicolls, who married a Leicestershire
squire, named William Purefoy. Five hundred pounds was left in
trust for him, and delivered to him when he came of age; a sum

equivalent to almost as many thousand to-day. At the school to which he was sent he gained a fair knowledge of Latin, but he was soon taken from it to become a page in the family of William Lord Compton, afterward the Earl of Northumberland.

His studies were continued, and in time he became a clerk of his kinsman, "Judge Nicholls," whose name appears in letters, and who was a sergeant-at-law. Such legal knowledge as came to him here was of service through all his later life, but law gave place to arms, the natural bias of most Englishmen at that date, and he became captain of eighty volunteers "raised in and about Northhampton, and forming part of the force collected by order of Queen Elizabeth to assist Henry IV. of France, in the war against Philip II. of Spain," He was at the siege of Amiens in 1597, and returned home when it ended, having, though barely of age, already gained distinction as a soldier, and acquired the courtesy of manner which distinguished him till later life, and the blandness of which often blinded unfamiliar acquaintances to the penetration and acumen, the honesty and courage that were the foundations of his character. As his belief changed, and the necessity for free speech was laid upon him, he ceased to disguise his real feelings and became even too out-spoken, the tendency strengthening year by year, and doing much to diminish his popularity, though his qualities were too sterling to allow any lessening of real honor and respect. But he was still the courtier, and untitled as he was, prestige enough came with him to make his marriage to "a gentlewoman whose Extract and Estate were Considerable," a very easy matter, and though we know her only as Dorothy Dudley, no record of her maiden name having been preserved, the love borne her by both husband and daughter is sufficient evidence of her character and influence.

Puritanism was not yet an established fact, but the seed had been sown which later became a tree so mighty that thousands gathered under its shadow. The reign of Elizabeth had brought not only power but peace to England, and national unity had no further peril of existence to dread. With peace, trade established itself on sure foundations and increased with every year. Wealth flowed into the country and the great merchants of London whose growth amazed and troubled the royal Council, founded hospitals, "brought the New River from its springs at Chadwell and Amwell to supply the city with pure water," and in many ways gave of their increase for the benefit of all who found it less easy to earn. The smaller land-owners came into a social power never owned before, and "boasted as long a rent-roll and wielded as great an influence as many of the older nobles.... In wealth as in political consequence the merchants and country gentlemen who formed the bulk of the House of Commons, stood far above the mass of the peers."

Character had changed no less than outward circumstances. "The nation which gave itself to the rule of the Stewarts was another nation from the panic-struck people that gave itself in the crash of social and religious order to the guidance of the Tudors." English aims had passed beyond the bounds of England, and every English "squire who crossed the Channel to flesh his maiden sword at Ivry or Ostend, brought back to English soil, the daring temper, the sense of inexhaustable resources, which had bourn him on through storm and battle field." Such forces were not likely to settle into a passive existence at home. Action had become a necessity. Thoughts had been stirred and awakened once for all. Consciously for the few, unconsciously for the many, "for a hundred years past, men had been living in the midst of a spiritual revolution. Not only the world about them, but the world within every breast had been utterly transformed. The work of the sixteenth century had wrecked that tradition of religion, of knowledge, of political and social order, which had been accepted without question by the Middle Ages. The sudden freedom of the mind from these older bonds brought a consciousness of power such as had never been felt before; and the restless energy, the universal activity of the Renaissance were but outer expressions of the pride, the joy, the amazing self-confidence, with which man welcomed this revelation of the energies which had lain slumbering within him."

This was the first stage, but another quickly and naturally followed, and dread took the place of confidence. With the deepening sense of human individuality, came a deepening conviction of the boundless capacities of the human soul. Not as a theological dogma, but as a human fact man knew himself to be an all but infinite power, whether for good or for ill. The drama towered into sublimity as it painted the strife of mighty forces within the breasts of Othello or Macbeth. Poets passed into metaphysicians as they strove to unravel the workings of conscience within the soul. From that hour one dominant influence told on human action; and all the various energies that had been called into life by the age that was passing away were seized, concentrated and steadied to a definite aim by the spirit of religion. Among the myriads upon whom this change had come, Thomas Dudley was naturally numbered, and the ardent preaching of the well-known Puritan ministers, Dodd and Hildersham, soon made him a Non-conformist and later an even more vigorous dissenter from ancient and established forms. As thinking England was of much the same mind, his new belief did not for a time interfere with his advancement, for, some years after his marriage he became steward of the estate of the Earl of Lincoln, and continued so for more than ten years. Plunged in debt as the estate had been by the excesses of Thomas, Earl of Lincoln, who left the property to his son Theophilus, so encumbered that it was well nigh worthless, a few years of Dudley's skillful management freed it entirely, and he became the dear and trusted friend of the entire family. His first child had been born in 1610, a son named Samuel, and in 1612 came the daughter whose delicate infancy and childhood gave small hint of the endurance shown in later years. Of much the same station and training as Mrs. Lucy Hutchinson, Anne Dudley could undoubtedly have written in the same words as that most delightful of chroniclers: "By the time I was four years old I read English perfectly, and having a great memory I was carried to sermons.... When I was about seven years of age, I remember I had at one time eight tutors in several qualities, languages, music, dancing, writing and needle work; but my genius was quite averse from all but my book, and that I was so eager of, that my mother thinking it prejudiced my health, would moderate me in it; yet this rather animated me than kept me back, and every moment I could steal from my play I would employ in any book I could find when my own were locked up from me."

It is certain that the little Anne studied the Scriptures at six or seven, with as painful solicitude as her elders, for she writes

in the fragmentary diary which gives almost the only clue to her
real life:

"In my young years, about 6 or 7, as I take it, I began to make
conscience of my wayes, and what I knew was sinful, as lying,
disobedience to Parents, etc., I avoided it. If at any time I was
overtaken with the like evills, it was a great Trouble. I could
not be at rest 'till by prayer I had confest it unto God. I was
also troubled at the neglect of Private Duteys, tho' too often
tardy that way. I also found much comfort in reading the
Scriptures, especially those places I thought most concerned my
Condition, and as I grew to have more understanding, so the more
solace I took in them.

"In a long fitt of sickness which I had on my bed, I often
communed with my heart and made my supplication to the most High,
who sett me free from that affliction."

For a childhood which at six searches the Scriptures to find
verses applicable to its condition, there cannot have been much if
any natural child life, and Mrs. Hutchinson's experience again was
probably duplicated for the delicate and serious little Anne.
"Play among other children I despised, and when I was forced to
entertain such as came to visit me, I tried them with more grave
instruction than their mothers, and plucked all their babies to
pieces, and kept the children in such awe, that they were glad when
I entertained myself with elder company, to whom I was very
acceptable, and living in the house with many persons that had a
great deal of wit, and very profitable serious discourses being
frequent at my father's table and in my mother's drawing room, I
was very attentive to all, and gathered up things that I would
utter again, to great admiration of many that took my memory and
imitation for wit.... I used to exhort my mother's words much, and
to turn their idle discourses to good subjects."

Given to exhortation as some of the time may have been, and drab-
colored as most of the days certainly were, there were, bright
passages here and there, and one reminiscence was related in later
years, in her poem "In Honour of Du Bartas," the delight of
Puritan maids and mothers;

"My muse unto a Child I may compare,
Who sees the riches of some famous Fair,
He feeds his eyes but understanding lacks,
To comprehend the worth of all those knacks;
The glittering plate and Jewels he admires,
The Hats and Fans, the Plumes and Ladies' tires,
And thousand times his mazed mind doth wish
Some part, at least, of that brave wealth was his;
But seeing empty wishes nought obtain,
At night turns to his Mother's cot again,
And tells her tales (his full heart over glad),
Of all the glorious sights his eyes have had;
But finds too soon his want of Eloquence,
The silly prattler speaks no word of sense;
But seeing utterance fail his great desires,
Sits down in silence, deeply he admires."

It is probably to one of the much exhorted maids that she owed

this glimpse of what was then a rallying ground for the jesters
and merry Andrews, and possibly even a troop of strolling players,
frowned upon by the Puritan as children of Satan, but still
secretly enjoyed by the lighter minded among them. But the burden
of the time pressed more and more heavily. Freedom which had
seemed for a time to have taken firm root, and to promise a better
future for English thought and life, lessened day by day under the
pressure of the Stuart dynasty, and every Nonconformist home was
the center of anxieties that influenced every member of it from
the baby to the grandsire, whose memory covered more astonishing
changes than any later day has known.

The year preceding Anne Dudley's birth, had seen the beginning of
the most powerful influence ever produced upon a people, made
ready for it, by long distrust of such teaching as had been
allowed. With the translation of the Bible into common speech, and
the setting up of the first six copies in St. Pauls, its
popularity had grown from day to day. The small Geneva Bibles soon
appeared and their substance had become part of the life of every
English family within an incredibly short space of time. Not only
thought and action but speech itself were colored and shaped by
the new influence. We who hold to it as a well of English
undefiled, and resent even the improvements of the new Version as
an infringement on a precious possession, have small conception of
what it meant to a century which had had no prose literature and
no poetry save the almost unknown verse of Chaucer.

"Sunday after Sunday, day after day, the crowds that gathered
round the Bible in the nave of St. Pauls, or the family group that
hung on its words in the devotional exercises at home, were
leavened with a new literature. Legend and annal, war song and
psalm, State-roll and biography, the mighty voices of prophets,
the parables of Evangelists, stories of mission-journeys, of
perils by the sea and among the heathens, philosophic arguments,
apocalyptic visions, all were flung broadcast over minds
unoccupied for the most part by any rival learning. The disclosure
of the stores of Greek literature had wrought the revolution of
Renaissance. The disclosure of the older mass of Hebrew literature,
wrought the revolution of the Reformation. But the one revolution
was far deeper and wider in its effects than the other.
No version could transfer to another tongue the peculiar charm of
language which gave their value to the authors of Greece and Rome.
Classical letters, therefore, remained in the possession of the
learned, that is, of the few, and among these, with the exception
of Colet and More, or of the pedants who revived a Pagan worship
in the gardens of the Florentine Academy, their direct influence
was purely intellectual. But the language of the Hebrew, the idiom
of the Hellenistic Greek, lent themselves with a curious felicity
to the purposes of translation. As a mere literary monument the
English version of the Bible remains the noblest example of the
English tongue, while its perpetual use made it from the instant
of its appearance, the standard of our language.

"One must dwell upon this fact persistently, before it will become
possible to understand aright either the people or the literature of
the time. With generations the influence has weakened, though the
best in English speech has its source in one fountain. But the
Englishman of that day wove his Bible into daily speech, as we weave
Shakespeare or Milton or our favorite author of a later day. It was

neither affectation nor hypocrisy but an instinctive use that made the
curious mosaic of Biblical words and phrases which colored English
talk two hundred years ago. The mass of picturesque allusion and
illustration which we borrow from a thousand books, our fathers were
forced to borrow from one; and the borrowing was the easier and the
more natural, that the range of the Hebrew literature fitted it
for the expression of every phase of feeling. When Spencer poured
forth his warmest love-notes in the 'Epithalamion,' he adopted the
very words of the Psalmist, as he bade the gates open for the
entrance of his bride. When Cromwell saw the mists break over the
hills of Dunbar, he hailed the sun-burst with the cry of David: 'Let
God arise, and let his enemies be scattered. Like as the smoke
vanisheth so shalt thou drive them away!' Even to common minds this
familiarity with grand poetic imagery in prophet and apocalypse,
gave a loftiness and ardor of expression that with all its tendency
to exaggeration and bombast we may prefer to the slip-shod
vulgarisms of today."

Children caught the influence, and even baby talk was half
scriptural, so that there need be no surprise in finding Anne
Bradstreet's earliest recollections couched in the phrases of
psalms learned by heart as soon as she could speak, and used, no
doubt, half unconsciously. Translate her sentences into the
thought of to-day, and it is evident, that aside from the morbid
conscientiousness produced by her training, that she was the
victim of moods arising from constant ill-health. Her
constitution seems to have been fragile in the extreme, and there
is no question but that in her case as in that of many another
child
born into the perplexed and troubled time, the constant anxiety of
both parents, uncertain what a day might bring forth, impressed
itself on the baby soul. There was English fortitude and courage,
the endurance born of faith, and the higher evolution from English
obstinacy, but there was for all of them, deep self-distrust and
abasement; a sense of worthlessness that intensified with each
generation; and a perpetual, unhealthy questioning of every
thought and motive. The progress was slow but certain, rising
first among the more sensitive natures of women, whose lives held
too little action to drive away the mists, and whose motto was
always, "look in and not out"--an utter reversal of the teaching
of to-day. The children of that generation lost something that had
been the portion of their fathers. The Elizabethan age had been
one of immense animal life and vigor, and of intense capacity for
enjoyment, and, deny it as one might, the effect lingered and had
gone far toward forming character. The early Nonconformist still
shared in many worldly pleasures, and had found no occasion to
condense thought upon points in Calvinism, or to think of himself
as a refugee from home and country.

The cloud at first no bigger than a man's hand, was not dreaded,
and life in Nonconformist homes went on with as much real
enjoyment as if their ownership were never to be questioned.
Serious and sad, as certain phases come to be, it is certain that
home life developed as suddenly as general intelligence. The
changes in belief in turn affected character. "There was a sudden
loss of the passion, the caprice, the subtle and tender play of
feeling, the breath of sympathy, the quick pulse of delight, which
had marked the age of Elizabeth; but on the other hand life gained
in moral grandeur, in a sense of the dignity of manhood, in
orderliness and equable force. The larger geniality of the age

that had passed away was replaced by an intense tenderness within
the narrower circle of the home. Home, as we now conceive it, was
the creation of the Puritan. Wife and child rose from mere
dependants on the will of husband or father, as husband or father saw
in them saints like himself, souls hallowed by the touch of a divine
spirit and called with a divine calling like his own. The
sense of spiritual fellowship gave a new tenderness and refinement
to the common family affections."

The same influence had touched Thomas Dudley, and Dorothy Dudley
could have written of him as Lucy Hutchinson did of her husband:
"He was as kind a father, as dear a brother, as good a master, as
faithful a friend as the world had." In a time when, for the
Cavalier element, license still ruled and lawless passion was
glorified by every play writer, the Puritan demanded a
different standard, and lived a life of manly purity in strange
contrast to
the grossness of the time. Of Hutchinson and Dudley and thousands
of their contemporaries the same record held good: "Neither in
youth nor riper years could the most fair or enticing woman draw him
into unnecessary familiarity or dalliance. Wise and virtuous women
he loved, and delighted in all pure and holy and unblameable
conversation with them, but so as never to excite scandal or
temptation. Scurrilous discourse even among men he abhorred; and
though he sometimes took pleasure in wit and mirth, yet that
which was mixed with impurity he never could endure."

Naturally with such standards life grew orderly and methodical.
"Plain living and high thinking," took the place of high living
and next to no thinking. Heavy drinking was renounced. Sobriety
and self-restraint ruled here as in every other act of life, and
the division between Cavalier and Nonconformist became daily more
and more marked. Persecution had not yet made the gloom and
hardness which soon came to be inseparable from the word Puritan,
and children were still allowed many enjoyments afterward totally
renounced. Milton could write, even after his faith had settled
and matured:

"Haste then, nymph, and bring with thee
Jest and youthful jollity,
Quips and Cranks and wanton Wiles,
Nods and becks and wreathed Smiles,
Such as hang on Hebe's cheek
And love to live in dimple sleek;
Sports that wrinkled care derides
And Laughter holding both his sides."

Cromwell himself looked on at masques and revels, and Whitelock, a
Puritan lawyer and his ambassador to Sweden, left behind him a
reputation for stately and magnificent entertaining, which his
admirers could never harmonize with his persistent refusal to
conform to the custom of drinking healths. In the report of this
embassy printed after Whitelock's return and republished some
years ago, occurs one of the best illustrations of Puritan social
life at that period. "How could you pass over their very long
winter nights?" was one of the questions asked by the Protector at
the first audience after his return from The embassy.

"I kept my people together," was the reply, "and in action and
recreation, by having music in my house, and encouraging that and

the exercise of dancing, which held them by the eyes and ears, and gave them diversion without any offence. And I caused the gentlemen to have disputations in Latin, and declamations upon words which I gave them." Cromwell, "Those were very good diversions, and made your house a little academy."

Whitelock, "I thought these recreations better than gaming for money, or going forth to places of debauchery."

Cromwell, "It was much better."

In the Earl of Lincoln's household such amusements would be common, and it was not till many years later, that a narrowing faith made Anne write them down as "the follyes of youth." Through that youth, she had part in every opportunity that the increased respect for women afforded.

Many a Puritan matron shared her husband's studies, or followed her boys in their preparation for Oxford or Cambridge, and Anne Bradstreet's poems and the few prose memorials she left, give full evidence of an unusually broad training, her delicacy of health making her more ready for absorption in study. Shakespeare and Cervantes were still alive at her birth, and she was old enough, with the precocious development of the time, to have known the sense of loss and the general mourning at their death in 1616. It is doubtful if the plays of the elder dramatists were allowed her, though there are hints in her poems of some knowledge of Shakespeare, but by the time girlhood was reached, the feeling against them had increased to a degree hardly comprehensible save in the light of contemporaneous history. The worst spirit of the time was incorporated in the later plays, and the Puritans made no discrimination. The players in turn hated them, and Mrs. Hutchinson wrote: "Every stage and every table, and every puppet-play, belched forth profane scoffs upon them, the drunkards made them their songs, and all fiddlers and mimics learned to abuse them, as finding it the most gameful way of fooling."

If, however, the dramatists were forbidden, there were new and inexhaustible sources of inspiration and enjoyment, in the throng of new books, which the quiet of the reign of James allowed to appear in quick succession. Chapman's magnificent version of Homer was delighting Cavalier and Puritan alike. "Plutarch's Lives," were translated by Sir Thomas North and his book was "a household book for the whole of the seventeenth century." Montaigne's Essays had been "done into English" by John Florio, and to some of them at least Thomas Dudley was not likely to take exception. Poets and players had, however, come to be classed together and with some reason, both alike antagonizing the Puritan, but the poets of the reign of James were far more simple and natural in style than those of the age of Elizabeth, and thus, more likely to be read in Puritan families. Their numbers may be gauged by their present classification into "pastoral, satirical, theological, metaphysical and humorous," but only two of them were in entire sympathy with the Puritan spirit, or could be read without serious shock to belief and scruples.

For the sake of her own future work, deeper drinking at these springs was essential, and in rejecting them, Anne Dudley lost the influence that must have moulded her own verse into much more

agreeable form for the reader of to-day, though it would probably have weakened her power in her own day. The poets she knew best hindered rather than helped development. Wither and Quarles, both deeply Calvinistic, the former becoming afterward one of Cromwell's major-generals, were popular not only then but long afterward, and Quarles' "Emblems", which appeared in 1635, found their way to New England and helped to make sad thought still more dreary. Historians and antiquaries were at work. Sir Walter Raleigh's "History of the World," must have given little Anne her first suggestion of life outside of England, while Buchanan, the tutor of King James, had made himself the historian and poet of Scotland. Bacon had just ended life and labor; Hooker's Ecclesiastical Polity was before the world, though not completed until 1632, and the dissensions of the time had given birth to a "mass of sermons, books of devotion, religious tracts and controversial pamphlets." Sermons abounded, those of Archbishop Usher, Andrews and Donne being specially valued, while "The Saint's Cordial," of Dr. Richard Sibbs, and the pious meditations of Bishop Hall were on every Puritan bookshelf. But few strictly sectarian books appeared, "the censorship of the press, the right of licensing books being almost entirely arrogated to himself by the untiring enemy of the Nonconformists, Laud, Bishop of London, whose watchful eye few heretical writings could escape... . Many
of the most ultra pamphlets and tracts were the prints of foreign presses secretly introduced into the country without the form of a legal entry at Stationers' Hall."

The same activity which filled the religious world, was found also in scientific directions and Dr. Harvey's discovery of the circulation of the blood, and Napier's introduction of logarithms, made a new era for both medicine and mathematics.

That every pulse of this new tide was felt in the castle at Lempingham is very evident, in all Anne Bradstreet's work. The busy steward found time for study and his daughter shared it, and when he revolted against the incessant round of cares and for a time resigned the position, the leisure gained was devoted to the same ends. The family removed to Boston in Lincolnshire, and there an acquaintance was formed which had permanent influence on the minds of all.

Here dwelt the Rev. John Cotton, vicar of the parish and already obnoxious to the Bishops.

No man among the Nonconformists had had more brilliant reputation before the necessity of differing came upon him, and his personal influence was something phenomenal. To the girl whose sensitive, eager mind reached out to every thing high and noble he must have seemed of even rarer stuff than to-day we know him to have been.

At thirteen he had entered Emmanuel College at Cambridge, and adding distinction to distinction had come at last to be dean of the college to which he belonged. His knowledge of Greek was minute and thorough, and he conversed with ease in either Latin or Hebrew. As a pulpit orator he was famous, and crowds thronged the ancient church of St. Mary in Cambridge whenever he preached. Here he gave them "the sort of sermons then in fashion--learned, ornate, pompous, bristling with epigrams, stuffed with conceits, all set off dramatically by posture, gesture and voice."

The year in which Anne Dudley was born, had completed the change which had been slowly working in him and which Tyler describes in his vivid pages on the theological writers of New England:

"His religious character had been deepening into Puritanism. He had come to view his own preaching as frivolous, Sadducean, pagan." He decided to preach one sermon which would show what changes had come, and the announcement of his intention brought together the usual throng of under-graduates, fellows and professors who looked for the usual entertainment. Never was a crowd more deceived. "In preparing once more to preach to this congregation of worldly and witty folk, he had resolved to give them a sermon intended to exhibit Jesus Christ rather than John Cotton. This he did. His hearers were astonished, disgusted. Not a murmur of applause greeted the several stages of his discourse as before. They pulled their shovel caps down over their faces, folded their arms, and sat it out sullenly, amazed that the promising John Cotton had turned lunatic or Puritan."

Nearly twenty years passed before his energies were transferred to New England, but the ending of his university career by no means hampered his work elsewhere. As vicar of St. Botolphs at Boston his influence deepened with every year, and he grew steadily in knowledge about the Bible, and in the science of God and man as seen through the dim goggles of John Calvin.

His power as a preacher was something tremendous, but he remained undisturbed until the reign of James had ended and the "fatal eye of Bishop Laud" fell upon him. "It was in 1633 that Laud became primate of England; which meant, among other things, that nowhere within the rim of that imperial island was there to be peace or safety any longer for John Cotton. Some of his friends in high station tried to use persuasive words with the archbishop on his behalf, but the archbishop brushed aside their words with an insupportable scorn. The Earl of Dorset sent a message to Cotton, that if he had only been guilty of drunkenness or adultery, or any such minor ministerial offence, his pardon could have been had; but since his crime was Puritanism, he must flee for his life. So, for his life he fled, dodging his pursuers; and finally slipping out of England, after innumerable perils, like a hunted felon; landing in Boston in September, 1633."

Long before this crisis had come, Thomas Dudley had been recalled by the Earl of Lincoln, who found it impossible to dispense with his services, and the busy life began again. Whether Anne missed the constant excitement the strenuous spiritual life enforced on all who made part of John Cotton's congregation, there is no record, but one may infer from a passage in her diary that a reaction had set in, and that youth asserted itself.

"But as I grew up to bee about fourteen or fifteen I found my heart more carnall and sitting loose from God, vanity and the follys of youth take hold of me.

"About sixteen, the Lord layd his hand sore upon me and smott mee with the small-pox. When I was in my affliction, I besought the Lord, and confessed my Pride and Vanity and he was entreated of me, and again restored me. But I rendered not to him according to ye benefit received."

Here is the only hint as to personal appearance. "Pride and
Vanity," are more or less associated with a fair countenance, and
though no record gives slightest detail as to form or feature,
there is every reason to suppose that the event, very near at hand,
which altered every prospect in life, was influenced in degree, at
least, by considerations slighted in later years, but having full
weight with both. That Thomas Dudley was a "very personable
man," we know, and there are hints that his daughter resembled
him, though it was against the spirit of the time to record mere
accidents of coloring or shape. But Anne's future husband was a
strikingly handsome man, not likely to ignore such advantages in
the wife he chose, and we may think of her as slender and dark,
with heavy hair and the clear, thoughtful eyes,
which may be seen in the potrait of Paul Dudley to-day. There were
few of what we consider the typical Englishmen among these Puritan
soldiers and gentry. Then, as now, the reformer and liberal was
not likely to be of the warm, headlong Saxon type, fair-haired, blue-
eyed, and open to every suggestion of pleasure loving temperament. It
was the dark-haired men of the few districts who made up Cromwell's
regiment of Ironsides, and who from what Galton calls, "their
atrabilious and sour temperament," were likely to
become extremists, and such Puritan portraits as remain to us,
have most of them these characteristics. The English type of face
altered steadily for many generations, and the Englishmen of the
eighteenth century had little kinship with the race reproduced in
Holbein's portraits, which show usually, "high cheek-bones, long
upper lips, thin eyebrows, and lank, dark hair. It would be
impossible ... for the majority of modern Englishmen so to dress
themselves and clip and arrange their hair, as to look like the
majority of these portraits."

The type was perpetuated in New England, where for a hundred
years, there was not the slightest admixture of foreign blood,
increased delicacy with each generation setting it farther and
farther apart from the always grosser and coarser type in Old
England. Puritan abstinence had much to do with this, though even
for them, heavy feeding, as compared with any modern standard was
the rule, its results being found in the diaries of what they
recorded and believed to be spiritual conflicts. Then, as now,
dyspepsia often posed as a delicately susceptible temperament, and
the "pasty" of venison or game, fulfilled the same office as the
pie into which it degenerated, and which is one of the most
firmly established of American institutions. Then, as occasionally
even to day, indigestion counted as "a hiding of the Lord's face,"
and
a bilious attack as "the hand of the Lord laid heavily on one for
reproof and correction." Such "reproof and correction" would
often follow if the breakfasts of the Earl of Lincoln and his
household were of the same order as those of the Earl of
Northumberland, in whose house "the family rose at six and took
breakfast at seven. My Lord and Lady sat down to a repast of two
pieces of salted
fish, and half a dozen of red herrings, with four fresh ones, or a
dish of sprats and a quart of beer and the same measure of wine ...
At other seasons, half a chine of mutton or of boiled beef, graced
the board. Capons at two-pence apiece and plovers (at Christmas),
were deemed too good for any digestion that was not carried on in
a noble stomach."

With the dropping of fasts and meager days, fish was seldom used, and the Sunday morning breakfast of Queen Elizabeth and her retinue in one of her "progresses" through the country, for which three oxen and one hundred and forty geese were furnished, became the standard, which did not alter for many generations. A diet more utterly unsuited to the child who passed from one fit of illness to another, could hardly be imagined, and the gloom discoverable in portions of her work was as certainly dyspepsia as she imagined it to be "the motion and power of ye Adversary." Winthrop had encountered the same difficulty and with his usual insight and common sense, wrote in his private dairy fifteen years before he left England, "Sep: 8, 1612. ffinding that the variety of meates drawes me on to eate more than standeth with my healthe I have resolved not to eat of more than two dishes at any one meale, whither fish, fleshe, fowle or fruite or whitt-meats, etc; whither at home or abroade; the lord give me care and abilitie to perform it." Evidently the flesh rebelled, for later he writes: "Idlenesse and gluttonie are the two maine pillars of the flesh his kingdome," but he conquered finally, both he and Simon Bradstreet being singularly abstinent.

Her first sixteen years of life were, for Anne Dudley, filled with the intensest mental and spiritual activity--hampered and always in leading strings, but even so, an incredible advance on anything that had been the portion of women for generations. Then came, for the young girl, a change not wholly unexpected, yet destined to alter every plan, and uproot every early association. But to the memories of that loved early life she held with an English tenacity, not altered by transplanting, that is seen to-day in countless New Englanders, whose English blood is of as pure a strain as any to be found in the old home across the sea.

CHAPTER II.

UPHEAVAL

S.

Though the long engagement which Mr. Ruskin demands as a necessity in lessening some of the present complications of the marriage question may not have been the fortune of Simon and Anne Bradstreet, it is certain that few couples have ever had better opportunity for real knowledge of one another's peculiarities and habits of thought. Circumstances placed them under the same roof for years before marriage, and it would have been impossible to preserve any illusions, while every weakness as well as every virtue had fullest opportunity for disclosure. There is no hint of other suitors, nor detail of the wooing, but the portrait of Governor Bradstreet, still to be seen in the Senate Chamber of the Massachusetts State House, shows a face that even in middle life, the time at which the portrait was painted, held an ardor, that at twenty-five must have made him irresistible. It is the head of Cavalier rather than Roundhead--the full though delicately curved lips and every line in the noble face showing an eager, passionate, pleasure-loving temperament. But the broad, benignant forehead, the clear, dark eyes, the firm, well-cut nose, hold strength as well as sweetness, and prepare one for the reputation

which the old Colonial records give him. The high breeding, the
atmosphere of the whole figure, comes from a marvellously well-
balanced nature, as well as from birth and training. There is a
sense of the keenest life and vigor, both mental and physical, and
despite the Puritan garb, does not hide the man of whom his wife
might have written with Mrs. Hutchinson: "To sum up, therefore,
all that can be said of his outward frame and disposition, we must
truly conclude that it was a very handsome and well-furnished
lodging prepared for the reception of that prince who, in the
administration of all excellent virtues, reigned there a while,
till he was called back to the palace of the universal emperor."

Simon Bradstreet's father, "born of a wealthy family in Suffolk,
was one of the first fellows of Emanuel College, and highly
esteemed by persons distinguished for learning." In 1603 he was
minister at Horbling in Lincolnshire, but was never anything but a
nonconformist to the Church of England. Here in 1603 Simon
Bradstreet was born, and until fourteen years old was educated in
the grammar school of that place, till the death of his father
made some change necessary. John Cotton was the mutual friend of
both Dudley and the elder Bradstreet, and Dudley's interest in the
son may have arisen from this fact. However this may be, he was
taken at fifteen into the Earl of Lincoln's household, and trained
to the duties of a steward by Dudley himself. Anne being then a
child of nine years old, and probably looking up to him with the
devotion that was shared by her older brother, then eleven and
always the friend and ally of the future governor.

His capacity was so marked that Dr. Preston, another family friend
and a noted Nonconformist, interested himself in his further
education, and succeeded in entering him at Emanuel College,
Cambridge, in the position of governor to the young Lord Rich, son
of the Earl of Warwick. For some reason the young nobleman failed
to come to college and Bradstreet's time was devoted to a brother
of the Earl of Lincoln, who evidently shared the love of idleness
and dissipation that had marked his grandfather's career. It was all
pleasant and all eminently unprofitable, Bradstreet wrote in later
years, but he accomplished sufficient study to secure his
bachelor's degree in 1620. Four years later, while holding the
position of steward to the Earl of Lincoln, given him by Dudley
on the temporary removal to Boston, that of Master of Arts was
bestowed upon him, making it plain that his love of study had
continued. With the recall of Dudley, he became steward to the
countess of Warwick, which position he held at the time of his
marriage in 1628.

It was in this year that Anne, just before her marriage recorded,
when the affliction had passed: "About 16, the Lord layde his hand
sore upon me and smott me with the small-pox." It is curious that
the woman whose life in many points most resembles her own--Mrs.
Lucy Hutchinson--should have had precisely the same experience,
writing of herself in the "Memoirs of Colonel Hutchinson": "That
day that the friends on both sides met to conclude the marriage,
she fell sick of the small-pox, which was in many ways a great
trial upon him. First, her life was in almost desperate hazard,
and then the disease, for the present, made her the most deformed
person that could be seen, for a great while after she recovered;
yet he was nothing troubled at it, but married her as soon as she
was able to quit the chamber, when the priest and all that saw her

were affrighted to look on her; but God recompensed his justice
and constancy by restoring her, though she was longer than
ordinary before she recovered to be as well as before."

Whether disease or treatment held the greater terror, it would be hard
to say. Modern medical science has devised many alleviations, and
often restores a patient without spot or blemish. But to have lived at
all in that day evidenced extraordinary vitality.
Cleanliness was unknown, water being looked upon as deadly poison
whether taken internally or applied externally. Covered with
blankets, every window tightly sealed, and the moaning cry for
water answered by a little hot ale or tincture of bitter herbs,
nature often gave up the useless struggle and released the
tortured and delirious wretch. The means of cure left the
constitution irretrievably weakened if not hopelessly ruined, and
the approach of the disease was looked upon with affright and
regarded usually as a special visitation of the wrath of God.

That Anne Dudley so viewed it is evident from the passage in her
diary, already quoted; that the Lord "smott" her, was unquestioned,
and she cast about in her girlish mind for the shadow of the
sin that had brought such judgment, making solemn resolutions,
not only against any further indulgence in "Pride and Vanity,"
but all other offences, deciding that self-abnegation was the only
course, and possibly even beginning her convalescence with a
feeling that love itself should be put aside, and all her heart be
"sett upon God." But Simon Bradstreet waited, like Colonel
Hutchinson, only till "she was fit to leave her chamber," and
whether "affrighted" or not, the marriage was consummated
early in 1628.

Of heavier, stouter frame than Colonel Hutchinson, and of a far
more vigorous constitution, the two men had much in common. The
forces that moulded and influenced the one, were equally potent
with the other. The best that the time had to give entered into
both, and though Hutchinson's name and life are better known, it
is rather because of the beauty and power with which his story was
told, by a wife who worshipped him, than because of actually
greater desert. But the first rush of free thought ennobled many men
who in the old chains would have lived lives with nothing in
them worth noting, and names full of meaning are on every page of
the story of the time.

We have seen how the whole ideal of daily life had altered, as the
Puritan element gained ground, and the influence affected the
thought and life--even the speech of their opponents. A writer on
English literature remarks: "In one sense, the reign of James is
the most religious part of our history; for religion was then
fashionable. The forms of state, the king's speeches, the debates
in parliament and the current literature, were filled with
quotations from Scripture and quaint allusions to sacred things."

Even the soldier studied divinity, and Colonel Hutchinson, after
his "fourteen months various exercise of his mind, in the pursuit
of his love, being now at rest in the enjoyment of his wife,"
thought it the most natural thing in the world to make "an
entrance upon the study of school divinity, wherein his father was
the most eminent scholar of any gentleman in England and had a
most choice library.... Having therefore gotten into the house

with him an excellent scholar in that kind of learning, he for
two years made it the whole employment of his time."

Much of such learning Simon Bradstreet had taken in unconsciously
in the constant discussions about his father's table, as well as
in the university alive to every slightest change in doctrine,
where freer but fully as interested talk went on. Puritanism had
as yet acquired little of the bitterness and rigor born of
persecution, but meant simply emancipated thought, seeking
something better than it had known, but still claiming all the
good the world held for it. Milton is the ideal Puritan of the
time, and something of the influences that surrounded his youth
were in the home of every well-born Puritan. Even much farther
down in the social scale, a portrait remains of a London house
mother, which may stand as that of many, whose sons and daughters
passed over at last to the new world, hopeless of any quiet or
peace in the old. It is a turner in Eastcheap, Nehemiah Wallington,
who writes of his mother: "She was very loving and obedient to
her parents, loving and kind to her husband, very tender-hearted to
her children, loving all that were godly, much misliking the
wicked and profane. She was a pattern of sobriety unto many, very
seldom was seen abroad except at church; when
others recreated themselves at holidays and other times, she would
take her needle-work and say--'here is my recreation'.... God had
given her a very pregnant wit and an excellent memory. She was
very ripe and perfect in all stories of the Bible, likewise in all
the stories of the Martyrs, and could readily turn to them; she
was also perfect and well seen in the English Chronicles, and in
the descents of the Kings of England. She lived in holy wedlock
with her husband twenty years, wanting but four days."

If the influence of the new thought was so potent with a class who
in the Tudor days had made up the London mob, and whose signature,
on the rare occasions when anybody wanted it, had been a mark, the
middle class, including professional men, felt it infinitely more.
In the early training with many, as with Milton's father, music
was a passion; there was nothing illiberal or narrow. In Milton's
case he writes: "My father destined me while yet a little boy to
the study of humane letters; which I seized with such eagerness
that from the twelth year of my age I scarcely ever went from my
lessons to my bed before midnight." "To the Greek, Latin and
Hebrew learned at school the scrivener advised him to add Italian
and French. Nor were English letters neglected. Spencer gave the
earliest turn to the boy's poetic genius. In spite of the war
between playwright and precisian, a Puritan youth could still in
Milton's days avow his love of the stage, 'if Jonson's learned
sock be on, or sweetest Shakspeare Fancy's child, warble his
native wood-notes wild' and gather from the 'masques and antique
pageantry,' of the court revels, hints for his own 'Comus' and
'Arcades'."

Simon Bradstreet's year at Cambridge probably held much the same
experience, and if a narrowing faith in time taught him to write
it down as "all unprofitable," there is no doubt that it helped to
broaden his nature and establish the Catholic-mindedness which in
later years, in spite of every influence against it, was one of
his distinguishing characteristics. In the meantime he was a
delightful companion. Cut off by his principles from much
that passed as enjoyment, hating the unbridled licentiousness,
the

"ornate beastliness," of the Stuart reign, he like others of the same faith took refuge in intellectual pleasures. Like Colonel Hutchinson--and this portrait, contrary in all points to the preconceived idea, is a typical one--he "could dance admirably well, but neither in youth nor riper years made any practice of it; he had skill in fencing such as became a gentleman; he had great love to music and often diverted himself with a viol, on which he played masterly; he had an exact ear and judgment in other music; he shot excellently in bows and guns, and much used them for his exercise; he had great judgment in paintings, graving, sculpture, and all liberal arts, and had many curiosities of value in all kinds; he took great delight in perspective glasses, and, for his other rarities was not so much affected with the antiquity as the merit of the work; he took much pleasure in improvement of grounds, in planting groves and walks and fruit trees, in opening springs, and making fish-ponds."

All these tastes were almost indispensable to anyone filling the position which, alike, Dudley and Bradstreet held. "Steward" then, had a very different meaning from any associated with it now, and great estates were left practically in the hands of managers while the owners busied themselves in other directions, relying upon the good taste as well as the financial ability of the men who, as a rule, proved more than faithful to the trust.

The first two years of marriage were passed in England, and held the last genuine social life and intellectual development that Anne Bradstreet was to enjoy. The love of learning was not lost in the transition from one country to another, but it took on more and more a theological bias, and embodied itself chiefly in sermons and interminable doctrinal discussions. Even before the marriage, Dudley had decided to join the New England colony, but Simon Bradstreet hesitated and lingered, till forced to a decision by the increasing shadow of persecution. Had they remained in England, there is little doubt that Anne Bradstreet's mind, sensitively alive as it was to every fine influence, would have developed in a far different direction to that which it finally took. The directness and joyous life of the Elizabethan literature had given place to the euphuistic school, and as the Puritans put aside one author after another as "not making for godliness," the strained style, the quirks and conceits of men like Quarles and Withers came to represent the highest type of literary effort. But no author had the influence of Du Bartas, whose poems had been translated by Joshua Sylvester in 1605, under the title of "Du Bartas. His Duuine Weekes and Workes, with a Complete Collection of all the other most delightfull Workes, Translated and Written by ye famous Philomusus, Josvah Sylvester, Gent." He in turn was an imitator; a French euphuist, whose work simply followed and patterned after that of Ronsard, whose popularity for a time had convinced France that no other poet had been before him, and that no successor could approach his power. He chose to study classical models rather than nature or life, and his most formidable poem, merely a beginning of some five or six thousand verses on "the race of French kings, descended from Francion, a child of Hector and a Trojan by birth," ended prematurely on the death of Charles IX, but served as a model for a generation of imitators.

What spell lay in the involved and interminable pages the modern reader cannot decide, but Milton studied them, and affirmed that they had aided in forming his style, and Spenser wrote of him--

"And after thee, (du Bellay) 'gins
Barras hie to raise
His Heavenly muse, th' Almighty to adore.
Live, happy spirits! th' honor of your
name, And fill the world with never dying
fame."

Dryden, too, shared the infatuation, and in the Epistle Dedicatory
to "The Spanish Friar," wrote: "I remember when I was a boy, I
thought inimitable Spenser a mean poet, in comparison of
Sylvester's 'Dubartas,' and was wrapt into an ecstasy when I read
these lines:

"'Now when the winter's keener breath began
To crystallize the Baltic ocean;
To glaze the lakes, to bridle up the floods,
And periwig with snow (wool) the bald-pate woods.'

"I am much deceived if this be not abominable fustian." Van Lann
stigmatizes this poem, _Le Semaine ou Creation du Monde_, as "the
marriage-register of science and verse, written by a Gascon Moses,
who, to the minuteness of a Walt Whitman and the unction of a
parish-clerk, added an occasional dignity superior to anything
attained by the abortive epic of his master."

But he had some subtle, and to the nineteenth century mind,
inscrutable charm. Poets studied him and Anne Bradstreet did more
than study; she absorbed them, till such originality as had been
her portion perished under the weight. In later years she disclaimed
the charge of having copied from him, but the infection was too
thorough not to remain, and the assimilation had been so perfect that
imitation was unconscious. There was everything in the life of Du
Bartas to appeal to her imagination as well as her sympathy, and
with her minute knowledge of history she relished his detail while
reverencing his character. For Du Bartas was a French Puritan,
holding the same religious views as Henry IV, before he became
King of France, his strong religious nature appealing to every
English reader. Born in 1544, of noble parents, and brought up,
according to Michaud in the Biographic Universelle, to the
profession of arms, he distinguished himself as a soldier and
negotiater. Attached to the person of Prince Henry "in the capacity
of gentleman in ordinary of his bedchamber, he was successfully
employed by him on missions to Denmark, Scotland and England. He
was at the battle of Ivry and celebrated in song the victory which
he had helped to gain. He died four months after, in July, 1559, at
the age of forty-six, in consequence of some wounds which had been
badly healed. He passed all the leisure which his duties left him,
at his chateau du Bartas. It was there that he composed his long
and numerous poems.... His principal poem, _La Semaine,_ went
through more than thirty editions in less than six years, and was
translated into Latin, Italian, Spanish, English, German and
Dutch."

The influence was an unfortunate one. Nature had already been set
aside so thoroughly that, as with Dryden, Spenser was regarded as
common-place and even puerile, and the record of real life or
thought as no part of a poet's office. Such power of observation
as Anne Bradstreet had was discouraged in the beginning, and

though later it asserted itself in slight degree, her early work shows no trace of originality, being, as we are soon to see, merely a rhymed paraphrase of her reading. That she wrote verse, not included in any edition of her poems, we know, the earliest date assigned there being 1632, but the time she had dreaded was at hand, and books and study went the way of many other pleasant things.

With the dread must have mingled a certain thrill of hope and expectation common to every thinking man and woman who in that seventeenth century looked to the New World to redress every wrong of the Old, and who watched every movement of the little band that in Holland waited, for light on the doubtful and beclouded future.

The story of the first settlement needs no repetition here. The years in Holland had knit the little band together more strongly and lastingly than proved to be the case with any future company, their minister, John Robinson, having infused his own intense and self-abnegating nature into every one. That the Virginian colonies had suffered incredibly they knew, but it had no power to dissuade them. "We are well weaned," John Robinson wrote, "from the delicate milk of the mother-country, and inured to the difficulties of a strange land; the people are industrious and frugal. We are knit together as a body in a most sacred covenant of the Lord, of the violation whereof we make great conscience, and by virtue whereof, we hold ourselves strictly tied to all care of each other's good and of the whole. It is not with us, as with men whom small things can discourage."

By 1629, the worst difficulties had been overcome, and the struggle for mere existence had ended. The little colony, made up chiefly of hard working men, had passed through every phase of suffering. Sickness and famine had done their worst. The settlers were thoroughly acclimated, and as they prospered, more and more the eyes of Puritan England turned toward them, with a longing for the same freedom. Laud's hand was heavy and growing heavier, and as privileges lessened, and one after another found fine, or pillory, or banishment awaiting every expression of thought, the eagerness grew and intensified. As yet there had been no separation from the Mother Church. It had simply "divided into two great parties, the Prelatical or Hierarchical, headed by Laud, and the Nonconformist or Puritan." For the latter, Calvin had become the sole authority, and even as early as 1603, their preachers made up more than a ninth of the clergy. The points of disagreement increased steadily, each fresh severity from the Prelatical party being met by determined resistance, and a stubborn resolution never to yield an inch of the new convictions. No clearer presentation of the case is to be found anywhere than in Mason's life of Milton, the poet's life being absolutely contemporaneous with the cause, and his own experience came to be that of hundreds. From his childhood he had been set apart for the ministry, but he was as he wrote in later life, with a bitterness he never lost, "Church-outed by the prelates." "Coming to some maturity of years, and perceiving what tyranny had invaded in the Church, that he who would take orders, must subscribe slave, and take an oath withal, which, unless he took with a conscience that would retch, he must either straight perjure or split his faith, I thought it better to prefer a blameless silence before the sacred office of speaking, bought and begun with servitude and forswearing."

Each year of the increasing complications found a larger body
enrolled on his side, and with 1629, Simon Bradstreet resigned any
hope of life in England, and cast in his fortunes once for all
with the projected colony. In dissolving his third Parliament
Charles had granted the charter for the Massachusetts Colony, and
seizing upon this as a "Providential call," the Puritans at once
circulated "conclusions" among gentry and traders, and full
descriptions of Massachusetts. Already many capitalists deemed
encouragement of the emigration an excellent speculation, but the
prospective emigrants had no mind to be ruled by a commercial
company at home, and at last, after many deliberations, the old
company was dissolved; the officers resigned and their places were
filled by persons who proposed to emigrate.

Two days before this change twelve gentlemen met at Cambridge and
"pledged themselves to each other to embark for New England with
their families for a permanent residence."

"Provided always, that, before the last of September next, the
whole government, together with the patent for the said
plantation, be first legally transferred." Dudley's name was one
of the twelve, and at another meeting in October he was also
present, with John Winthrop, who was shortly chosen governor. A
day or two later, Dudley was made assistant governor, and in the
early spring of 1630, but a few days before sailing Simon
Bradstreet was elected to the same office in the place of Mr.
Thomas Goffe. One place of trust after another was filled by the
two men, whose history henceforward is that of New England. Dudley
being very shortly made "undertaker," that is, to be one of those
having "the sole managinge of the joynt stock, wth all things
incydent theronto, for the space of 7 years."

Even for the sternest enthusiasts, the departure seemed a
banishment, though Winthrop spoke the mind of all when he wrote,
"I shall call that my country where I may most glorify God and
enjoy the presence of my dearest friends."

For him the dearest were left behind for a time, and in all
literature there is no tenderer letter than that in which his last
words go to the wife whom he loved with all the strength of his
nature, and the parting from whom, was the deepest proof that
could have been of his loyalty to the cause he had made his own.

As he wrote the Arbella was riding at anchor at Cowes, waiting for
favorable winds. Some of the party had gone on shore, and all
longed to end these last hours of waiting which simply prolonged a
pain that even the most determined and resolute among them, felt
to be almost intolerable. Many messages went back carried by
friends who lingered at Cowes for the last look at the vanishing
sails, but none better worth record than the words which hold the
man's deep and tender soul.

"And now, my sweet soul, I must once again take my last farewell
of thee in old England. It goeth very near to my heart to leave
thee, but I know to whom I have committed thee, even to Him, who
loves thee much better than any husband can; who hath taken
account of the hairs of thy head, and puts all thy tears in his

bottle; who can, and (if it be for his glory) will, bring us
together again with peace and comfort. Oh, how it refresheth my
heart to think, that I shall yet again see thy sweet face in the
land of the living; that lovely countenance that I have so much
delighted in, and beheld with so great content! I have hitherto
been so taken up with business, as I could seldom look back to my
former happiness; but now when I shall be at some leisure, I shall
not avoid the remembrance of thee, nor the grief for thy absence.
Thou hast thy share with me, but I hope the course we have agreed
upon will be some ease to us both. Mondays and Fridays at five
o'clock at night we shall meet in spirit till we meet in person.
Yet if all these hopes should fail, blessed be our God, that we
are assured we shall meet one day, if not as husband and wife, yet
in a better condition. Let that stay and comfort thine heart.
Neither can the sea drown thy husband, nor enemies destroy, nor
any adversity deprive thee of thy husband or children. Therefore I
will only take thee now and my sweet children in mine arms, and
kiss and embrace you all, and so leave you with God. Farewell,
farewell. I bless you all in the name of the Lord Jesus."

"Farewell, dear England!" burst from the little group on that 8th
of April, 1630, when at last, a favorable wind bore them out to
sea, and Anne Bradstreet's voice had part in that cry of pain and
longing, as the shores grew dim and "home faded from their sight.
But one comfort or healing remained for them, in the faith that
had been with all from the beginning, one record being for them
and the host who preceded and followed their flight. So they left
that goodly and pleasant city which had been their resting
place; ... but they knew they were pilgrims and looked not much on
those things, but lift up their eyes to the heavens, their dearest
country, and quieted their spirits."

CHAPTER III.

THE

VOYAGE.

It is perhaps the fault of the seventeenth century and its firm
belief that a woman's office was simply to wait such action as man
might choose to take, that no woman's record remains of the long
voyage or the first impressions of the new country.

For the most of them writing was by no means a familiar task, but
this could not be said of the women on board the Arbella, who had
known the highest cultivation that the time afforded. But poor
Anne Bradstreet's young "heart rose," to such a height that
utterance may have been quite stifled, and as her own family were
all with her, there was less need of any chronicle.

For all details, therefore, we are forced to depend on the journal
kept by Governor Winthrop, who busied himself not only with
this, making the first entry on that Easter Monday which found
them riding at anchor at Cowes, but with another quite as
characteristic piece of work. A crowded storm-tossed ship, is
hardly a point to which one looks for any sustained or fine literary
composition,
but the little treatise, "A Model of Christian Charity," the fruit

of long and silent musing on the new life awaiting them, holds
the highest thought of the best among them, and was undoubtedly
read with the profoundest feeling and admiration, as it took shape
in the author's hands. There were indications even in the first
fervor of the embarkation, that even here some among them
thought "every man upon his own," while greater need of
unselfishness and self-renunciation had never been before
a people. "Only by mutual love and help," and "a grand, patient, self-
denial," was there the slightest hope of meeting the demands bound
up with the new conditions, and Winthrop wrote--"We must be knit
together in this work as one man. We must entertain each
other in brotherly affection. We must be willing to
abridge ourselves of our superfluities for the supply of
others'
necessities. We must uphold a familiar commerce together, in all
meekness, gentleness, patience and liberality. We must delight in
each other; make others' conditions our own; rejoice together,
mourn together, labor and suffer together, always having before
our eyes, our commission and community in the work as members of
the same body."

A portion of this body were as closely united as if forming but one
family. The lady Arbella, in compliment to whom the ship, which
had been first known as The Eagle, had been re-christened, had
married Mr. Isaac Johnson, one of the wealthiest members of the
party. She was a sister of the Earl of Lincoln who had come to the
title in 1619, and whose family had a more intimate connection
with the New England settlements than that of any other English
nobleman. Her sister Susan had become the wife of John Humfrey,
another member of the company, and the close friendship between
them and the Dudleys made it practically a family party. Anne
Bradstreet had grown up with both sisters, and all occupied
themselves in such ways as their cramped quarters would allow.
Space was of the narrowest, and if the Governor and his deputies
indulged themselves in spreading out papers, there would be small
room for less important members of the expedition. But each had
the little Geneva Bible carried by every Puritan, and read it with
a concentrated eagerness born of the sense that they had just
escaped its entire loss, and there were perpetual religious
exercises of all varieties, with other more secular ones recorded in
the Journal. In the beginning there had been some expectation
that several other ships would form part of the expedition, but
they were still not in sailing order and thus the first entry
records "It was agreed, (it being uncertain when the rest of the
fleet would be ready) these four ships should consort together;
the Arbella to be Admiral, the Talbot Vice-Admiral, the
Ambrose
Rear-Admiral, and the Jewel a Captain; and accordingly articles of
consortship were drawn between the said captains and masters."

The first week was one of small progress, for contrary winds drove
them back persistently and they at last cast anchor before
Yarmouth, and with the feeling that some Jonah might be in their
midst ordered a fast for Friday, the 2d of April, at which time
certain light-minded "landmen, pierced a runlet of strong water,
and stole some of it, for which we laid them in bolts all the
night, and the next morning the principal was openly whipped, and
both kept with bread and water that day."

Nothing further happened till Monday, when excitement was afforded
for the younger members of the party at least, as "A maid of Sir

Robert Saltonstall fell down at the grating by the cook-room, but the carpenter's man, who unwittingly, occasioned her fall caught hold of her with incredible nimbleness, and saved her; otherwise she had fallen into the hold."

Tuesday, finding that the wind was still against them, the captain drilled the landmen with their muskets, "and such as were good shot among them were enrolled to serve in the ship if occasion should be"; while the smell of powder and the desire, perhaps, for one more hour on English soil, made the occasion for another item: "The lady Arbella and the gentlewomen, and Mr. Johnson and some others went on shore to refresh themselves."

The refreshment was needed even then. Anne Bradstreet was still extremely delicate, never having fully recovered from the effects of the small-pox, and the Lady Arbella's health must have been so also, as it failed steadily through the voyage, giving the sorest anxiety to her husband and every friend on board.

It is evident from an entry in Anne Bradstreet's diary after reaching New England that even the excitement of change and the hope common to all of a happy future, was not strong enough to keep down the despondency which came in part undoubtedly from her weak health. The diary is not her own thoughts or impressions of the new life, but simply bits of religious experience; an autobiography of the phase with which we could most easily dispense. "After a short time I changed my condition and was married, and came into this country, where I found a new world and new manners at which my heart rose. But after I was convinced it was the will of God I submitted to it and joined to the church at Boston."

This rebellion must have been from the beginning, for every inch of English soil was dear to her, but she concealed it so thoroughly, that no one suspected the real grief which she looked upon as rebellion to the will of God. Conservative in thought and training, and with the sense of humor which might have lightened some phases of the new dispensation, almost destroyed by the Puritan faith, which more and more altered the proportions of things, making life only a grim battle with evil, and the days doings of absolute unimportance save as they advanced one toward heaven, she accepted discomfort or hardship with quiet patience.

There must have been unfailing interest, too, in the perpetual chances and changes of the perilous voyage. They had weighed anchor finally on the 8th of April, and were well under way on the morning of the 9th, when their journey seemed suddenly likely to end then and there. The war between Spain and England was still going on, and privateers known as Dunkirkers, were lying in wait before every English harbor. Thus there was reason enough for apprehension, when, "In the morning we descried from the top, eight sail astern of us.... We supposing they might be Dunkirkers, our captain caused the gun room and gun deck to be cleared; all the hammocks were taken down, our ordnance loaded, and our powder chests and fireworks made ready, and our landmen quartered among the seamen, and twenty-five of them appointed for muskets, and every man written down for his quarter.

"The wind continued N. with fair weather, and after noon it

calmed, and we still saw those eight ships to stand towards us; having more wind than we, they came up apace, so as our captain and the masters of our consorts were more occasioned to think they might be Dunkirkers, (for we were told at Yarmouth, that there were ten sail of them waiting for us); whereupon we all prepared to fight with them, and took down some cabins which were in the way of our ordnance, and out of every ship were thrown such bed matters as were subject to take fire, and we heaved out our long boats and put up our waste cloths, and drew forth our men and armed them with muskets and other weapons, and instruments for fireworks; and for an experiment our captain shot a ball of wild fire fastened to an arrow out of a cross bow, which burnt in the water a good time. The lady Arbella and the other women and children, were removed into the lower deck, that they might be out of danger. All things being thus fitted, we went to prayer upon the upper deck. It was much to see how cheerful and comfortable all the company appeared; not a woman or child that shewed fear, though all did apprehend the danger to have been great, if things had proved as might well be expected, for there had been eight against four, and the least of the enemy's ships were reported to carry thirty brass pieces; but our trust was in the Lord of Hosts; and the courage of our captain, and his care and diligence did much to encourage us.

"It was now about one of the clock, and the fleet seemed to be within a league of us; therefore our captain, because he would show he was not afraid of them, and that he might see the issue before night should overtake us, tacked about and stood to meet them, and when we came near we perceived them to be our friends-- the little Neptune, a ship of some twenty pieces of ordnance, and her two consorts, bound for the Straits, a ship of Flushing, and a Frenchman and three other English ships bound for Canada and Newfoundland. So when we drew near, every ship (as they met) saluted each other, and the musketeers discharged their small shot, and so (God be praised) our fear and danger was turned into mirth and friendly entertainment. Our danger being thus over, we espied two boats on fishing in the channel; so every one of our four ships manned out a skiff, and we bought of them great store of excellent fresh fish of divers sorts."

It is an astonishing fact, that no line in Anne Bradstreet's poems has any reference to this experience which held every alternation of hope and fear, and which must have moved them beyond any other happening of the long voyage. But, inward states, then as afterward, were the only facts that seemed worthy of expression, so far as she personally was concerned, and they were all keyed to a pitch which made danger even welcome, as a test of endurance and genuine purpose. But we can fancy the dismay of every house-wife as the limited supply of "bed matters," went the way of many other things "subject to take fire." Necessarily the household goods of each had been reduced to the very lowest terms, and as the precious rugs and blankets sunk slowly, or for a time defied the waves and were tossed from crest to crest, we may be sure that the heart of every woman, in the end at least, desired sorely that rescue might be attempted. Sheets had been dispensed with, to avoid the accumulation of soiled linen, for the washing of which no facilities could be provided, and Winthrop wrote of his boys to his wife in one of his last letters, written as they rode at anchor before Cowes, "They lie both with me, and sleep as soundly in a rug (for we use no sheets here) as ever they did at Groton; and so I do myself, (I praise God)."

Among minor trials this was not the least, for the comfort we associate with English homes, had developed, under the Puritan love of home, to a degree that even in the best days of the Elizabethan time was utterly unknown. The faith which demanded absolute purity of life, included the beginning of that cleanliness which is "next to godliness," if not an inherent part of godliness itself, and fine linen on bed and table had become more and more a necessity. The dainty, exquisite neatness that in the past has been inseparable from the idea of New England, began with these Puritan dames, who set their floating home in such order as they could, and who seized the last opportunity at Yarmouth of going on shore, not only for refreshment, but to wash neckbands and other small adornments, which waited two months for any further treatment of this nature.

There were many resources, not only in needlework and the necessary routine of each day, but in each other. The two daughters of Sir Robert Saltonstall, Mrs. Phillips the minister's wife, the wives of Nowell, Coddington and others made up the group of gentlewomen who dined with Lady Arbella in "the great cabin," the greatness of which will be realized when the reader reflects that the ship was but three hundred and fifty tons burden and could carry aside from the fifty or so sailors, but thirty passengers, among whom were numbered various discreet and reputable "young gentlemen" who, as Winthrop wrote, "behave themselves well, and are conformable to all good orders," one or two of whom so utilized their leisure that the landing found them ready for the marriage bells that even Puritan asceticism still allowed to be rung.

Disaster waited upon them, even when fairly under way. Winthrop, whose family affection was intense, and whose only solace in parting with his wife had been, that a greatly loved older son, as well as two younger ones were his companions, had a sore disappointment, entered in the journal, with little comment on its personal bearings. "The day we set sail from Cowes, my son Henry Winthrop went on shore with one of my servants, to fetch an ox and ten wethers, which he had provided for our ship, and there went on shore with him Mr. Pelham and one of his servants. They sent the cattle aboard, but returned not themselves. About three days after my servant and a servant of Mr. Pelham's came to us in Yarmouth, and told us they were all coming to us in a boat the day before, but the wind was so strong against them as they were forced on shore in the night, and the two servants came to Yarmouth by land, and so came on shipboard, but my son and Mr. Pelham (we heard) went back to the Cowes and so to Hampton. We expected them three or four days after, but they came not to us, so we have left them behind, and suppose they will come after in Mr. Goffe's ships. We were very sorry they had put themselves upon such inconvenience when they were so well accommodated in our ship."

A fresh gale on the day of this entry encouraged them all; they passed the perils of Scilly and looked for no further delay when a fresh annoyance was encountered which, for the moment, held for the women at least, something of the terror of their meeting with supposed "Dunkirkers."

"About eight in the morning, ... standing to the W. S. W. we met two small ships, which falling in among us, and the Admiral coming under our lee, we let him pass, but the Jewel and Ambrose, perceiving the other to be a Brazilman, and to take the wind of us, shot at them, and made them stop and fall after us, and sent a skiff aboard them to know what they were. Our captain, fearing lest some mistake might arise, and lest they should take them for enemies which were friends, and so, through the unruliness of the mariners some wrong might be done them, caused his skiff to be heaved out, and sent Mr. Graves, one of his mates and our pilot (a discreet man) to see how things were, who returned soon after, and brought with him the master of one of the ships, and Mr. Lowe and Mr. Hurlston. When they were come aboard to us, they agreed to send for the captain, who came and showed his commission from the Prince of Orange. In conclusion he proved to be a Dutchmen, and his a man of war from Flushing, and the other ship was a prize he had taken, laden with sugar and tobacco; so we sent them aboard their ships again, and held on our course. In this time (which hindered us five or six leagues) the Jewel and the Ambrose came foul of each other, so as we much feared the issue, but, through God's mercy, they came well off again, only the Jewel had her foresail torn, and one of her anchors broken. This occasion and the sickness of our minister and people, put us all out of order this day, so as we could have no sermons."

No words hold greater force of discomfort and deprivation than that one line, "so as we could have no sermons," for the capacity for this form of "temperate entertainment," had increased in such ratio, that the people sat spell bound, four hours at a stretch, both hearers and speaker being equally absorbed. Winthrop had written of himself at eighteen, in his "Christain Experience": "I had an insatiable thirst after the word of God; and could not misse a good sermon, though many miles off, especially of such as did search deep into the conscience," and to miss this refreshment even for a day, seemed just so much loss of the needed spiritual food.

But the wind, which blew "a stiffe gale," had no respect of persons, and all were groaning together till the afternoon of the next day, when a device occurred to some inventive mind, possibly that of Mistress Bradstreet herself, which was immediately carried out. "Our children and others that were sick and lay groaning in the cabins, we fetched out, and having stretched a rope from the steerage to the main mast, we made them stand, some of one side and some of the other, and sway it up and down till they were warm, and by this means they soon grew well and merry."

The plan worked well, and three days later, when the wind which had quieted somewhat, again blew a "stiffe gale," he was able to write: "This day the ship heaved and set more than before, yet we had but few sick, and of these such as came up upon the deck and stirred themselves, were presently well again; therefore our captain set our children and young men, to some harmless exercises, which the seamen were very active in, and did our people much good, though they would sometimes play the wags with them."

Wind and rain, rising often till the one was a gale and the other

torrents, gave them small rest in that first week. The fish they
had secured at Yarmouth returned to their own element, Winthrop
mourning them as he wrote: "The storm was so great as it split our
foresail and tore it in pieces, and a knot of the sea washed our
tub overboard, wherein our fish was a-watering." The children had
become good sailers, and only those were sick, who, like "the
women kept under hatches." The suffering from cold was constant,
and for a fortnight extreme, the Journal reading: "I wish,
therefore, that all such as shall pass this way in the spring have care
to provide warm clothing; for nothing breeds more trouble and
danger of sickness, in this season, than cold."

From day to day the little fleet exchanged signals, and now and
then, when calm enough the masters of the various ships dined in
the round-house of the Arbella, and exchanged news, as that, "all
their people were in health, but one of their cows was dead." Two
ships in the distance on the 24th of April, disturbed them for a
time, but they proved to be friends, who saluted and "conferred
together so long, till his Vice Admiral was becalmed by our sails,
and we were foul one of another, but there being little wind and
the sea calm, we kept them asunder with oars, etc., till they
heaved out their boat, and so towed their ship away. They told us
for certain, that the king of France had set out six of his own
ships to recover the fort from them."

Here was matter for talk among the travellers, whose interest in
all that touched their future heightened day by day, and the item,
with its troublous implications may have been the foundation of
one of the numerous fasts recorded.

May brought no suggestion of any quiet, though three weeks out,
they had made but three hundred leagues, and the month opened with
"a very great tempest all the night, with fierce showers of rain
intermixed, and very cold.... Yet through God's mercy, we were
very comfortable and few or none sick, but had opportunity to keep
the Sabbath, and Mr. Phillips preached twice that day."

Discipline was of the sharpest, the Puritan temper brooking no
infractions of law and order. There were uneasy and turbulent
spirits both among the crew and passengers, and in the beginning
swift judgment fell upon two young men, who, "falling at odds
and fighting, contrary to the orders which we had published and
set up in the ship, were adjudged to walk upon the deck till night,
with
their hands bound behind them, which accordingly was executed; and
another man for using contemptuous speeches in our presence, was
laid in bolts till he submitted himself and promised open
confession of his offence."

Impressive as this undoubtedly proved to the "children and youth
thereby admonished," a still greater sensation was felt among them
on the discovery that "a servant of one of our company had
bargained with a child to sell him a box worth three-pence for
three biscuits a day all the voyage, and had received about forty
and had sold them and many more to some other servants. We caused
his hands to be tied up to a bar, and hanged a basket with stones
about his neck, and so he stood two hours."

Other fights are recorded, the cause a very evident one. "We
observed it a common fault in our young people that they gave

themselves to drink hot waters very immoderately."

Brandy then as now was looked upon as a specific for sea-sickness, and "a maid servant in the ship, being stomach sick, drank so much strong water, that she was senseless, and had near killed herself."

The constant cold and rain, the monotonous food, which before port was reached had occasioned many cases of scurvy and reduced the strength of all, was excuse enough for the occasional lapse into overindulgence which occurred, but the long penance was nearly ended. On the 8th of June Mount Mansell, now Mt. Desert, was passed, an enchanting sight for the sea-sad eyes of the travellers. A "handsome gale" drove them swiftly on, and we may know with what interest they crowded the decks and gazed upon these first glimpses of the new home. As they sailed, keeping well in to shore, and making the new features of hill and meadow and unfamiliar trees, Winthrop wrote: "We had now fair sunshine weather, and so pleasant a sweet air as did much refresh us, and there came a smell off the shore like the smell of a garden."

Peril was past, and though fitful winds still tormented them, the 12th of May saw the long imprisonment ended, and they dropped anchor "a little within the islands," in the haven where they would be.

CHAPTER IV.

BEGINNINGS

.

There are travellers who insist that, as they near American shores in May or early June, the smell of corn-blossom is on the wind, miles out at sea, a delicate, distinct, penetrating odor, as thoroughly American as the clearness of the sky and the pure, fine quality in the air. The wild grape, growing as profusely to-day on the Cape as two hundred years ago, is even more powerful, the subtle, delicious fragrance making itself felt as soon as one approaches land. The "fine, fresh smell like a garden," which Winthrop notes more than once, came to them on every breeze from the blossoming land. Every charm of the short New England summer waited for them. They had not, like the first comers to that coast to disembark in the midst of ice and snow, but green hills sloped down to the sea, and wild strawberries were growing almost at high-tide mark. The profusion of flowers and berries had rejoiced Higginson in the previous year, their men rowing at once to "Ten Pound Island," and bringing back, he writes: "ripe strawberries and gooseberries and sweet single roses. Thus God was merciful to us in giving us a taste and smell of the sweet fruit, as an earnest of his bountiful goodness to welcome us at our first arrival."

But no fairness of Nature could undo the sad impression of the first hour in the little colony at Salem, where the Arbella landed, three days before her companions reached there. Their own cares would have seemed heavy enough, but the winter had been a terrible one, and Dudley wrote later in his letter to the Countess of Lincoln: "We found the Colony in a sad and unexpected condition, above eighty of them being dead the winter before; and many of those alive, weak and sick; all the corn and bread amongst them all, hardly sufficient to feed them a fortnight, insomuch that the remainder of a hundred and eighty servants we had the two years before sent over, coming to us for victuals to sustain them, we found ourselves wholly unable to feed them, by reason that the provisions shipped for them were taken out of the ship they were put in, and they who were trusted to ship them in another, failed us and left them behind; whereupon necessity enforced us, to our extreme loss, to give them all liberty, who had cost us about L16 or L20 a person, furnishing and sending over."

Salem holding only discouragement, they left it, exploring the Charles and the Mystic Rivers, and finally joining the settlement at Charlestown, to which Francis Higginson had gone the previous year, and which proved to be in nearly as desperate case as Salem. The Charlestown records as given in Young's "Chronicles of Massachusetts," tell the story of the first days of attempt at organization. The goods had all been unshipped at Salem and were not brought to Charlestown until July. In the meantime, "The Governor and several of the Patentees dwelt in the great house which was last year built in this town by Mr. Graves and the rest of their servants. The multitude set up cottages, booths and tents about the Town Hill. They had long passage; some of the ships were seventeen, some eighteen weeks a coming. Many people arrived sick of the scurvy, which also increased much after their arrival, for want of houses, and by reason of wet lodging in their cottages, etc. Other distempers also prevailed; and although [the] people were generally very loving and pitiful, yet the sickness did so prevail, that the whole were not able to tend the sick as they should be tended; upon which many perished and died, and were buried about the Town Hill."

Saddest of all among these deaths must have been that of the Lady Arbella, of whom Mather in a later day, wrote: "She came from a paradise of plenty and pleasure, in the family of a noble earldom, into a wilderness of wants, and took New England in her way to heaven." There had been doubt as to the expediency of her coming, but with the wife of another explorer she had said: "Whithersoever your fatal destiny shall drive you, either by the waves of the great ocean, or by the manifold and horrible dangers of the land, I will surely bear you company. There can no peril chance to me so terrible, nor any kind of death so cruel, that shall not be much easier for me to abide, than to live so far separate from you."

Weakened by the long voyage and its perpetual hardships, and dismayed, if may be at the sadness and privations of what they had hoped might hold immediate comfort, she could not rally, and Anne Bradstreet's first experience of New England was over the grave, in which they laid one of the closest links to childhood and that England both had loved alike.

Within a month, Winthrop wrote in his journal: "September 30. About two in the morning, Mr. Isaac Johnson died; his wife, the lady Arbella, of the house of Lincoln, being dead about one month before. He was a holy man and wise, and died in sweet peace, leaving some part of his substance to the Colony."

"He tried
To live without her, liked it not and died."

Still another tragedy had saddened them all, though in the press
of overwhelming business, Winthrop wrote only: "Friday, July 2.
My son Henry Winthrop drowned at Salem," and there is no other
mention of himself till July 16, when he wrote the first letter to
his wife from America.

The loss was a heavy one to the colony as well as the father, for
Henry Winthrop, though but twenty-two, had already had experience
as a pioneer, having gone out to Barbadoes at eighteen, and became
one of the earliest planters in that island. Ardent, energetic,
and with his fathers deep tenderness for all who depended on him,
he was one who could least be spared. "A sprightly and hopeful
young gentleman he was," says Hubbard, and another chronicle gives
more minute details. "The very day on which he went on shore in
New England, he and the principal officers of the ship,
walking out to a place now called by the Salemites, Northfield,
to view the Indian wigwams, they saw on the other side of the
river a
small canoe. He would have had one of the company swim over and
fetch it, rather than walk several miles on foot, it being very
hot weather; but none of the party could swim but himself; and so
he plunged in, and, as he was swimming over, was taken with the
cramp a few roods from the shore and drowned."

The father's letter is filled with an anguish of pity for the
mother and the young wife, whose health, like that of the elder
Mrs. Winthrop, had made the journey impossible for both.

"I am so overpressed with business, as I have no time for these or
other mine own private occasions. I only write now that thou
mayest know, that yet I live and am mindful of thee in all my
affairs. The larger discourse of all things thou shalt receive
from my brother Downing, which I must send by some of the last
ships. We have met with many sad and discomfortable things as thou
shalt hear after; and the Lord's hand hath been heavy upon myself
in some very near to me. My son Henry! My son Henry! Ah, poor
child! Yet it grieves me much more for my dear daughter. The
Lord strengthen and comfort her heart to bear this cross patiently. I
know thou wilt not be wanting to her in this distress."

Not one of the little colony was wanting in tender offices in
these early days when a common suffering made them "very pitiful
one to another," and as the absolutely essential business was
disposed of they hastened to organize the church where free
worship should make amends for all the long sorrow of its search.

A portion of the people from the Arbella had remained in Salem,
but on Friday, July 30th, 1630, Winthrop, Dudley, Johnson and
Wilson entered into a church covenant, which was signed two days
after by Increase Nowell and four others--Sharpe, Bradstreet, Gager
and Colborne.

It is most probable that Anne Bradstreet had been temporarily
separated from her husband, as Johnson in his "Wonder-working
Providence," writes, that after the arrival at Salem, "the lady
Arrabella and some other godly women aboad at Salem, but their

husbands continued at Charles Town, both for the settling the
Civill Government and gathering another Church of Christ." The
delay was a short one, for her name stands thirteenth on the list.
Charlestown, however, held hardly more promise of quiet life than
Salem. The water supply was, curiously enough, on a peninsula
which later gave excellent water, only "a brackish spring in the
sands by the water side ... which could not supply half the
necessities of the multitude, at which time the death of so many
was concluded to be much the more occasioned by this want of good
water."

Heat was another evil to the constitutions which knew only the
equable English temperature, and could not face either the intense
sun, or the sudden changes of the most erratic climate the earth
knows. In the search for running-water, the colonists scattered,
moving from point to point, "the Governor, the Deputy-Governor
and all the assistants except Mr. Nowell going across the river to
Boston at the invitation of Mr. Blaxton, who had until then
been its only white inhabitant."

Even the best supplied among them were but scantily provided with
provisions. It was too late for planting, and the colony already
established was too wasted and weakened by sickness to have cared
for crops in the planting season. In the long voyage "there was
miserable damage and spoil of provisions by sea, and divers came
not so well provided as they would, upon a report, whilst they
were in England, that now there was enough in New England." Even
this small store was made smaller by the folly of several who
exchanged food for beaver skins, and, the Council suddenly finding
that famine was imminent "hired and despatched away Mr. William
Pearce with his ship of about two hundred tons, for Ireland to buy
more, and in the mean time went on with their work of settling."

The last month of the year had come before they could decide where
the fortified town, made necessary by Indian hostilities, should
be located. The Governor's house had been partly framed at
Charlestown, but with the removal to Boston it was taken down, and
finally Cambridge was settled upon as the most desirable point,
and their first winter was spent there. Here for the first time it was
possible for Anne Bradstreet to unpack their household belongings,
and seek to create some semblance of the forsaken home. But even
for the Dudleys, among the richest members of the party there was a
privation which shows how sharply it must have fared with the
poorer portion, and Dudley wrote, nine months after their arrival,
that he "thought fit to commit to memory our
present condition, and what hath befallen us since our arrival
here; which I will do shortly, after my usual manner, and must do
rudely, having yet no table, nor other room to write in than by
the fireside upon my knee, in this sharp winter; to which my
family must have leave to resort, though they break good manners,
and make me many times forget what I would say, and say what I
would not."

No word of Mistress Dudley's remains to tell the shifts and
strivings for comfort in that miserable winter which, mild as
it
was, had a keenness they were ill prepared to face. Petty miseries
and deprivations, the least endurable of all forms of suffering,
surrounded them like a cloud of stinging insects, whose attacks,
however intolerable at the moment, are forgotten with the passing,

and either for this reason, or from deliberate purpose, there is
not a line of reference to them in any of Anne Bradstreet's
writings. Scarcity of food was the sorest trouble. The Charlestown
records show that "people were necessitated to live upon clams and
muscles and ground nuts and acorns, and these got with much
difficulty in the winter-time. People were very much tried and
discouraged, especially when they heard that the Governor himself
had the last batch of bread in the oven."

All fared alike so far as possible, the richer and more provident
distributing to the poor, and all watching eagerly for the ship
sent back in July in anticipation of precisely such a crisis. Six
months had passed, when, on the fifth of February, 1631, Mather
records that as Winthrop stood at his door giving "the last
handful of meal in the barrel unto a poor man distressed by the
wolf at the door, at that instant, they spied a ship arrived at
the harbor's mouth with provisions for them all." The Fast day just
appointed became one of rejoicing, the first formal proclamation
for Thanksgiving Day being issued, "by order of the Governour
and Council, directed to all the plantations, and though the stores
held little reminder of holiday time in Old England, grateful hearts
did not stop to weigh differences. In any case the worst was past
and early spring brought the hope of substantial comfort, for the
town was 'laid out in squares, the streets intersecting each other at
right-angles,' and houses were built
as rapidly as their small force of carpenters could work.
Bradstreet's house was at the corner of 'Brayntree' and Wood
Streets, the spot now occupied by the familiar University Book-
store of Messrs. Sever and Francis on Harvard Square, his plot of
ground being 'aboute one rood,' and Dudley's on a lot of half an
acre was but a little distance from them at the corner of the
present Dunster and South Streets." Governor Winthrop's decision
not to remain here, brought about some sharp correspondence
between Dudley and himself, but an amicable settlement followed
after a time, and though the frame of his house was removed to
Boston, the town grew in spite of its loss, so swiftly that in
1633, Wood wrote of it:

"This is one of the neatest and best compacted Towns in New
England, having many fair structures, with many handsome contrived
streets. The inhabitants most of them are very rich and well
stored with Cattell of all sorts."

Rich as they may have appeared, however, in comparison with many
of the settlements about them, sickness and want were still
unwelcome guests among them, so that Dudley wrote: "there is not a
house where there is not one dead and in some houses many. The
natural causes seem to be in the want of warm lodging and good
diet, to which Englishmen are habituated at home, and in the
sudden increase of heat which they endure that are landed here in
summer, the salt meats at sea having prepared their bodies thereto;
for those only these two last years died of fevers who landed in
June and July; as those of Plymouth, who landed in winter, died of
the scurvey, as did our poorer sort, whose houses and bedding kept
them not sufficiently warm, nor their diet sufficiently in heart."

Thus far there were small inducements for further emigration. The
tide poured in steadily, but only because worse evils were behind

than semi-starvation in New England. The fairest and fullest
warning was given by Dudley, whose letter holds every strait and
struggle of the first year, and who wrote with the intention of
counteracting the too rosy statements of Higginson and Graves: "If
any come hither to plant for worldly ends that can live well at
home, he commits an error, of which he will soon repent him; but
if for spiritual, and that no particular obstacle hinder his
removal, he may find here what may well content him, viz.,
materials to build, fuel to burn, ground to plant, seas and rivers
to fish in, a pure air to breathe in, good water to drink till
wine or beer can be made; which together with the cows, hogs and
goats brought hither already, may suffice for food; for as for
fowl and venison, they are dainties here as well as in England. For
clothes and bedding, they must bring them with them, till time
and industry produce them here. In a word, we yet enjoy little to
be envied, but endure much to be pitied in the sickness and
mortality of our people. And I do the more willingly use this open
and plain dealing, lest other men should fall short of their
expectations when they come hither, as we to our great prejudice
did, by means of letters sent us from hence into England, wherein
honest men, out of a desire to draw over others to them, wrote
something hyperbolically of many things here. If any godly men,
out of religious ends, will come over to help us in the good work
we are about, I think they cannot dispose of themselves nor their
estates more to God's glory and the furtherance of their own
reckoning. But they must not be of the poorer sort yet, for divers
years; for we have found by experience that they have hindered,
not furthered the work. And for profane and debauched persons,
their oversight in coming hither is wondered at, where they shall
find nothing to content them."

This long quotation is given in full to show the fair temper of
the man, who as time went on was slightly less in favor than in
the beginning. No one questioned his devotion to the cause, or the
energy with which he worked for it, but as he grew older he lost
some portion of the old urbanity, exchanging it disastrously for
traits which would seem to have been the result of increasing
narrowness of religious faith rather than part of his real self.
Savage writes of him: "a hardness in publick and ridgidity in
private life, are too observable in his character, and even an
eagerness for pecuniary gain, which might not have been expected
in a soldier and a statesman." That the impression was general is
evident from an epitaph written upon him by Governor Belcher,
who may, however, have had some personal encounter with this
"rigidity," which was applied to all without fear or favor.

"Here lies Thomas Dudley, that trusty old stud,
A bargain's a bargain and must be made good."

Whatever his tendencies may have been they did not weigh heavily
on his family, who delighted in his learning and devoted spirit,
and whose affection was strong enough to atone for any criticism
from outsiders.

Objectionable as his methods may sometimes have been--sour as his
compatriots now and then are said to have found him, "the world it
appears, is indebted for much of its progress, to uncomfortable
and even grumpy people," and Tyler whose analysis of the Puritan
character has never been surpassed, writes of them: "Even some of

the best of them, perhaps, would have seemed to us rather
pragmatical and disputatious persons, with all the edges and
corners of their characters left sharp, with all their opinions
very definitely formed, and with their habits of frank
utterance
quite thoroughly matured. Certainly ... they do not seem to have
been a company of gentle, dreamy and euphemistical saints, with a
particular aptitude for martyrdom and an inordinate development of
affability."

They argued incessantly, at home and abroad, and "this exacting
and tenacious propensity of theirs, was not a little criticized by
some who had business connections with them." Very probably
Governor Belcher had been worsted in some wordy battle, always
decorously conducted, but always persistent, but these minor
infelicities did not affect the main purposes of life, and the
settlement grew in spite of them; perhaps even, because of them,
free speech being, as yet, the privilege of all, though as the
answering became in time a little too free, means were taken to
insure more discretion.

In the meantime Cambridge grew, and suddenly arose a complaint,
which to the modern mind is preposterous. "Want of room" was the
cry of every citizen and possibly with justice, as the town had
been set within fixed limits and had nearly doubled in size
through the addition in August, 1632, of the congregation of the
Rev. Thomas Hooker at Chelmsford in the county of Essex, England,
who had fallen under Laud's displeasure, and escaped with
difficulty, being pursued by the officers of the High Commission
from one county to another, and barely eluding them when he took
ship for New England.

One would have thought the wilderness at their doors afforded
sense of room enough, and that numbers would have been a welcome
change, but the complaint was serious enough to warrant their
sending out men to Ipswich with a view of settling there. Then
for a time the question dropped, much to the satisfaction, no
doubt,
of Mistress Dudley and her daughter, to whom in 1633, or '34, the
date being uncertain, came her first child, the son Samuel, who
graduated at Harvard College in 1653, and of whom she wrote long
after in the little diary of "Religious Experiences":

"It pleased God to keep me a long time without a child, which was a
great greif to me, and cost mee many prayers and tears before I
obtained one, and after him gave mee many more of whom I now take
the care."

Cambridge still insisting that it had not room enough, the town
was enlarged, but having accomplished this, both Dudley and
Bradstreet left it for Ipswich, the first suggestion of which had
been made in January, 1632, when news came to them that "the
French had bought the Scottish plantation near Cape Sable, and
that the fort and all the amunition were delivered to them, and
that the cardinal, having the managing thereof, had sent many
companies already, and preparation was made to send many more the
next year, and divers priests and Jesuits among them---called the
assistants to Boston, and the ministers and captains, and some
other chief men, to advise what was fit to be done for our safety,
in regard the French were like to prove ill neighbors, (being
Papists)."

Another change was in store for the patient women who followed the path laid open before them, with no thought of opposition, desiring only "room for such life as should in the ende return them heaven for an home that passeth not away," and with the record in Winthrop's journal, came the familiar discussion as to methods, and the decision which speedily followed.

Dudley and Bradstreet as "assistants" both had voice in the conclusions of the meeting, the record of which has just been given, though with no idea, probably, at that time, that their own movements would be affected. It was settled at once that "a plantation and a fort should be begun at Natascott, partly to be some block in an enemy's way (though it could not bar his entrance), and especially to prevent an enemy from taking that passage from us.... Also, that a plantation be begun at Agawam (being the best place in the land for tillage and cattle), least an enemy, finding it void should possess and take it from us. The governor's son (being one of the assistants) was to undertake this, and to take no more out of the bay than twelve men; the rest to be supplied, at the coming of the next ships."

That they were not essential to Cambridge, but absolutely so at this weak point was plain to both Dudley and Bradstreet, who forthwith made ready for the change accomplished in 1634, when at least one other child, Dorothy, had come to Anne Bradstreet.
Health, always delicate and always fluctuating, was affected more seriously than usual at this time, no date being given, but the period extending over several years, "After some time, I fell into a lingering sickness like a consumption, together with a lameness, which correction I saw the Lord sent to humble and try me and do me Good: and it was not altogether ineffectual."

Patient soul! There were better days coming, but, self-distrust was, after her affections, her strongest point, and there is small hint of inward poise or calmness till years had passed, though she faced each change with the quiet dauntlessness that was part of her birthright. But the tragedy of their early days in the colony still shadowed her. Evidently no natural voice was allowed to speak in her, and the first poem of which we have record is as destitute of any poetic flavor, as if designed for the Bay Psalm-book. As the first, however, it demands place, if only to show from what she afterward escaped. That she preserved it simply as a record of a mental state, is evident from the fact, that it was never included in any edition of her poems, it having been found among her papers after her death.

UPON A FIT OF SICKNESS, _Anno_. 1632.
Aetatis suce, 19.

Twice ten years old not fully told
    since nature gave me breath,
My race is run, my thread is spun, lo! here
    is fatal Death.
All men must dye, and so must I, this cannot
    be revoked,
For Adam's sake, this word God spake, when he
    so high provoke'd.
Yet live I shall, this life's but small, in

place of highest bliss,
Where I shall have all I can crave, no life is
     like to this.
For what's this life but care and strife? since
     first we came from womb,
Our strength doth waste, our time doth hast and
     then we go to th' Tomb.
O Bubble blast, how long can'st last? that
     always art a breaking,
No sooner blown, but dead and gone ev'n as a
     word that's speaking,
O whil'st I live this grace me give, I doing
     good may be,
Then death's arrest I shall count best because
     it's thy degree.
Bestow much cost, there's nothing lost to make
     Salvation sure,
O great's the gain, though got with pain, comes
     by profession pure.
The race is run, the field is won, the victory's
     mine, I see,
For ever know thou envious foe the foyle belongs
     to thee.

This is simply very pious and unexceptionable doggerel and no one
would admit such fact more quickly than Mistress Anne herself,
who laid it away in after days in her drawer, with a smile at the
metre and a sigh for the miserable time it chronicled. There were
many of them, for among the same papers is a shorter burst of
trouble:

UPON SOME DISTEMPER OF BODY.

In anguish of my heart repleat with woes,
And wasting pains, which best my body knows,
In tossing slumbers on my wakeful bed,
Bedrencht with tears that flow from mournful
head, Till nature had exhausted all her store,
Then eyes lay dry disabled to weep more;
And looking up unto his Throne on high,
Who sendeth help to those in misery;
He chas'd away those clouds and let me see,
My Anchor cast i' th' vale with safety,
He eas'd my soul of woe, my flesh of pain,
And brought me to the shore from troubled Main.

The same brooding and saddened spirit is found in some verses of
the same period and written probably just before the birth of her
third child, the latter part containing a touch of jealous
apprehension that has been the portion of many a young mother, and
that indicates more of human passion than could be inferred from
anything in her first attempt at verse.

All things within this fading world hath
end, Adversity doth still our joys attend;
No tyes so strong, no friends so dear and sweet
But with death's parting blow is sure to meet.
The sentence past is most irrevocable
A common thing, yet oh, inevitable;

How soon, my Dear, death may my steps attend,
How soon 't may be thy Lot to lose thy friend!
We both are ignorant, yet love bids me
These farewell lines to recommend to thee,
That when that knot's untyed that made us one, I
may seem thine, who in effect am none.
And if I see not half my dayes that's due,
What nature would, God grant to yours and you;
The many faults that well you know I have,
Let be interred in my oblivious
grave; If any worth or virtue were in
me,
Let that live freshly in thy memory,
And when thou feel'st no grief as I no harms,
Yet love thy dead, who long lay in thine arms:
And when thy loss shall be repaid with gains
Look to my little babes my dear remains,
And if thou love thyself, or loved'st me,
These O protect from step-Dames injury.
And if chance to thine eyes shall bring this verse,
With some sad sighs honor my absent Herse;
And kiss this paper for thy love's dear sake
Who with salt tears this last farewell did take.
                    --_A. B._

CHAPTER V.

OLD FRIENDS AND NEW.

In spite of the fits of depression evident in most of the quotations
thus far given, there were many alleviations, as life settled into
more tolerable conditions, and one chief one was now very near.
Probably no event in the first years of Anne
Bradstreet's life in the little colony had as much significance
for her as the arrival at Boston in 1633, of the Rev. John Cotton,
her father's friend, and one of the strongest influences in the
lives of both English and American Puritans. She was still living
in Cambridge and very probably made one of the party who went in
from there to hear his first sermon before the Boston church. He had
escaped from England with the utmost difficulty, the time of
freedom allowed him by King James who admired his learning, having
ended so thoroughly that he was hunted like an escaped convict.
Fearless and almost reckless, the Colonial ministers wondered at
his boldness, a brother of Nathaniel Ward saying as he and some
friends "spake merrily" together: "Of all men in the world, I envy
Mr. Cotton of Boston, most; for he doth nothing in way of
conformity, and yet hath his liberty, and I do everything in that
way and cannot enjoy mine."

The child born on the stormy passage over, and who in good time
became Anne Bradstreet's son-in-law, marrying her daughter Dorothy
in 1654, appeared with the father and mother at the first public
service after his arrival, and before it was positively decided
that he should remain in Boston. The baptism, contrary to the
usual custom of having it take place, not later than ten days
after birth, had been delayed, and Winthrop gives a characteristic

picture of the scene: "The Lord's day following, he (Mr. Cotton) exercised in the afternoon, and being to be admitted, he signified his desire and readiness to make his confession according to order, which he said might be sufficient in declaring his faith about baptism (which he then desired for their child, born in their passage, and therefore named Seaborn). He gave two reasons why he did not baptize it at sea (not for want of fresh water, for he held sea-water would have served): 1st, because they had no settled congregation there; 2d, because a minister hath no power to give the seals, but in his own congregation."

Some slight question, as to whether Boston alone, or the colony at large should be taxed for his support was settled with little difficulty, and on Sept. 10, another gathering from all the neighboring towns, witnessed his induction into the new church a ceremony of peculiar solemnity, preceded by a fast, and followed by such feasting as the still narrow stores of the people admitted.

No one can estimate the importance of this occasion, who does not realize what a minister meant in those first days, when the sermon held for the majority the sole opportunity of intellectual stimulus as well as spiritual growth. The coming of John Cotton to Boston, was much as if Phillips Brooks should bestow himself upon the remotest English settlement in Australia, or a missionary station in northern Minnesota, and a ripple of excitement ran through the whole community. It meant keener political as well as religious life, for the two went side by side. Mather wrote later of New England: "It is a country whose interests were most remarkably and generally enwrapped in its ecclesiastical circumstances," and he added: "The gospel has evidently been the making of our towns."

It was the deacons and elders who ruled public affairs, always under direction of well-nigh supreme authority vested in the minister. There was reason for such faith in them. "The objects of much public deference were not unaware of their authority; they seldom abused it; they never forgot it. If ever men, for real worth and greatness, deserved such pre-eminence, they did; they had wisdom, great learning, great force of will, devout consecration, philanthropy, purity of life. For once in the history of the world, the sovereign places were filled by the sovereign men. They bore themselves with the air of leaderships; they had the port of philosophers, noblemen and kings. The writings of our earliest times are full of reference to the majesty of their looks, the awe inspired by their presence, the grandeur and power of their words."

New England surely owes something of her gift of "ready and commanding speech," to these early talkers, who put their whole intellectual force into a sermon, and who thought nothing of a prayer lasting for two hours and a sermon for three or even four. Nathaniel Ward, whose caustic wit spared neither himself nor the most reverend among his brethren, wrote in his "Simple Cobbler": "We have a strong weakness in New England, that when we are speaking, we know not how to conclude. We make many ends, before we make an end.... We cannot help it, though we can; which is the arch infirmity in all morality. We are so near the west pole, that our longitudes are as long as any wise man would wish and somewhat longer. I scarce know any adage more grateful than '_Grata brevitas_'."

Mr. Cotton was no exception to this rule, but his hearers would not have had him shorter. It was, however, the personality of the man that carried weight and nothing that he has left for a mocking generation to wonder over gives slightest hint of reason for the spell he cast over congregations, under the cathedral towers, or in the simple meeting house in the new Boston. The one man alive, who, perhaps, has gone through his works conscientiously and hopefully, Moses Coit Tyler, writes of John Cotton's works: "These are indeed clear and cogent in reasoning; the language is well enough, but that is all. There are almost no remarkable merits in thought or style. One wanders through these vast tracts and jungles of Puritanic discourse--exposition, exhortation, logic- chopping, theological hair-splitting--and is unrewarded by a single passage of eminent force or beauty, uncheered even by the felicity of a new epithet in the objurgation of sinners, or a new tint in the landscape-painting of hell."

Hubbard wrote, while he still lived: "Mr. Cotton had such an insinuating and melting way in his preaching, that he would usually carry his very adversary captive, after the triumphant chariot of his rhetoric," but "the chariot of his rhetoric ceased to be triumphant when the master himself ceased to drive it," and we shall never know the spell of his genius. For one who had shown himself so uncompromising in action where his own beliefs were concerned, he was singularly gentle and humble. Followed from his church one day, by a specially sour and peevish fanatic, who announced to him with a frown that his ministry had become dark and flat, he replied:

"Both, brother--it may be both; let me have your prayers that it may be otherwise."

Such a nature would never revolt against the system of spiritual cross-questioning that belonged to every church, and it is easy to see how his hold on his congregation was never lost, even at the stormiest episode in his New England career.

The people flocked to hear him, and until the removal to Ipswich, there is no doubt that Anne Bradstreet and her husband met him often, and that he had his share in confirming her faith and stimulating her thought. Dudley and he remained friends to the end, and conferred often on public as well as private matters, but there are no family details save the record of the marriage in later years, which united them all more closely, than even their common suffering had done.

Health alone, or the want of it, gave sufficient reason for at least a shadow of gloom, and there were others as substantial, for fresh changes were at hand, and various circumstances had brought her family under a general criticism against which Anne Bradstreet always revolted. Minute personal criticism was the order of the day, considered an essential in holding one another in the straight path, and the New England relish for petty detail may have had its origin in this religious gossip. As usual the first trouble would seem to have arisen from envy, though undoubtedly its originator strenuously denied any such suspicion. The houses at Cambridge had gradually been made more and more comfortable, though even in the beginning, they were the rudest of structures, the roofs covered with thatch, the fire-places generally made of rough stones and the chimneys of boards plastered with clay. To shelter was the only requisite demanded, but Dudley, who desired something more, had already come under public censure, the governor and other assistants joining in the reproach that "he did not well to bestow such cost about wainscotting and adorning his house in the beginning of a plantation, both in regard to the expense, and the example."

This may have been one of the "new customs" at which poor Anne's "heart rose, for none of the company, not even excepting the governor, had come from as stately and well-ordered a home as theirs, the old castle still testifying to the love of beauty in its ancient owners." Dudley's excuse was, however, accepted, "that it was for the warmth of his house, and the charge was but little, being but clapboards nailed to the wall in the form of wainscot."

The disagreement on this question of adornment was not the only reason why a removal to Ipswich, then known as Agawam, may have seemed desirable. Dudley, who was some thirteen years older than the Governor, and whose capacity for free speech increased with every year, had criticised sharply the former's unexpected removal to Boston, and placable as Winthrop always was, a little feeling had arisen, which must have affected both families. The first open indication of Dudley's money-loving propensities had also been made a matter of discussion, and was given "in some bargains he had made with some poor members of the same congregation, to whom he had sold seven bushels and a half of corn, to receive ten for it after harvest, which the governor and some others held to be oppressing usury."

Dudley contested the point hotly, the governor taking no "notice of these speeches, and bore them with more patience than he had done upon a like occasion at another time," but the breach had been made, and it was long before it ceased to trouble the friends of both. With all his self-sacrifice, Dudley desired leadership, and the removal to Ipswich gave him more fully the position he craved, as simply just acknowledgment of his services to the Colony, than permanent home at Cambridge could have done. Objections were urged against the removal, and after long discussion waxing hotter and hotter Dudley resigned, in a most Puritan fit of temper, leaving the council in a passion and "clapping the door behind him." Better thoughts came to all. The gentle temper of both wife and daughter quieted him, and disposed him to look favorably upon the letter in which the council refused to accept his resignation, and this was the last public occasion upon which such scandal arose. But Ipswich was a safe harbor, and life there would hold fewer thorns than seemed sown in the Cambridge surroundings, and we may feel sure, that in spite of hardships, the long-suffering Anne and her mother welcomed the change, when it had once been positively decided upon.

The most serious objection arose from the more exposed situation of Ipswich and the fact that the Indians were becoming more and more troublesome. The first year, however, passed in comparative quiet. A church was organized, sermons being the first necessity thought of for every plantation, and "Mr. Wilson, by leave of the congregation of Boston whereof he was pastor, went to Agawam to teach the people of that plantation, because they had yet no minister," to be succeeded shortly by Nathaniel Ward, a man of most intense nature and personality, who must have had marked effect on every mind brought under his influence. A worker of prodigious energy, he soon broke down, and after two years of pastorship, left Ipswich to become a few years later, one of the commission appointed to frame laws for the Colony and to write gradually one of the most distinctive books in early American literature, "The Simple Cobbler of Agawam." That he became the strong personal friend of the Bradstreet family was natural, for not only were they of the same social status, but sympathetic in many points, though Simon Bradstreets' moderation and tolerant spirit undoubtedly fretted the uncompromising Puritan whose opinions were as stiff and incisive as his way of putting them. An extensive traveller, a man of ripe culture, having been a successful lawyer before the ministry attracted him, he was the friend of Francis Bacon, of Archbishop Usher and the famous Heidelberg theologian, David Pareus. He had travelled widely and knew men and manners, and into the exhortations and expoundings of his daily life, the unfoldings of the complicated religious experience demanded of every Puritan, must have crept many a reminiscence of old days, dear to the heart of Anne Bradstreet, who, no matter what theory she deemed it best to follow, was at heart, to the end of her life a monarchist. We may know with what interest she would listen, and may fancy the small Simon and Dorothy standing near as Puritan discipline allowed, to hear tales of Prince Rupert, whom Nathaniel Ward had held as a baby in his arms, and of whom he wrote what we may be sure he had often said: "I have had him in my arms; . . . I wish I had him there now. If I mistake not, he promised then to be a good prince; but I doubt he hath forgot it. If I thought he would not be angry with me, I would pray hard to his Maker to make him a right Roundhead, a wise-hearted Palatine, a thankful man to the English; to forgive all his sins, and at length to save his soul, notwithstanding all his God-damn-me's."

Even in these early days, certain feminine pomps and vanities had emigrated with their owners, and much disconcerted the energetic preacher. Anne Bradstreet had no share in them, her gentle simplicity making her always choose the least obtrusive form of speech and action, as well as dress, but she must have smiled over the fierceness with which weaker sisters were attacked, and perhaps have sought to change the attitude of this chronic fault- finder; "a sincere, witty and valiant grumbler," but always a grumbler, to whom the fashions of the time seemed an outrage on common sense. He devotes a separate section of his book to them, and the delinquencies of women in general because they were "deficients or redundants not to be brought under any rule," and therefore not entitled to "pester better matter with such stuff," and then announces that he proposes, "for this once to borrow a little of their loose-tongued liberty, and mis-spend a word or two upon their long-waisted but short-skirted patience." "I honor the woman that can honor herself with her attire," he goes on, his wrath rising as he writes; "a good text always deserves a fair margent, but as for a woman who lives but to ape the newest court-fashions, I look at her as the very gizzard of a trifle, the product of a quarter of a cipher, the epitome of nothing; fitter to be kicked, if she were of a kickable substance, than either

honored or humored. To speak moderately, I truly confess, it is
beyond the ken of my understanding to conceive how those women
should have any true grace or valuable virtue, that have so little
wit as to disfigure themselves with such exotic garbs, as not only
dismantles their native, lovely lustre, but transclouts them into
gaunt bar-geese, ill-shapen, shotten shell-fish, Egyptian
hieroglyphics, or at the best into French flirts of the pastry,
which a proper English woman should scorn with her heels. It is no
marvel they wear trails on the hinder part of their heads; having
nothing it seems in the forepart but a few squirrels' brains to
help them frisk from one ill-favored fashion to another.... We
have about five or six of them in our colony; if I see any of
them accidentally, I cannot cleanse my fancy for a month
after.... If any man think I have spoken rather merrily than
seriously, he is much mistaken; I have written what I write, with
all the indignation I can, and no more than I ought."

Let it be remembered, that these ladies with "squirrels brains,"
are the "grandmothers" whose degenerate descendants we are daily
accused of being. It is an old tune, but the generations have
danced to it since the world began, each with a profound
conviction of its newness, and their own success in following its
lead. Nor was he alone in his indignation, for even in the midst
of discussions on ordnance, and deep perplexities over unruly
settlers, the grave elders paused, and as Winthrop records:

"At the lecture in Boston a question was propounded about veils. Mr.
Cotton concluded, that where (by the custom of the place) they were
not a sign of the woman's subjection, they were not commanded by the
apostle. Mr. Endecott opposed, and did maintain it by the general
arguments brought by the apostle. After some debate, the governor,
perceiving it to grow to some earnestness, interposed,
and so it brake off." Isaiah had protested, before Nathaniel Ward or
the Council echoed him, but if this is the attitude the sturdy preacher
held toward the women of his congregation, he must have found it
well to resign his place to his successor, also a
Nathaniel, Nathaniel Rogers, one of the row of "nine small
children," still to be seen in the New England Primer, gazing upon
the martyr, John Rogers, the famous preacher of Dedham, whose
gifts of mind and soul made him a shining mark for persecution,
and whose name is still honored in his descendants.

Of less aggressive and incisive nature than Nathaniel Ward, he was
a man of profound learning, his son and grandson succeeding him at
Ipswich, and the son, who had accompanied him from England
becoming the President of Harvard College. His sympathy with Simon
Bradstreet's moderate and tolerant views, at once brought them
together, and undoubtedly made him occasionally a thorn in the
side of Governor Dudley, who felt then, precisely the same
emotions as in later life were chronicled in his one attempt at
verse:

"Let men of God in Courts and Churches watch,
O'er such as do a Toleration hatch,
Lest that ill egg bring forth a cockatrice
To poison all with Heresie and Vice."

Nathaniel Rogers has left no written memorial save a tract in the
interest of this most objectionable toleration, in which, while

favoring liberty and reformation, he censured those who had brought false charges against the king, and as a result, was accused of being one of the king's agents in New England. Anne Bradstreet's sympathies were even more strongly with him than those of her husband, and in the quiet listening to the arguments which went on, she had rarest opportunity for that gradual accumulation of real worldly wisdom to be found in many of her "Reflections" in prose.

At present there was more room for apprehension than reflection. Indian difficulties were more and more pressing, and in Sept., 1635, the General Court had included Ipswich in the order that no dwelling-house should be more than half a mile from the meeting-house, it being impossible to guard against the danger of coming and going over longer space. The spring of 1636-7 brought still more stringent care. Watches were kept and no one allowed to travel without arms. The Pequot war was the culmination for the time, the seed of other and more atrocious conflicts to come, and whatever the judgment of to-day may be on the causes which brought such results, the terror of the settlers was a very real and well-grounded fact. As with Deerfield at a later date, they were protected from Indian assaults, only by "a rude picketted fort. Sentinels kept guard every night; even in the day time, no one left his door-steps without a musket; and neighborly communication between the houses was kept up principally by underground passages from cellar to cellar."

Mr. Daniel Dennison, who had married Anne Bradstreet's sister, was chosen captain for Ipswich and remained so for many years. As the Indians were driven out, they concentrated in and about New Hampshire, which, being a frontier colony, knew no rest from peril day and night, but it was many years before any Massachusetts settler dared move about with freedom, and the perpetual apprehension of every woman who dreaded the horrible possibilities of Indian outrage, must have gone far toward intensifying and grinding in the morbid sensitiveness which even to-day is part of the genuine New England woman's character. The grim details of expeditions against them were known to every child. The same impatience of any word in their favor was shown then, as we find it now in the far West, where their treachery and barbarity is still a part of the story of to-day, and Johnson, in his "Wonder-Working Providence," gives one or two almost incredible details of warfare against them with a Davidic exultation over the downfall
of so pestilent an enemy, that is more Gothic than Christian.

"The Lord in mercy toward his poor churches, having thus destroyed these bloody, barbarous Indians, he returns his people in safety to their vessels, where they take account of their prisoners. The squaws and some young youths they brought home with them; and finding the men to be deeply guilty of the crimes they undertook the war for, they brought away only their heads."

Such retribution seemed just and right, but its effect on Puritan character was hardly softening, and was another unconscious factor in that increasing ratio of hatred against all who opposed them, whether in religious belief, or in the general administration of affairs. In these affairs every woman was interested to a degree that has had no parallel since, unless it may be, on the Southern side during our civil war. Politics and religion were one, and

removal to Ipswich had not deadened the interest with which they
watched and commented on every fluctuation in the stormy situation
at "home," as they still called England, Cotton taking active part
in all discussions as to Colonial action.

It was at this period that she wrote the poem, "A Dialogue between
Old England and New," which holds the political situation at that
time. Many of the allusions in the first edition, were altered in
the second, for as Charles II. had then begun his reign, loyalty
was a necessity, and no strictures upon kings could be allowed.
The poem, which is rather a summary of political difficulties,
has its own interest, as showing how thoroughly she had caught
the spirit of the time, as well as from the fact that it was quoted
as authority by the wisest thinkers of the day, and regarded with
an awe and admiration we are hardly likely to share, as the
phenomenal work of a phenomenal woman.

A DIALOGUE BETWEEN OLD ENGLAND AND
NEW, CONCERNING THEIR PRESENT
TROUBLES.
Anno, 1642.

NEW ENGLAND.

Alas, dear Mother, fairest Queen and best,
With honour, wealth and peace happy and blest;
What ails thee hang thy head and cross thine arms?
And sit i' th' dust, to sigh these sad alarms?
What deluge of new woes thus overwhelme
The glories of thy ever famous Realme?
What means this wailing tone, this mournful guise?
Ah, tell thy daughter, she may sympathize.

OLD ENGLAND.

Art ignorant indeed of these my woes?
Or must my forced tongue my griefs disclose?
And must myself dissect my tatter'd state,
Which mazed Christendome stands wond'ring at?
And thou a child, a Limbe, and dost not feel
My fainting weakened body now to reel?
This Physick purging portion I have taken,
Will bring Consumption, or an Ague
quaking, Unless some Cordial, thou fetch
from high, Which present help may ease my
malady.
If I decease, dost think thou shalt survive?
Or by my wasting state dost think to thrive?
Then weigh our case, if't be not justly sad;
Let me lament alone, while thou art glad.

NEW ENGLAND.

And thus (alas) your state you much deplore,
In general terms, but will not say wherefore;
What medicine shall I seek to cure this woe
If th' wound so dangerous I may not know?
But you, perhaps, would have me ghess it out,
What hath some Hengist like that Saxon stout,
By fraud or force usurp'd thy flow'ring crown,
Or by tempestuous warrs thy fields trod down?

Or hath Canutus, that brave valiant Dane,
The Regal peacefull Scepter from the tane?
Or is't a Norman, whose victorious hand
With English blood bedews thy conquered land?
Or is't Intestine warrs that thus offend?
Do Maud and Stephen for the crown contend?
Do Barons rise and side against their King,
And call in foreign aid to help the thing?
Must Edward be deposed? or is't the hour
That second Richard must be clapt i' th' tower?
Or is't the fatal jarre again begun
That from the red white pricking roses sprung?
Must Richmond's aid, the Nobles now implore,
To come and break the Tushes of the Boar?
If none of these, dear Mother, what's your woe?
Pray do you fear Spain's bragging Armado?
Doth your Allye, fair France, conspire your
wrack, Or do the Scots play false behind your
back? Doth Holland quit you ill for all your love?
Whence is the storm from Earth or Heaven above?
Is't drought, is't famine, or is't pestilence,
Dost feel the smart or fear the Consequence?
Your humble Child intreats you, shew your
grief, Though Arms nor Purse she hath for your
relief, Such is her poverty; yet shall be found
A Suppliant for your help, as she is bound.

OLD ENGLAND.

I must confess, some of those sores you name,
My beauteous body at this present maime;
But forreign foe, nor feigned friend I fear,
For they have work enough, (thou knowst) elsewhere.
Nor is it Alce's Son nor Henrye's daughter,
Whose proud contention cause this slaughter;
Nor Nobles siding to make John no King,
French Jews unjustly to the Crown to bring;
No Edward, Richard, to lose rule and life,
Nor no Lancastrians to renew old strife;
No Duke of York nor Earl of March to soyle
Their hands in kindred's blood whom they did
foil. No crafty Tyrant now usurps the Seat,
Who Nephews slew that so he might be great;
No need of Tudor Roses to unite,
None knows which is the Red or which the White;
Spain's braving Fleet a second time is sunk,
France knows how oft my fury she hath drunk;
By Edward third, and Henry fifth of fame
Her Lillies in mine Arms avouch the same,
My sister Scotland hurts me now no more,
Though she hath been injurious heretofore;
What Holland is I am in some suspence,
But trust not much unto his excellence.
For wants, sure some I feel, but more I fear,
And for the Pestilence, who knows how near
Famine and Plague, two Sisters of the Sword,
Destruction to a Land doth soon afford.
They're for my punishment ordain'd on high,
Unless our tears prevent it speedily.

But yet I answer not what you demand
To shew the grievance of my troubled Land?
Before I tell the Effect I'le shew the Cause,
Which are my sins, the breach of sacred Laws,
Idolatry, supplanter of a nation,
With foolish Superstitious Adoration,
Are liked and countenanced by men of might
The gospel trodden down and hath no right;
Church offices were sold and bought for gain,
That Pope had hoped to find Rome here again;
For Oaths and Blasphemies did ever Ear
From Belzebub himself such language hear?
What scorning of the saints of the most high,
What injuries did daily on them lye,
What false reports, what nick-names did they take
Not for their own but for their Master's sake?

And thou, poor soul, wert jeer'd among the rest,
Thy flying for the truth was made a jest
For Sabbath-breaking, and for drunkenness,
Did ever loud profaneness more express?
From crying blood yet cleansed am not I,
Martyrs and others, dying causelessly.
How many princely heads on blocks laid down
For nought but title to a fading crown!
'Mongst all the crueltyes by great ones done,
Of Edward's youths, and Clarence hapless son,
O Jane, why didst thou dye in flow'ring prime?
Because of royal stem, that was thy crime.
For bribery, Adultery and lyes,
Where is the nation I can't parallize?
With usury, extortion and oppression,
These be the Hydraes of my stout transgression.
These be the bitter fountains, heads and roots,
Whence flowed the source, the sprigs, the boughs, and fruits,
Of more than thou canst hear or I relate,
That with high hand I still did perpetrate;
For these were threatened the woful day
I mockt the Preachers, put it far away;
The Sermons yet upon Record do stand
That cri'd destruction to my wicked land;
I then believed not, now I feel and see,
The plague of stubborn incredulity.

Some lost their livings, some in prison pent, Some
fin'd from house and friends to exile went. Their
silent tongues to heaven did vengeance cry, Who
saw their wrongs, and hath judg'd righteously, And
will repay it seven fold in my lap;
This is forerunner of my After clap.
Nor took I warning by my neighbors'
falls, I saw sad Germany's dismantled
walls,
I saw her people famish'd, nobles slain,
The fruitful land a barren Heath remain.
I saw immov'd her Armyes foil'd and fled,
Wives forc'd, babes toss'd, her houses calimed. I
saw strong Rochel yielded to her Foe,
Thousands of starved Christians there also

I saw poor Ireland bleeding out her last,
Such crueltyes as all reports have passed;
Mine heart obdurate stood not yet aghast.
Now sip I of that cup, and just't may be
The bottome dreggs reserved are for me.

NEW ENGLAND.

To all you've said, sad Mother, I assent,
Your fearful sins great cause there's to lament,
My guilty hands in part, hold up with you,
A Sharer in your punishment's my due.
But all you say amounts to this affect,
Not what you feel but what you do expect, Pray
in plain terms what is your present grief? Then
let's joyn heads and hearts for your relief.

OLD ENGLAND.

Well to the matter then, there's grown of late
'Twixt King and Peers a Question of State,
Which is the chief, the law or else the King.
One said, it's he, the other no such thing.
'Tis said, my beter part in Parliament
To ease my groaning land, shew'd their intent,
To crush the proud, and right to each man deal,
To help the Church, and stay the Common-weal
So many obstacles came in their way,
As puts me to a stand what I should say;
Old customes, new prerogatives stood on,
Had they not held Law fast, all had been gone;
Which by their prudence stood them in such stead
They took high Strafford lower by the head.
And to their Land be't spoke, they held i' th' tower
All England's Metropolitane that hour;
This done, an act they would have passed fain
No Prelate should his Bishoprick retain;
Here tugged they hard (indeed), for all men saw
This must be done by Gospel, not by law.
Next the Militia they urged sore,
This was deny'd (I need not say wherefore),
The King displeas'd at York himself absents,
They humbly beg return, shew their intents;
The writing, printing, posting too and fro,
Shews all was done, I'll therefore let it go;

But now I come to speak of my disaster,
Contention grown, 'twixt Subjects and their Master;
They worded it so long, they fell to blows,
That thousands lay on heaps, here bleeds my woes; I
that no wars so many years have known,
Am now destroy'd and slaughter'd by mine own;
But could the Field alone this strife decide,
One Battle two or three I might abide.
But these may be beginnings of more woe
Who knows but this may be my overthrow?
Oh, pity me in this sad Perturbation,
My plundered Towns, my houses devastation,
My weeping Virgins and my young men slain;

My wealthy trading fall'n, my dearth of grain,
The seed times come, but ploughman hath no hope
Because he knows not who shall inn his Crop!
The poor they want their pay, their Children bread,
Their woful--Mothers' tears unpittied.
If any pity in thy heart remain,
Or any child-like love thou dost retain,
For my relief, do what there lyes in thee,
And recompence that good I've done to thee.

NEW ENGLAND.

Dear Mother, cease complaints and wipe your eyes,
Shake off your dust, chear up and now arise,
You are my Mother Nurse, and I your flesh,
Your sunken bowels gladly would refresh,
Your griefs I pity, but soon hope to see,
Out of your troubles much good fruit to be; To
see those latter days of hop'd for good, Though
now beclouded all with tears and blood; After
dark Popery the day did clear,
But now the Sun in's brightness shall appear;
Blest be the Nobles of thy Noble Land,
With ventur'd lives for Truth's defence that stand;
Blest be thy Commons, who for common good,
And thy infringed Laws have boldly stood;
Blest be thy Counties, who did aid thee still,
With hearts and States to testifie their will;
Blest be thy Preachers, who did chear thee on,
O cry the Sword of God and Gideon;
And shall I not on them with Mero's curse,
That help thee not with prayers, Arms and purse?
And for myself let miseries abound,
If mindless of thy State I ere be found.
These are the dayes the Churches foes to crush, To
root out Popelings, head, tail, branch and rush;
Let's bring Baals' vestments forth to make a fire,
Their Mytires, Surplices, and all their Tire,
Copes, Rotchets, Crossiers, and such empty trash,
And let their Names consume, but let the flash
Light Christendome, and all the world to see,
We hate Romes whore, with all her trumpery.

Go on, brave Essex, with a Loyal heart,
Not false to King, nor to the better part;
But those that hurt his people and his Crown,
As duty binds, expel and tread them down,
And ye brave Nobles, chase away all fear,
And to this hopeful Cause closely adhere;
O Mother, can you weep and have such Peers,
When they are gone, then drown yourself in tears,
If now you weep so much, that then no more
The briny Ocean will o'erflow your shore.
These, these are they I trust, with Charles our King,
Out of all mists, such glorious days shall bring;
That dazzled eyes beholding much shall wonder,
At that thy settled peace, thy wealth and splendor.
Thy Church and weal establish'd in such manner,
That all shall joy, that then display'st thy Banner;

And discipline erected so I trust,
That nursing Kings shall come and lick thy dust.

Then justice shall in all thy courts take place,
Without respect of person, or of case;
Then Bribes shall cease, and Suits shall not stick long
Patience and purse of Clients oft to wrong;
Then high Commissions shall fall to decay,
And Pursivants and Catchpoles want their pay.
So shall thy happy nation ever flourish,
When truth and righteousness they thus shall nourish,
When thus in peace, thine Armies brave send out,
To sack proud Rome, and all her Vassals rout;
There let thy name, thy fame and glory shine,
As did thine Ancestors in Palestine;
And let her spoyls full pay with Interest be,
Of what unjustly once she poll'd from thee,
Of all the woes thou canst, let her be sped
And on her pour the vengeance threatened;
Bring forth the Beast that rul'd the World with 's
beck, And tear his flesh, and set your feet on 's neck;
And make his filthy Den so desolate,
To th' astonishment of all that knew his state.
This done, with brandish'd Swords to Turky goe,
For then what is 't, but English blades dare do?
And lay her waste for so 's the sacred Doom,
And to Gog as thou hast done to Rome.
Oh Abraham's seed lift up your heads on high,
For sure the day of your Redemption 's nigh;
The Scales shall fall from your long blinded eyes,
And him you shall adore who now despise,
Then fulness of the Nations in shall flow,
And Jew and Gentile to one worship go;
Then follows days of happiness and rest;
Whose lot doth fall, to live therein is
blest.
No Canaanite shall then be found i' th' Land,
And holiness on horses bell's shall stand;
If this make way thereto, then sigh no more,
But if it all, thou did'st not see 't before;
Farewell, dear Mother, rightest cause prevail
And in a while, you'll tell another tale.

This, like all her earlier work, is heavy reading, the account
given by "Old Age" in her "Four Ages of Man," of what he has
seen and known of Puritan affairs, being in somewhat more lively
strain. But lively was an adjective to which Mistress Anne had a
rooted objection. Her contemporaries indulged in an occasional
solemn pun, but the only one in her writings is found in the
grim turn on Laud's name, in the "Dialogue" just quoted, in
which is also a sombre jest on the beheading of Strafford.

"Old Age" recalls the same period, opening with a faint--very
faint--suggestion of Shakespeare's thought in his "Seven Ages."

"What you have been, even such have I before
And all you say, say I, and somewhat more,
Babe's innocence, youth's wildness I have seen,
And in perplexed middle Age have been;
Sickness, dangers and anxieties have past,

And on this stage am come to act my last,
I have been young and strong and wise as you;
But now _Bis pueri senes,_ is too true.
In every age I've found much vanity
An end of all perfection now I see.
It's not my valour, honor, nor my gold,
My ruined house now falling can uphold,
It's not my learning Rhetorick wit so
large,
Hath now the power, death's warfare to discharge,
It's not my goodly state, nor bed of downs
That can refresh, or ease, if Conscience frown,
Nor from Alliance can I now have hope,
But what I have done well that is my prop;
He that in youth is Godly, wise and sage,
Provides a staff then to support his Age.
Mutations great, some joyful and some sad,
In this short pilgrimage I oft have had;
Sometimes the Heavens with plenty smiled on me,
Sometime again rain'd all Adversity,
Sometimes in honor, sometimes in disgrace,
Sometime an Abject, then again in place.
Such private changes oft mine eyes have seen,
In various times of state I've also been,
I've seen a Kingdom nourish like a tree,
When it was ruled by that Celestial she;
And like a Cedar, others so surmount,
That but for shrubs they did themselves account.
Then saw I France and Holland say'd Cales won,
And Philip and Albertus half undone,
I saw all peace at home, terror to foes,
But oh, I saw at last those eyes to close.
And then methought the clay at noon grew dark,
When it had lost that radiant Sunlike Spark;
In midst of griefs I saw our hopes revive,

(For 'twas our hopes then kept our hearts alive)
We changed our queen for king under whose rayes
We joy'd in many blest and prosperous dayes.
I've seen a Prince, the glory of our land
In prime of youth seiz'd by heaven's angry hand,
Which fil'd our hearts with fears, with tears our eyes,
Wailing his fate, and our own destinies.
I've seen from Rome an execrable thing,
A Plot to blow up nobles and their King,
But saw their horrid fact soon disappointed,
And Land Nobles say'd with their annointed.
I've Princes seen to live on others' lands;
A royal one by gifts from strangers' hands
Admired for their magnanimity,
Who lost a Prince-dome and a Monarchy.
I've seen designs for Ree and Rochel crost,
And poor Palatinate forever lost.
I've seen unworthy men advanced high,
And better ones suffer extremity;
But neither favour, riches, title, State,
Could length their days or once reverse their fate.

I've seen one stab'd, and some to loose their heads,
And others fly, struck both with gilt and dread;

I've seen and so have you, for tis but late
The desolation of a goodly state,
Plotted and acted so that none can tell
Who gave the counsel, but the Prince of hell.
Three hundred thousand slaughtered innocents
By bloody, Popish, hellish miscreants;
Oh, may you live, and so you will I trust,
To see them swill in blood until they
burst.

I've seen a King by force thrust from his thrones
And an Usurper subt'ly mount thereon;
I've seen a state unmoulded, rent in twain,
But ye may live to see't made up again.
I've seen it plunder'd, taxt and soaked in blood,
But out of evill you may see much good.
What are my thoughts, this is no time to say.
Men may more freely speak another day;
These are no old-wives tales, but this is truth,
We old men love to tell what's done in
youth."

Though this is little more than rhymed chronology, there are
curious reminders here and there of the spirit of the time. Gentle
as was Anne Bradstreet's nature, it seemed to her quite natural to
write of the "bloody, Popish, hellish miscreants"--

"Oh may you live, and so you will I trust,
To see them swill in blood untill they burst."

There was reason it was true; the same reason that brings the same
thought to-day to women on the far Western frontiers, for the
Irish butcheries had been as atrocious as any Indian massacre our
own story holds. The numbers butchered were something appaling,
and Hume writes: "By some computations, those who perished by all
these cruelties are supposed to be a hundred and fifty or two
hundred thousand; by the most moderate, and probably the most
reasonable account, they are made to amount to forty thousand---if
this estimation itself be not, as is usual in such cases, somewhat
exaggerated."

Irish ferocity was more than matched by English brutality.
Puritanism softened many features of the Saxon character, but even
in the lives of the most devoted, there is a keen relish for
battle whether spiritual or actual, and a stern rejoicing in any
depth of evil that may have overtaken a foe. In spite of the
tremendous value set upon souls, indifference to human life still
ruled, and there was even a certain relish, if that life were an
enemy's, in turning it over heartily and speedily to its proper
owner, Satan. Anne Bradstreet is no exception to the rule, and her
verses hold various fierce and unexpected outbursts against enemies
of her faith or country. The constant discussion of mooted points by
the ministers as well as people, made each man the judge of
questions that agitated every mind, and problems of all natures from
national down to town meeting debates, were pondered over in every
Puritan home. Cotton's interest in detail never flagged, and
his influence was felt at every point in the Colony, and though
Ipswich, both in time and facilities for reaching it, was more
widely separated from Boston than Boston now is from the remotest
hamlet on Cape Cod, there is no doubt that Nathaniel Ward and Mr.
Cotton occasionally met and exchanged views if not pulpits, and

that the Bradstreet family were not entirely cut off from
intercourse. When Nathaniel Ward became law-maker instead of
settled minister, it was with John Cotton that he took counsel,
and Anne undoubtedly thought of the latter what his grandson
Cotton Mather at a later day wrote. "He was indeed a most
universal scholar, and a living system of the liberal arts and a
walking library."

Walking libraries were needed, for stationary ones were very
limited. Governer Dudley's, one of the largest in the Colony,
contained between fifty and sixty books, chiefly on divinity and
history, and from the latter source Anne obtained the minute
historical knowledge shown in her rhymed account of "The Four
Monarchies." It was to her father that she owed her love of books.
She calls him in one poem, "a magazine of history," and at other
points, her "guide," and "instructor," writing:

"Most truly honored and as truly dear,
If worth in me, or ought I do appear,
Who can of right better demand the same?
Then may your worthy self from whom it came?"

As at Cambridge, and in far greater degree, she was cut off from
much that had held resources there. At the worst, only a few miles
had separated them from what was fast becoming the center and soul
of the Colony. But Ipswich shut them in, and life for both
Mistress Dudley and her daughter was an anxious one. The General
Court called for the presence of both Dudley and Bradstreet, the
latter spending much of his time away, and some of the tenderest and
most natural of Anne Bradstreet's poems, was written at this time,
though regarded as too purely personal to find place in any edition of
her poems. The quiet but fervent love between them had deepened
with every year, and though no letters remain, as with Winthrop, to
evidence the steady and intense affection of both,
the "Letter to her Husband, absent upon some Publick employment,"
holds all the proof one can desire.

"My head, my heart, mine Eyes, my life, my
more, My joy, my Magazine of earthly store.
If two be one as surely thou and I,
How stayest thou there, whilst I at Ipswich lie?
So many steps, head from the heart to sever,
If but a neck, soon would we be together;
I like the earth this season mourn in black
My Sun is gone so far in 's Zodiack,
Whom whilst I joyed, nor storms nor frosts I
felt, His warmth such frigid colds did cause to
melt. My chilled limbs now nummed lye
forlorn, Return, return sweet Sol, from
Capricorn;
In this dead time, alas, what can I more
Than view those fruits which through thy heat I bore?
Which sweet contentment yield me for a space,
True, living Pictures of their Father's face.
O strange effect! now thou art Southward gone,
I weary grow, the tedious day so long;
But when thou Northward to me shalt return,
I wish my Sun may never set but burn
Within the Cancer of my glowing breast.
The welcome house of him my dearest guest.

Where ever, ever stay, and go not thence
Till nature's sad decree shall call thee hence;
Flesh of thy flesh, bone of thy bone,
I here, thou there, yet both are one."

A second one is less natural in expression, but still holds the
same longing.

Phoebus, make haste, the day's too long, be gone,
The silent nights, the fittest time for moan;
But stay this once, unto my suit give ear,
And tell my griefs in either Hemisphere.
(And if the whirling of thy wheels don't
drown'd) The woeful accents of my doleful
sound,
If in thy swift Carrier thou canst make stay, I
crave this boon, this Errand by the way,
Commend me to the man more lov'd than life,
Shew him the sorrows of his widowed wife;
My dumpish thoughts, my groans, my brakish tears,
My sobs, my longing hopes, my doubting fears,
And if he love, how can he there abide?
My Interest's more than all the world beside.
He that can tell the Starrs or Ocean sand,
Or all the grass that in the Meads do stand,
The leaves in th' woods, the hail or drops of rain,
Or in a corn field number every grain,
Or every mote that in the sunshine hops,
May count my sighs, and number all my drops:
Tell him, the countless steps that thou dost trace,
That once a day, thy Spouse thou mayst embrace;
And when thou canst not treat by loving mouth,
Thy rays afar salute her from the south.
But for one month I see no day (poor soul)
Like those far scituate under the pole,
Which day by day long wait for thy arise,
O, how they joy, when thou dost light the skyes.
O Phoebus, hadst thou but thus long from thine,
Restrained the beams of thy beloved shine,
At thy return, if so thou could'st or durst
Behold a Chaos blacker than the first.
Tell him here's worse than a confused matter,
His little world's a fathom under water,
Nought but the fervor of his ardent beams
Hath power to dry the torrent of these streams
Tell him I would say more but cannot well,
Oppressed minds, abruptest tales do tell.
Now post with double speed, mark what I says
By all our loves, conjure him not to stay."

In the third and last, there is simply an imitation of much of the
work of the seventeenth century; with its conceits and twisted
meanings, its mannerisms and baldness, but still the feeling is
there, though Mistress Bradstreet has labored painfully to make it
as unlike nature as possible.

"As loving Hind that (Hartless) wants her Deer,
Scuds through the woods and Fern with hearkening ear,
Perplext, in every bush and nook doth pry,
Her dearest Deer might answer ear or eye;

So doth my anxious soul, which now doth miss,
A dearer Deer (far dearer Heart) than this.
Still wait with doubts and hopes and failing eye;
His voice to hear or person to descry.
Or as the pensive Dove doth all alone
(On withered bough) most uncouthly bemoan
The absence of her Love and Loving Mate,
Whose loss hath made her so unfortunate;
Ev'n thus doe I, with many a deep sad groan,
Bewail my turtle true, who now is gone,
His presence and his safe return, still wooes
With thousand doleful sighs and mournful Cooes.
Or as the loving Mullet that true Fish,
Her fellow lost, nor joy nor life do wish,
But lanches on that shore there for to dye,
Where she her captive husband doth espy,
Mine being gone I lead a joyless life,
I have a living sphere, yet seem no wife;
But worst of all, to him can't steer my course,
I here, he there, alas, both kept by force;
Return, my Dear, my Joy, my only Love,
Unto thy Hinde, thy Mullet and thy Dove,
Who neither joys in pasture, house nor streams,
The substance gone, O me, these are but dreams,
Together at one Tree, O let us brouse,
And like two Turtles roost within one
house. And like the Mullets in one River
glide,
Let's still remain one till death
divide. Thy loving Love and Dearest
Dear,
At home, abroad and everywhere.
                    _A.B._"

Of a far higher order are a few lines, written at the same time,
and with no suspicion of straining or of imitation in the quiet
fervor of the words, that must have carried a thrill of deep and
exquisite happiness to the heart of the man, so loved and honored.

  "To my dear and loving Husband:
If ever two were one then surely we,
If ever man were loved by wife, then thee;
If ever wife was happy in a man,
Compare with me ye women if you can.
I prize thy love more than whole Mines of
Gold, Or all the riches that the East doth hold.
My love is such that Rivers cannot quench,
Nor ought but love from thee give recompense.
Thy love is such I can no way repay,
The heavens reward thee, manifold I pray.
Then while we live in love let's so persevere,
That when we live no more, we may live ever."

The woman who could feel such fervor as these lines express, owed
the world something more than she ever gave, but every influence
tended, as we have seen, to silence natural expression. One must
seek, however, to discover why she failed even when admitting that
failure was the only thing to be expected, and the causes are in
the nature of the time itself, the story of literary development
for that period being as complicated as politics, religion and
every other force working on the minds of men.

CHAPTER VI.

A THEOLOGICAL TRAGEDY.

It was perhaps Anne Bradstreet's youth, and a sense that she could
hardly criticise a judgment which had required the united forces
of every church in the Colony to pronounce, that made her ignore
one of the most stormy experiences of those early days, the trial
and banishment of Anne Hutchinson. Her silence is the more
singular, because the conflict was a purely spiritual one, and
thus in her eyes deserving of record. There can be no doubt that
the effect on her own spiritual and mental life must have been
intense and abiding. No children had as yet come to absorb her
thoughts and energies, and the events which shook the Colony to
the very center could not fail to leave an ineffaceable
impression. No story of personal experience is more confounding to
the modern reader, and none holds a truer picture of the time.
Governor Dudley and Simon Bradstreet were both concerned in the
whole course of the matter, which must have been discussed at home
from day to day, and thus there is every reason for giving it full
place in these pages as one of the formative forces in Anne
Bradstreet's life; an inspiration and then a warning. There are
hints that Anne resented the limitations that hedged her in, and
had small love of the mutual criticism, which made the corner
stone of Puritan life. That she cared to write had already excited
the wonder of her neighbors and Anne stoutly asserted her right to
speak freely whatever it seemed good to say, taking her stand
afterwards given in the Prologue to the first edition of her
poems, in which she wrote:

"I am obnoxious to each carping tongue
Who says my hand a needle better fits,
A Poet's pen all scorn I should thus wrong,
For such despite they cast on Female wits;
If what I do prove well, it won't advance,
They'l say it's stol'n, or else it was by chance.

"But sure the antique Greeks were far more mild,
Else of our Sexe, why feigned they those Nine
And poesy made Callippi's own Child;
So 'mongst the rest they placed the Arts Divine,
But this weak knot they will full soon untie,
The Greeks did nought but play the fools and lye."

This has a determined ring which she hastens to neutralize by a
tribute and an appeal; the one to man's superior force, the other
to his sense of justice.

"Let Greeks be Greeks, and women what they are,
Men have precedency and still excell,
It is but vain unjustly to wage warrs;
Men can do best and women know it well,
Preheminence in all and each is yours;
Yet grant some small acknowledgement of ours."

Plain speaking was a Dudley characteristic, but the fate of Anne Hutchinson silenced all save a few determined spirits, willing to face the same consequences. In the beginning, however, there could have been only welcome for a woman, whose spiritual gifts and unusual powers had made her the friend of John Cotton, and who fascinated men and woman alike. There was reason, for birth and training meant every gift a woman of that day was likely to possess. Her father, Thomas Marbury, was one of the Puritan ministers of Lincolnshire who afterward removed to London; her mother, a sister of Sir Erasmus Dryden. She was thus related in the collateral line to two of the greatest of English intellects. Free thinking and plain speaking were family characteristics, for John Dryden the poet, her second cousin, was reproached with having been an Anabaptist in his youth, and Johnathan Swift, a more distant connection, feared nothing in heaven or earth. It is no wonder, then, that even an enemy wrote of her as "the masterpiece of women's wit," or that her husband followed her lead with a devotion that never swerved. She had married him at Alford in Lincolnshire, and both were members of Mr. Cotton's congregation at Boston.

Mr. Hutchinson's standing among his Puritan contemporaries was of the highest. He had considerable fortune, and the gentlest and most amiable of dispositions. The name seems to have meant all good gifts, for the same devoted and tender relation existed between this pair as between Colonel Hutchinson and his wife. From the quiet and happy beginning of their married life to its most tragic ending, they clung together, accepting all loss as part of the cross they had taken up, when they left the ease of Lincolnshire behind, and sought in exile the freedom which intolerance denied.

It is very probable that Anne Hutchinson may have known the Dudley family after their return to Lincolnshire, and certainly in the first flush of her New England experiences was likely to have had intimate relations with them. Her opinions, so far as one can disentangle them from the mass of testimony and discussion, seem to have been in great degree, those held by the early Quakers, but they had either not fully developed in her own mind before she left England, or had not been pronounced enough to attract attention. In any case the weariness of the long voyage seems to have been in part responsible for much that followed. Endless discussions of religious subtleties were their chief occupation on board, and one of the company, the Rev. Mr. Symmes, a dogmatic and overbearing man, found himself often worsted by the quick wit of this woman, who silenced all objections, and who, with no conception of the rooted enmity she was exciting, told with the utmost freedom, past and present speculations and experiences. The long fasts, and continuous religious exercises, worked upon her enthusiast's temper, and excited by every circumstance of time and place, it is small wonder that she supposed a direct revelation had come to her, the nature of which Winthrop mentions in his History.

"One Mrs. Hutchinson, a member of the church of Boston, a woman of a ready wit and bold spirit, brought over with her two dangerous errours:

"1. That the person of the Holy Ghost dwells in a justified person.

"2. That no sanctification can help to evidence to us our justification. From these two, grew many branches; as, 1st, Our union with the Holy Ghost, so as a Christian remains dead to every spiritual action, and hath no gifts nor graces, other than such as are in hypocrites, nor any other sanctification but the Holy Ghost himself. There joined with her in these opinions a brother of hers, one Mr. Wheelwright, a silenced minister sometime in England."

Obnoxious as these doctrines came to be, she had been in New England two years before they excited special attention. Her husband served in the General Court several elections as representative for Boston, until he was excused at the desire of the church, and she herself found constant occupation in a round of kindly deeds. She denied the power of works as any help toward justification, but no woman in the Colony, gave more practical testimony of her faith or made herself more beloved. Though she had little children to care for, she found time to visit and nurse the sick, having special skill in all disorders of women. Her presence of mind, her warm sympathy and extraordinary patience made her longed for at every sick bed, and she very soon acquired the strongest influence. Dudley had made careful inquiries as to her religious standing, and must have been for the time at least, satisfied, and unusual attention was paid her by all the colonists; the most influential among them being her chief friends. Coddington, who had built the first brick house in Boston, received them warmly. Her public teaching began quietly, her ministrations by sick beds attracting many, and it is doubtful if she herself realized in the least the extent of her influence.

Governor Vane, young and ardent, the temporary idol of the Colony, who had taken the place Governor Winthrop would have naturally filled, visited her and soon became one of her most enthusiastic supporters. Just and unprejudiced as Winthrop was, this summary setting aside by a people for whom he had sacrificed himself steadily, filled him with indignation, though the record in his Journal is quiet and dignified. But naturally, it made him a sterner judge, when the time for judgment came. In the beginning, however, her work seemed simply for good. It had been the custom for the men of the Boston church to meet together on Thursday afternoons, to go over the sermon of the preceding Sunday, of which notes had been taken by every member. No women were admitted, and believing that the same course was equally desirable for her own sex, Anne Hutchinson appointed two days in the week for this purpose, and at last drew about her nearly a hundred of the principal women of the Colony. Her lovely character and spotless life, gave immense power to her words, and her teaching at first was purely practical. We can imagine Anne Bradstreet's delight in the tender and searching power of this woman, who understood intuitively every womanly need, and whose sympathy was as unfailing as her knowledge. Even for that time her Scriptural knowledge was almost phenomenal, and it is probable that, added to this, there was an unacknowledged satisfaction in an assembly from which men were excluded, though many sought admission. Mrs. Hutchinson was obliged at last to admit the crowd who believed her gifts almost divine, but refused to teach, calling upon the ministers to do this, and confining herself simply to conversation. But Boston at last seemed to have gone over wholly to her views, while churches at other points opposed them fiercely. Up to this time there had been no attempt to define the character of the Holy Ghost, but now a powerful opposition to her theory arose, and furious discussions were held in meetings and out. The very children caught the current phrases, and jeered one another as believers in the "Covenant of Grace," or the "Covenant of Works," and the year 1636 came and passed with the Colony at swords points with one another. Every difficulty was aggravated by Vane, whose youth and inexperience made it impossible for him to understand the temper of the people he ruled. The rise of differences had been so gradual that no one suspected what mischief might come till the results suddenly disclosed themselves. That vagaries and eccentricities were to be expected, never entered the minds of this people, who accepted their own departure from authority and ancient ordinances as just and right, but could never conceive that others might be justified in acting on the same principle.

To understand even in slight degree the conflict which followed, one must remember at every turn, that no interests save religious interests were of even momentary importance. Every member of the Colony had hard, laborious work to do, but it was hurried through with the utmost speed, in order to have time for the almost daily lectures and expoundings that made their delight. Certain more worldly minded among them had petitioned for a shortening of these services, but were solemnly reproved, and threatened with the "Judgment of God on their frowardness."

With minds perpetually concentrated on subtle interpretations, agreement was impossible. Natural life, denied and set aside at every point, gave place to the unnatural, and every colonist was, quite unconsciously, in a state of constant nervous tension and irritability. The questions that to us seem of even startling triviality, were discussed with a fervor and earnestness it is well nigh impossible to comprehend. They were a slight advance on the scholastic disputations of the preceding century, but they meant disagreement and heart-burnings, and the more intolerant determined on stamping out all variations from their own convictions.

Any capacity for seeking to carry out Robinson's injunction in his final sermon at Leyden seems to have died once for all, in the war of words. "I beseech you," he had said, "remember that it is an article of your church covenant, that you be ready to receive whatever truth shall be made known to you from the written word of God." There was small remnant of this spirit even among the most liberal.

Dudley was one of the chief movers in the course resolved upon, and mourned over Cotton, who still held to Anne Hutchinson, and wrote and spoke of her as one who "was well beloved, and all the faithful embraced her conference, and blessed God for her fruitful discourses."

Mr. Welde, on the contrary, one of her fiercest opponents, described her as "a woman of haughty and fierce carriage, of a nimble wit and active spirit, and a very voluble tongue, more bold than a man, though in understanding and judgment inferior to many women."

How far the object of all this confusion realized the real state of things cannot be determined. But by January, 1637, dissension had reached such a height that a fast was appointed for the Pequot war and the religious difficulties. The clergy had become her bitterest enemies, and with some reason, for through her means many of their congregations had turned against them. Mr. Wilson, once the most popular minister in Boston, had been superseded by her brother,--Mr. Wheelwright, and Boston began the heretical career which has been her portion from that day to this.

Active measures were necessary. The General Court was still governed by the clergy, and by March had settled upon its future course, and summoned Wheelwright, who was censured and found guilty of sedition. Governor Vane opposed the verdict bitterly. The chief citizens of Boston sent in a "Remonstrance," and actual anarchy seemed before them. The next Court was held at Newtown to avoid the danger of violence at Boston, and a disorderly election took place in which the Puritan Fathers came to blows, set down by Winthrop as "a laying on of hands."

The grave and reverend Wilson, excited beyond all considerations of Puritanical propriety, climbed a tree, and made a vigorous speech to the throng of people, in which many malcontents were at work urging on an opposition that proved fruitless. Vane was defeated and Winthrop again made governor, his calm forbearance being the chief safety of the divided and unhappy colonists, who resented what they settled to be tyranny, and cast about for some means of redress. None was to be had. Exile, imprisonment and even death, awaited the most eminent citizens; Winthrop's entry into Boston was met by gloomy silence, and for it all, Welde and Symmes protested Anne Hutchinson to be responsible, and denounced her as a heretic and a witch.

She in the meantime seems to have been in a state of religious exaltation which made her blind and deaf to all danger. Her meetings continued, and she in turn denounced her opponents and believed that some revelation would be given to show the justice of her claims. There was real danger at last. If the full story of these dissensions were told in England, possession of charter, which had already been threatened, might be lost entirely. Dudley was worked up to the highest pitch of apprehension, believing that if the dissension went on, there might even be a repetition of the horrors of Munster. Divided as they were, concerted action against enemies, whether Indian or foreign, could not be expected. There was danger of a general league of the New England Indians, and "when a force was ordered to take the field for the salvation of the settlements, the Boston men refused to be mustered because they suspected the chaplain, who had been designated by lot to accompany the expedition, of being under a covenant of works."

Such a state of things, if known in full at home, would shut off all emigration. That men of character and means should join them was an essential to the continued life of the Colony. Setting aside any question of their own personal convictions, their leaders saw that the continuance among them of these disturbing elements meant destruction, and Winthrop, mild and reasonable as he sought to be, wrote: "He would give them one reason, which was a ground for his judgment, and that was, for that he saw that those brethren, etc., were so divided from the rest of the country in their judgment and practice, as it could not stand with the public peace, that they should continue amongst us. So by the example of Lot in Abraham's family, and after Hagar and Ishmael, he saw they must be sent away."

With August came the famous Synod of Cambridge, the first ever held in New England, in which the Church set about defining its own position and denouncing the Hutchinsonians. Eighty-two heresies were decided to have arisen, all of which were condemned, and this being settled, Cotton was admonished, and escaped exile only by meekly explaining away his errors. Wheelwright, refusing to yield, was sentenced to imprisonment and exile; Mrs. Hutchinson's meetings were declared seditious and disorderly, and prohibited, and the Synod separated, triumphant. The field was their own.

What they had really accomplished was simply to deepen the lines and make the walls of division still higher. In later years no one cared to make public the proceedings of the body, and there is still in existence a loose paper, described by the Rev. George E. Ellis in his "Life of Anne Hutchinson"; a petition from Mr. John Higginson, son of the Salem minister ... by which it appears that he was employed by the magistrates and ministers to take down in short hand, all the debates and proceedings of the Synod. He performed the work faithfully, and having written out the voluminous record, at "the expense of much time and pains," he presented it to the Court in May, 1639. The long time that elapsed may indicate the labor. The Court accepted it, and ordered that, if approved by the ministers, after they had viewed it, it should be printed, Mr. Higginson being entitled to the profits, which were estimated as promising a hundred pounds. The writer waited with patience while his brethren examined it, and freely took their advice. Some were in favor of printing it; but others advised to the contrary, "conceiving it might possibly be an occasion of further disputes and differences both in this country and other parts of the world."

Naturally they failed to agree. The unfortunate writer, having scruples which prevented his accepting an offer of fifty pounds for the manuscript, made probably by some Hutchinsonian, waited the pleasure of the brethren, reminding them at intervals of his claim, but so far as can be discovered, failing always to make it good, and the manuscript itself disappeared, carrying with it the only tangible testimony to the bitterness and intolerance of which even the owners were in after years ashamed.

In the meantime, Harry Vane, despairing of peaceful life among his enemies, had sailed for England early in August, to pass through every phase of political and spiritual experience, and to give up his life at last on the scaffold to which the treachery of the second Charles condemned him. With his departure, no powerful friend remained to Anne Hutchinson, whose ruin had been determined upon and whose family were seeking a new and safer home. Common prudence should have made her give up her public meetings and show some deference to the powers she had always defied. Even this, however, could not have saved her, and in November, 1637, the trial began which even to-day no New Englander can recall without shame; a trial in which civil, judicial, and ecclesiastical forces all united to crush a woman, whose deepest fault was a too enthusiastic belief in her own inspiration.

Winthrop conducted the prosecution, mild and calm in manner, but resolutely bent upon punishment, and by him sat Dudley, Endicott, Bradstreet, Nowell and Stoughton; Bradstreet and Winthrop being the only ones who treated her with the faintest semblance of courtesy. Welde and Symmes, Wilson and Hugh Peters, faced her with a curious vindictiveness, and in the throng of excited listeners, hardly a friendly face met her eyes, even her old friend, John Cotton, having become simply a timid instrument of her persecutors.

The building in which the trial took place was thronged. Hundreds who had been attracted by her power, looked on: magistrates and ministers, yeoman and military, the sad colored garments of the gentry in their broad ruffs and high crowned hats, bringing out the buff coats of the soldiers, and the bright bodices of the women, who clung to the vanities of color, and defied the tacit law that limited them to browns and drabs. Over all hung the gray November sky, and the chill of the dolorous month was in the air, and did its work toward intensifying the bitterness which ruled them all.

It is doubtful if Anne Bradstreet made one of the spectators. Her instinct would have been to remain away, for the sympathy she could not help but feel, could not betray itself, without at once ranking her in opposition to the judgment of both husband and father. Anne Hutchinson's condition was one to excite the compassion and interest of every woman, but it had no such effect on her judges, who forced her to stand till she nearly fell from exhaustion. Food was denied her; no counsel was allowed, or the presence of any friend who could have helped by presence, if in no other way.

Feeble in body, depressed and anxious in mind, one reacted on another, and the marvel is not that she here and there contradicted herself, or lost patience, but that any coherence or power of argument remained.

The records of the trial show both. Winthrop opened it by making a general charge of heresy, and Anne demanded a specific one, and when the charge of holding unlawful meetings was brought, denied it so energetically and effectually, that Winthrop had no more words and turned the case over to the less considerate Dudley, whose wrath at her presumption knew no bounds. Both he and the ministers who swore against her, used against her statements which she had made in private interviews with them, which she had supposed to be confidential, but which were now reported in detail. Naturally she reproached the witnesses with being informers, and they justified their course hotly. Mr. Cotton's testimony, given most reluctantly, confirmed their statements. The chief grievance was not her meetings, so much as the fact that she had publicly criticized the teaching and religious character of the ministers, insisting that Mr. Cotton alone had the full "thorough-furnishing" for such work. Deep but smothered feeling was apparent in every word the initiated witnesses spoke, and the magistrate, Mr. Coddington, in vain assured them, that even if she had said all this and more, no real harm had been done. Cotton sided with him, and spoke so powerfully that there was a slight diversion in her favor, rendered quite null by her claim of immediate inspiration in what she had done.

The records at this point, show none of the excitement, the hysterical ecstasy which marked the same declaration in the case of some among the Quakers who were afterward tried. Her calmness increased instead of lessening. On the score of contempt of the ministers it had become evident that she could not be convicted, but this claim to direct revelation, was an even more serious matter. Scripture might be twisted to the point of dismemberment, so long as one kept to the text, and made no pretence of knowledge beyond it; contention within these bounds was lawful and honorable, and the daily food of these argumentative Christians who gave themselves to the work of combining intellectual freedom and spiritual slavery, with perpetual surprise at any indication that the two were incompatible.

The belief in personal revelation, actually no more than a deep impression produced by long pondering over some passage, was really part of the Puritan faith, but the united company had no thought of discovering points of harmony, or brushing aside mere phrases which simply concealed the essential truth held by both. Such belief could come only from the direct prompting of Satan, and when she firmly and solemnly declared that whatever way their judgment went, she should be saved from calamity, that she was and should remain, in direct communion with God, and that they were simply pitiless persecutors of the elect, the wrath was instant and boundless. A unanimous vote condemned her at once, and stands in the records of Massachusetts as follows:

"Mrs. Hutchinson, the wife of Mr. William Hutchinson, being convicted for traducing the ministers and their ministry in the country, she declared voluntarily her revelations, and that she should be delivered, and the Court ruined with their posterity, and thereupon was banished, and in the meanwhile was committed to Mr. Joseph Welde (of Roxbury) until the Court shall dispose of her."

Her keeper for the winter was the brother of her worst enemy. She was to be kept there at the expense of her husband, but forbidden to pursue any of her usual occupations. Naturally she sunk into a deep melancholy, in no wise lessened by constant visits from the ministers, who insisted upon discussing her opinions, and who wrought upon her till she was half distracted. They accused her of falsehoods, declaring that she held "gross errors, to the number of thirty or thereabouts," and badgering the unhappy creature till it is miraculous that any spirit remained. Then came the church trial, more legitimate, but conducted with fully as much virulence as the secular one, the day of the weekly lecture, Thursday, being chosen, as that which brought together the greatest number of people.

The elders accused her of deliberate lying, and point by point, brought up the thirty errors. Of some she admitted her possible mistake; others she held to strenuously, but all were simply speculation, not one having any vital bearing on faith or life.

Public admonition was ordered, but before this her two sons had
been publicly censured for refusing to join in signing the paper
which excommunicated her, Mr. Cotton addressing them "most
pitifully and pathetically," as "giving way to natural affection
and as tearing the very bowels of their souls by hardening their
mother in sin." Until eight in the evening, an hour equivalent to
eleven o'clock with our present habits, the congregation listened
to question and answer and admonition, in which last, Mr. Cotton
"spake to the sisters of the church, and advised them to take heed
of her opinions, and to withhold all countenance and respect from
her, lest they should harden her in her sin."

Anne Bradstreet must have listened with a curious mixture of
feelings, though any evidence of them would naturally be
repressed. Once more all came together, and once more, Anne
Hutchinson, who faced them in this last encounter with a quiet
dignity, that moved the more sympathetic to pity, denied the
charges they brought, and the three years controversy which, as
Ellis writes, "had drawn nearly the whole of the believers in
Boston---magistrates, ministers, women, soldiers, and the common
multitude under the banners of a female leader, had changed the
government of the Colony, and spread its strange reports over
Protestant Europe, was thus brought to an issue, by imputing
deception about one of the most unintelligible tenets of faith to
her, who could not be circumvented in any other way."

The closest examination of her statements shows no ground for this
judgment. It was the inferences of her opponents, and no fact of
her real belief that made against her, but inference, then as now, made
the chief ground for her enemies. Excommunication followed at once,
and now, the worst having come, her spirits rose, and she
faced them with quiet dignity, but with all her old assurance,
glorying in the whole experience so that one of the indignant
ministers described her manner with deep disgust, and added: "God
giving her up, since the sentence of excommunication, to that
hardness of heart, as she is not affected with any remorse, but glories
in it, and fears not the vengeance of God which she lies under, as if
God did work contrary to his own word, and loosed
from heaven, while his church had bound upon earth."

Other ministers were as eager in denunciation, preaching against her
as "the American Jezebel," and even the saintly Hooker wrote: "The
expression of providence against this wretched woman hath
proceeded from the Lord's miraculous mercy, and his bare arm hath
been discovered therein from first to last, that all the churches
may hear and fear. I do believe such a heap of hideous errors at once
to be vented by such a self-deluding and deluded creature, no
history can record; and yet, after recantation of all, to be cast
out as unsavory salt, that she may not continue a pest to the
place, that will be forever marvellous in the eyes of all the
saints."

Even the lapse of several generations left the animus unchanged,
and Graham, usually so dispassionate and just in statement, wrote
of her almost vindictively:

"In the assemblies which were held by the followers of Mrs.
Hutchinson, there was nourished and trained a keen, contentious
spirit, and an unbridled license of tongue, of which the influence

was speedily felt in the serious disturbance, first of domestic happiness, and then of the public peace. The matrons of Boston were transformed into a synod of slanderous praters, whose inquisitional deliberations and audacious decrees, instilled their venom into the innermost recesses of society; and the spirits of a great majority of the citizen being in that combustible state in which a feeble spark will suffice to kindle a formidable conflagration, the whole Colony was inflamed and distracted by the incontinence of female spleen and presumption."

Amidst this rattle of theological guns there was danger that others might be heard. To subdue Boston was the first necessity, and an order for disarming the disaffected was issued. The most eminent citizens, if suspected of favoring her, had their firearms taken from them, and even Capt. John Underhill was forced to give up his sword. An account of the whole controversy was written by Mr. Welde and sent over to England for publication in order that the Colony might not suffer from slanderous reports, and that no "godly friends" might be prevented from coming over. For the winter of 1637, Boston was quiet, but it was an ominous quiet, in which destructive forces gathered, and though never visible on the surface, worked in evil ways for many, the heart of Anne Hutchinson's doctrine being really a belief in the "Inward Light," a doctrine which seems to have outraged every Puritan susceptibility for fully a hundred years, and until the reaction began, which has made individual judgment the only creed common to the people of New England. It was reasonable enough, however, that Massachusetts should dread a colony of such uneasy spirits, planted at her very doors, enfranchised and heretical to an appalling degree and considered quite as dangerous as so many malefactors, and an uneasy and constant watch was kept.

The Hutchinsons had sold their property in Boston and joined Coddington at Pocasset, of which Mr. Hutchinson soon became the chief magistrate. His wife, as before, was the master spirit. She even addressed an admonition to the church in Boston, turning the tables temporarily upon her enemies, though the end of her power was at hand. In 1642, her husband died, and various circumstances had before this made her influence feared and disliked. Freedom in any English settlement had ceased to be possible, and as Massachusetts grew more powerful, she resigned any hope of holding the place won by so many sacrifices and emigrated to the Dutch settlement, forming a small colony of sixteen persons at Pelham in Westchester County, New York, where a little river still bears her name.

One son had remained in Boston, and was the ancestor of the Tory Governor of Massachusetts during the Revolution, and a daughter also married and settled there, so that her blood is still found in the veins of more than one New England family, some of whose ancestors were most directly concerned in casting her out. But her younger children and a son-in-law were still with her, with a few of her most devoted followers, and she still anticipated peace and a quiet future. Both came at last, but not in the looked-for guise. No date remains of the fate of the little colony and only the Indian custom of preserving the names of those they killed, has made us know that Wampago himself, the owner of the land about Pelham, was the murderer of the woman, whose troubled but not unhappy life went out in the fire and blood of an Indian massacre.

To the Puritans in Boston, such fate seemed justice, and they rejoiced with a grim exultation. "The Lord," said Welde, "heard our groans to heaven, and freed us from our great and sore affliction." No tale was too gross and shameless to find acceptance, and popular feeling against her settled into such fixed enmity that even her descendant, the historian Hutchinson, dared not write anything that would seem to favor her cause. Yet, necessary as her persecution and banishment may have been to the safety of the Colony, the faith for which she gave her life has been stronger than her enemies. Mistaken as she often was, a truer Christianity dwelt with her than with them, and the toleration denied her has shown itself as the heart of all present life or future progress.

CHAPTER VII.

COLONIAL LITERARY DEVELOPMENT IN THE SEVENTEENTH CENTURY.

It was before the final charge from Ipswich to Andover, that the chief part of Anne Bradstreet's literary work was done, the ten years after her arrival in New England being the only fruitful ones. As daughter and wife of two of the chief magistrates, she heard the constant discussion of questions of policy as well as questions of faith, both strongly agitated by the stormy years of Anne Hutchinson's stay in Boston, and it is very probable that she sought refuge from the anxiety of the troubled days, in poetical composition, and in poring over Ancient History found consolation in the fact that old times were by no means better than the new. The literary life of New England had already begun, and it is worth while to follow the lines of its growth and development, through the colonial days, if only to understand better the curious limitations for any one who sought to give tangible form to thought, whether in prose or poetry. For North and South, the story was the same.

The points of divergence in the northern and southern colonies have been so emphasized, and the impression has become so fixed, that the divisions of country had as little in common as came later to be the fact, that any statement as to their essential agreement, is distrusted or denied. Yet even to-day, in a region where many causes have made against purity of blood, the traveller in the South is often startled, in some remote town of the Carolinas or of Virginia, at the sight of what can only be characterized as a Southern Yankee. At one's very side in the little church may sit a man who, if met in Boston, would be taken for a Brahmin of the Brahmins. His face is as distinctively a New England one as was Emerson's. High but narrow forehead, prominent

nose, thin lips, and cheek bones a trifle high; clear, cold blue
eyes and a slender upright figure Every line shows repressed
force, the possibility of passionate energy, of fierce enmity and
ruthless judgment on anything outside of personal experience.
Culture is equally evident, but culture refusing to believe in
anything modern, and resting its claims on little beyond the time
of Queen Anne. It is the Puritan alive again, and why not?
Descended directly from some stray member of the Cromwellian party
who fled at the Restoration, he chose Virginia rather than New
England, allured by the milder climate. But he is of the same
class, the same prejudices and limitations as the New England
Puritan, the sole difference being that he has stood still while
the other passed on unrestingly. But in 1635, it was merely a
difference of location, never of mental habit, that divided them.
For both alike, the description given by one of our most
brilliant writers, applied the English people of the seventeenth
century
being summed up in words quite as applicable to-day as then: "At
that time, though they were apparently divided into many classes,
they were really divided into only two---first, the disciples of
things as they are; second, the disciples of things as they ought
to be."

It was chiefly "the disciples of things as they ought to be" that
passed over from Old England to the New, and as such faith means
usually supreme discomfort for its holder, and quite as much for
the opposer, there was a constant and lively ebullition of forces on
either side. Every Puritan who came over waged a triple war--
first, with himself as a creature of malignant and desperate
tendencies, likely at any moment to commit some act born of hell;
second, with the devil, at times regarded as practically
synonymous with one's own nature, at others as a tangible and
audacious adversary; and last and always, with all who differed
from his own standard of right and wrong---chiefly wrong. The
motto of that time was less "Dare to do right," than "Do not dare
to do wrong." All mental and spiritual furnishings were shaken
out of the windows daily, by way of dislodging any chance seeds
of vice sown by the great adversary. One would have thought the
conflict with natural forces quite enough to absorb all
superfluous energy, every fact of climate, soil and natural
features being against them, but neither scanty harvests, nor
Indian wars, nor devastating disease, had the power to long
suppress this perpetual and unflinching self-discipline.

Unlike any other colony of the New World, the sole purpose and
motive of action was an ideal one. The Dutch sought peltries and
trade in general, and whereever they established themselves, at
once gave tokens of material comfort and prosperity. The more
Southern Colonies were this basis, adding to it the freedom of
life--the large hospitality possible where miles of land formed the
plantation, and service meant no direct outlay or expense. Here
and there a Southern Puritan was found, as his type may be found
to-day, resisting the charm of physical ease and comfort, and
constituting himself a missionary to the Indians of South Carolina,
or to settlements remote from all gospel privileges, but for the
most part the habits of an English squire-ruled country prevailed,
and were enlarged upon; each man in the centre of his great
property being practically king. Dispersion of forces was
the order, and thus many necessities of civilization were
dispensed with. The man who had a river at his door had no

occasion to worry over the making or improvement of roads, a boat carrying his supplies, and bridle-paths sufficing his horse and himself. With no need for strenuous conflict with nature or man, the power of resistance died naturally. Sharp lines softened; muscles weakened, and before many generations the type had so altered that the people who had left England as one, were two, once for all.

The law of dispersion, practical and agreeable to the Southern landholder, would have been destruction to his New England brethren. For the latter, concentration was the only safety. They massed together in close communities, and necessarily were forced to plan for the general rather than for the individual good. In such close quarters, where every angle made itself felt, and constant contact developed and implied criticism, law must work far more minutely than in less exacting communities. Every tendency to introspection and self-judging was strengthened to the utmost, and merciless condemnation for one's self came to mean a still sharper one for others. With every power of brain and soul they fought against what, to them, seemed the one evil for that or any time--toleration. Each man had his own thought, and was able to put it into strong words. No colony has ever known so large a proportion of learned men, there being more graduates of Cambridge and Oxford between the years 1630 and 1690 than it was possible to find in a population of the same size in the mother country. "In its inception, New England was not an agricultural community, nor a manufacturing community, nor a trading community; it was a thinking community---an arena and mart for ideas--its characteristic organ being not the hand, nor the heart, nor the pocket, but the brain."

The material for learning, we have seen, was of the scantiest, not only for Winthrop's Colony but for those that preceded it.

The three little ships that, on a misty afternoon in December, 1606, dropped down the Thames with sails set for an unknown country, carried any freight but that of books. Book-makers were there in less proportion than on board the solitary vessel that, in 1620, took a more northerly course, and cast anchor at last off the bleak and sullen shore of Massachusetts; but for both alike the stress of those early years left small energy or time for any composition beyond the reports that, at stated intervals, went back to the mother country. The work of the pioneer is for muscles first, brain having small opportunity, save as director; and it required more than one generation before authorship could become the business of any, not even the clergy being excepted from the stress of hard manual labor.

Yet, for the first departure, an enthusiasm of hope and faith filled many hearts. The England of that day had not been too kindly toward her men of letters, who were then, as now, also men of dreams, looking for something better than the best she had to offer, and who, in the early years of the seventeenth century, gathered in London as the centre least touched by the bigotry and narrowness of one party, the wild laxity and folly of the other. "The very air of London must have been electric with the daily words of those immortals whose casual talk upon the pavement by the street-side was a coinage of speech richer, more virile, more expressive than has been known on this planet since the great days

of Atheman poetry, eloquence and mirth." There were "wits,
dramatists, scholars, orators, singers, philosophers." For every
one of them was the faith of something undefined, yet infinitely
precious, to be born of all the mysterious influences in that new
land to which all eyes turned, and old Michael Drayton's
ringing ode on their departure held also a prophecy:

"In kenning of the shore,
  Thanks to God first given,
  O you, the happiest men,
  Be frolic then;
Let cannons roar,
  Frighting the wide heaven.

"And in regions far
  Such heroes bring ye forth
    As those from whom we came;
    And plant our name
Under that star
  Not known unto our north.

"And as there plenty grows
  Of laurel everywhere--
  Apollo's sacred tree--
    You, it may see,
  A poet's brows to crown
    That may sing there."

The men who, in passing over to America could not cease to be
Englishmen, were the friends and associates--the intellectual
equals in many points of this extraordinary assemblage of
brilliant and audacious intellects; and chief among them was the
man at whose name we are all inclined to smile--Captain John
Smith. So many myths have hid the real man from view--some of
them, it must be admitted, of his own making--that we forget how
vivid and resolute a personality he owned, and the pride we may
well have in him as the writer of the first distinctively American
book. His work was not only for Virginia, but for New England
as well. His life was given to the interests of both. Defeated
plans, baffled hopes, had no power to quench the absorbing love
that filled him to the end, and, at the very last, he wrote of the
American colonies: "By that acquaintance I have with them, I call
them my children; for they have been my wife, my hawks, hounds, my
cards, my dice, and, in total, my best content, as indifferent to
my heart as my left hand to my right."

Certain qualities, most prominent then, have, after a long
disappearance, become once more, in degree at least, characteristic of
the time. The book man of to-day is quite as likely to be also
the man of affairs, and the pale and cloistered student of the past
is rather a memory than a present fact. History thus repeats itself
as usual, and the story of the literary men of the nineteenth
century has many points in common with that of the seventeenth.

Smith's description of New England had had active circulation in
the Mother Country, and many a Puritan trusted it entirely, who
would have frowned upon the writer had he appeared in person to
testify of what he had seen. Certainly the Cavalier predominated
in him, the type to which he belonged being of the noble one "of

which the Elizabethan age produced so many examples--the man of action who was also the man of letters; the man of letters who was also a man of action; the wholesomest type of manhood anywhere to be found; body and brain both active, both cultivated; the mind not made fastidious and morbid by too much bookishness, nor coarse and dull by too little; not a doer who is dumb, not a speech-maker who cannot do; the knowledge that comes of books, widened and freshened by the knowledge that comes of experience; the literary sense fortified by common sense; the bashfulness and delicacy of the scholar hovering as a finer presence above the forceful audacity of the man of the world; at once bookman, penman, swordsman, diplomat, sailor, courtier, orator. Of this type of manhood, spacious, strong, refined and sane, were the best men of the Elizabethan time, George Gascoigne, Sir Philip Sidney, Sir Walter Raleigh, and, in a modified sense, Hakluyt, Bacon, Sackville, Shakespeare, Ben Johnson and nearly all the rest."

It would have been impossible to make John Smith a Puritan, but an ameliorated Puritan might easily have become a John Smith. It is worth while to recall his work and that of his fellow colonists, if only to note the wide and immediate departure of thought in the northern and southern colonies, even where the Puritan element entered in, nor can we understand Anne Bradstreet, without a thought of the forces at work in the new country, unconscious but potent causes of all phases of literary life in that early time.

The Virginia colonist had more knowledge of the world and less knowledge of himself, introspection, or any desire for it, being no part of his mental constitution or habit.

Intellectually, he demanded a spherical excellence, easier then than now, and attained by many a student of that day, and to this Captain John aspired, one at least of his contemporaries giving proof of faith that he had attained it in lines written on him and his book on the history of Virginia and New England:

"Like Caesar, now thou writ'st what them hast done.
These acts, this book, will live while there's a sun."

The history is picturesque, and often amusing. As a writer he was always "racy, terse, fearless," but, save to the special student, there is little value to the present student, unless he be a searcher after the spirit that moved not only the man, but, through him, the time he moulded. For such reader will still be felt "the impression of a certain personal largeness ... magnanimity, affluence, sense and executive force. Over all his personal associates in American adventure he seems to tower, by the natural loftiness and reach of the perception with which he grasped the significance of their vast enterprise and the means to its success.... He had the faults of an impulsive, irascible, egotistic and imaginative nature; he sometimes bought human praise at too high a price, but he had great abilities in word and deed; his nature was, upon the whole, generous and noble; and during the first two decades of the seventeenth century, he did more than any other Englishman to make an American nation and an American literature possible."

Behind the stockade at Jamestown, only the most persistent bent toward letters had chance of surviving. Joyful as the landing had been, the Colony had no sturdy backbone of practical workers. Their first summer was unutterably forlorn, the beauty and fertility that had seemed to promise to the sea-sad eyes a life of instant ease, bringing with it only a "horrible trail of homesickness, discord, starvation, pestilence and Indian hostility." No common purpose united them, as in the Northern Colony. Save for the leaders, individual profit had been the only ambition or intention. Work had no place in the scheme of life, and even when ship after ship discharged its load of immigrants matters were hardly mended. Perpetual discord became the law. Smith fled from the tumults which he had no power to quiet, and a long succession of soon-discouraged officers waged a species of hand-to-hand conflict with the wild elements that made up the Colony. One poet, George Sandys, whose name and work are still of meaning and value to the student, found leisure, borrowed from the night, for a translation of Ovid's "Metamorphoses," commended by both Dryden and Pope, and which passed at once through eight editions, but there were no others.

Twenty years of colonial life had ended when he returned to England, and the spirit of the early founders had well nigh disappeared. Literary work had died with it. A few had small libraries, chiefly Latin classics, but a curious torpor had settled down, the reasons for which are now evident. There was no constant intercourse, as in New England. The "policy of dispersion" was the law, for every man aspired to be a large land-owner, and, in the midst of his tract of half-cleared land, had small communication with any but his inferiors. Within fifty years any intellectual standard had practically ceased to exist. The Governor, Sir William Berkeley, whose long rule meant death to progress, thundered against the printing-press, and believed absolutely in the "fine old conservative policy of keeping subjects ignorant in order to keep them submissive." For thirty-six years his energies were bent in this direction. Protest of any sort simply intensified his purpose, and when 1670 dawned he had the happiness of making to the English Commissioners a reply that has become immortal, though hardly in the sense anticipated, when he wrote: "I thank God there are no free schools, nor printing; and I hope we shall not have these hundred years; for learning has brought disobedience and heresy and sects into the world, and printing has divulged them and libels against the best government. God keep us from both."

A dark prayer, and answered as fully as men's own acts can fulfill their prayers. The brilliant men who had passed from the scene had no successors. The few malcontents were silenced by a law which made "even the first thrust of the pressman's lever a crime," and until 1729 there was neither printing nor desire for printing in any general sense. The point where our literature began had become apparently its burial-place; the historians and poets and students of an earlier generation were not only unheeded but forgotten, and a hundred years of intellectual barrenness, with another hundred, before even partial recovery could be apparent, were the portion of Virginia and all the states she influenced or controlled. No power could have made it otherwise. "Had much literature been produced there, would it not have been a miracle? The units of the community isolated; little chance for mind to kindle mind; no schools; no literary institutions, high or low; no public libraries; no printing-press; no intellectual freedom; no

religious freedom; the forces of society tending to create two
great classes--a class of vast land-owners, haughty, hospitable,
indolent, passionate, given to field sports and politics; and a
class of impoverished white plebeians and black serfs; these
constitute a situation out of which may be evolved country
gentlemen, loud-lunged and jolly fox-hunters, militia heroes, men
of boundless domestic heartiness and social grace, astute and
imperious politicians, fiery orators, and, by and by, here and
there, perhaps after awhile, a few amateur literary men---but no
literary class, and almost no literature."

       *   *   *   *   *

The Northern Colony had known strange chances also, but every
circumstance and accident of its life fostered the literary spirit
and made the student the most honored member of the community. The
Mayflower brought a larger proportion of men with literary
antecedents and tendencies than had landed on the Virginia coast;
and though every detail of life was fuller of hard work, privation
and danger--climate being even more against them than Indians or
any other misery of the early years--the proportion remained much
the same. It is often claimed that this early environment was
utterly opposed to any possibility of literary development. On the
contrary, "those environments were, for a certain class of mind,
extremely wholesome and stimulating." Hawthorne has written
somewhere: "New England was then in a state incomparably more
picturesque than at present, or than it has been within the memory
of man." And Tyler, in his brilliant analysis of early colonial
forces, takes much the same ground: "There were about them many of
the tokens and forces of a picturesque, romantic and impressive
life; the infinite solitudes of the wilderness, its mystery, its
peace; the near presence of nature, vast, potent, unassailed; the strange
problems presented to them by savage character and savage life; their
own escape from great cities, from crowds, from mean competition;
the luxury of having room enough; the delight of
being free; the urgent interest of all the Protestant world in
their undertaking; the hopes of humanity already looking thither;
the coming to them of scholars, saints, statesmen, philosophers."

Yet even for these men there were restraints that to-day seem shameful
and degrading. Harvard College had been made responsible for the
good behavior of the printing-press set up in 1639, and
for twenty-three years this seemed sufficient. Finally two
official licensers were appointed, whose business was to read and
pronounce a verdict either for or against everything proposed for
publication. Anyone might consider these hindrances sufficient,
but intolerance gained with every year of restriction, and when
finally the officers were induced by arguments which must have
been singularly powerful, to allow the printing of an edition of
"Invitation of Christ," a howl arose from every council and
general assembly, whether of laws of divinity, and the unlucky
book was characterized as one written "by a popish minister,
wherein is contained some things that are less safe to be infused
amongst the people of this place"; and the authorities ordered not
only a revisal of its contents but a cessation of all work on the
printing-press. Common sense at length came to the rescue, but
legal restraints on printing were not abolished in Massachusetts
until twenty-one years before the Declaration of Independence.

As with Virginia the early years were most fertile in work of
any interest to the present time, and naturally so. Fresh from
the
life not only of books but of knowledge of "the central currents
of the world's best thinking," these influences could not die out
in the generation nearest them. For every writer some history of
the Colony was the first instinct, and William Bradford holds the
same relation to New England as Captain John Smith to Virginia--
the racy, incisive, picturesque diction of the latter being a key-
hole to their colonial life, as symbolical as the measured,
restrained and solemn periods of the Puritan writer. Argument had
become a necessity of life. It had been forced upon them in
England in the endeavor to define their position not only to the
Cavalier element but to themselves, and became finally so rooted a
mental habit that "even on the brink of any momentous enterprise
they would stop and argue the case if a suspicion occurred to them
that things were not right."

They were never meek and dreamy saints, but, on the contrary,
"rather pragmatical and disputatious persons, with all the edges
and corners of their characters left sharp, with all their
opinions very definitely formed, and with their habits of frank
utterance quite thoroughly matured." But for Bradford, and
Morton, and Johnson, and other equally worthy and honored
names, this disputatious tendency was a surface matter, and the
deeper traits were of an order that make petty peculiarities
forgotten. For Bradford especially, was "an untroubled command
of strong and manly speech.... The daily food of his spirit was
noble. He
uttered himself without effort, like a free man, a sage and a
Christian," and his voice was that of many who followed him.
Loving the mother country with passion, the sense of exile long
remained with them--a double exile, since they had first taken
firm hold in Leyden, and parted from its ease and prosperity with
words which hold the pathos and quiet endurance still the
undertone of much New England life, and which, though already
quoted, are the key note of the early days.

"So they left that goodly and pleasant city which had been their
resting-place near twelve years; but they knew they were pilgrims,
and looked not much on these things, but lift up their eyes to the

heavens, that dearest country, and quieted their spirits."

What John Winthrop's work was like, whether in private diary or
letter, or in more formal composition, we have already seen, but
there is one speech of his in 1645, which was of profoundest
interest to the whole Colony, and must have stirred Anne
Bradstreet to the very depths. This speech was made before the
general court after his acquittal of the charge of having exceeded
his authority as deputy governor. And one passage, containing his
statement of the nature of liberty, has been pronounced by both
English and American thinkers far beyond the definition of
Blackstone, and fully on a par with the noblest utterances of John
Locke or Algernon Sidney.

As time went on authorship passed naturally into the hands of the
clergy, who came to be the only class with much leisure for study.
The range of subjects treated dwindled more and more from year to
year. The breadth and vigor of the early days were lost, the
pragmatical and disputatious element gaining more and more ground.

Unfortunately, "they stood aloof with a sort of horror from
the richest and most exhilarating types of classic writing in
their
own tongue." The Hebrew Scriptures and many classics of Roman and
Greek literature were still allowed; but no genuine literary
development could take place where the sinewy and vital thought of
their own nation was set aside as unworthy of consideration. The
esthetic sense dwindled and pined. Standards of judgment altered.
The capacity for discrimination lessened. Theological quibbling
made much of the literature of the day, though there was much more
than quibbling. But the keenest minds, no matter how vivid and
beautiful their intelligence, were certain that neither man as a
body, nor the world as a home, were anything but lack evils,
ruined by the fall of Adam, and to be ignored and despised with
every power and faculty. Faith in God came to be faith in "a
microscopic and picayune Providence," governing the meanest detail
of the elect's existence, and faith in man had no place in any
scheme of life or thought. If a poem were written it came to be
merely some transcription from the Bible, or an epitaph or elegy
on some departed saint.

In spite of themselves, however, humor, the Saxon birthright,
refused to be suppressed, and asserted itself in unexpected ways, as in
Nathaniel Ward's "Simple Cobbler of Agawam," already mentioned.
What the cobbler saw was chiefly the theological difficulties of the
time. Discord and confusion seemed to have settled upon the earth,
and "looking out over English Christendom, he saw nothing but a
chaos of jangling opinions, upstart novelties, lawless manners,
illimitable changes in codes, institutions and creeds." He declaims
ferociously against freedom of opinion, and "the fathers of the
inquisition might have reveled over the first twenty-five pages of
this Protestant book, that actually blaze with the eloquent savagery
and rapture of religious intolerance." He laughed in the midst of
this declamation, but it was rather a sardonic laugh, and soon
checked by fresh consideration of man's vileness.

Liberty had received many a blow from the hands of these men, who
had fled from home and country to secure it, but it could not die
while their own principles were remembered, and constantly at one
point or another, irrepressible men and women rose up, bent upon
free thought and free speech, and shaming even the most determined
and intolerant spirit. One of such men, outspoken by nature,
recorded his mind in some two thousand printed pages, and Roger
Williams even to-day looms up with all the more power because we
have become "rather fatigued by the monotony of so vast a throng
of sages and saints, all quite immaculate, all equally prim and
stiff in their Puritan starch and uniform, all equally automatic
and freezing." It is most comfortable to find anyone defying the
rigid and formal law of the time, whether spoken or implied,
and we have positive "relief in the easy swing of this man's gait,
the limberness of his personal movement, his escape from the
pasteboard proprieties, his spontaneity, his impetuosity, his
indiscretions, his frank acknowledgements that he really had a few
things yet to learn." He demanded spiritual liberty, and though,
as time went on, he learned to use gentler phrases, he was always a
century or two ahead of his age. The mirthfulness of his early days
passed, as well it might, but a better possession--
cheerfulness--remained to the end. Exile never embittered him, and
the writings that are his legacy "show an habitual upwardness of
mental movement; they grow rich in all gentle, gracious, and

magnanimous qualities as the years increase upon him."

His influence upon New England was a profound one, and the seed
sown bore fruit long after his mortal body had crumbled into dust;
but it was chiefly in theological lines, to which all thought now
tended. Poetry, so far as drama or lyric verse was concerned, had
been forsworn by the soul of every true Puritan, but "of course
poetry was planted there too deep even for his theological grub-
hooks to root out. If, however, his theology drove poetry out of
many forms in which it has been used to reside, poetry itself
practiced a noble revenge by taking up its abode in his theology."
Stedman gives a masterly analysis of this time in the opening
essay of his "Victorian Poets," showing the shackles all minds
wore, and comparing the time when "even nature's laws were
compelled to bow to church fanaticism," to the happier day in
which "science, freedom of thought, refinement and material
progress have moved along together."

We have seen how the power of keen and delicate literary judgment
or discrimination died insensibly. The first era of literary
development passed with the first founders of the Republic, and
original thought and expression lay dormant, save in theological
directions. As with all new forms of life, the second stage was an
imitative one, and the few outside the clergy who essayed writing
at all copied the worst models of the Johnsonian period. Verse was
still welcome, and the verse-makers of the colonial time were
many. Even venerable clergymen like Peter Bulkley gave way to its
influence. Ostensible poems were written by more than one
governor; John Cotton yielded to the spell, though he hid the fact
discreetly by writing his English verses in Greek characters, and
confining them to the blank leaves of his almanac. Debarred from
ordinary amusements or occupations, the irrepressible need of
expression effervesced in rhymes as rugged and unlovely as the
writers, and ream upon ream of verse accumulated. Had it found
permanent form, our libraries would have been even more encumbered
than at present, but fortunately most of it has perished. Elegies
and epitaphs were its favorite method, and the "most elaborate and
painful jests," every conceivable and some inconceivable quirks
and solemn puns made up their substance. The obituary poet of the
present is sufficiently conspicuous in the daily papers which are
available for his flights, but the leading poets of to-day do not
feel that it is incumbent upon them to evolve stanzas in a casual
way on every mournful occasion. In that elder day allegories,
anagrams, acrostics--all intended to have a consolatory effect on
mourning friends--flowed from every clerical pen, adding a new
terror to death and a new burden to life, but received by the
readers with a species of solemn glee. Of one given to this habit
Cotton Mather writes that he "had so nimble a faculty of putting
his devout thoughts into verse that he signalized himself
by ... sending poems to all persons, in all places, on all occasions ...
wherein if the curious relished the piety sometimes rather than the
poetry, the capacity of the most therein to be accommodated must
be considered." Another poet had presently the opportunity to
"embalm his memory in some congenial verses," and wrote an
epitaph, and ended with a full description of--

"His care to guide his flock and feed his lambs,
By words, works, prayers, psalms, alms and anagrams."

To this period belongs a poetic phenomenon--a metrical horror
known as "The Bay Psalm Book," being the first English book ever
issued from an American printing-press. Tyler has given with his
accustomed happy facility of phrase the most truthful description
yet made of a production that formed for years the chief poetical
reading of the average New Englander, and undoubtedly did more to
lower taste and make inferior verse seem praiseworthy than any and
all other causes. He writes: "In turning over these venerable
pages, one suffers by sympathy something of the obvious toil of
the undaunted men who, in the very teeth of nature, did all this;
and whose appalling sincerity must, in our eyes, cover a multitude
of such sins as sentences wrenched about end for end, clauses
heaved up and abandoned in chaos, words disemboweled or split
quite in two in the middle, and dissonant combinations of sound
that are the despair of such poor vocal organs as are granted to
human beings. The verses seem to have been hammered out on an
anvil, by blows from a blacksmith's sledge. In all parts of the
book is manifest the agony it cost the writers to find two words
that would rhyme---more or less; and so often as this arduous feat
is achieved, the poetic athlete appears to pause awhile from sheer
exhaustion, panting heavily for breath. Let us now read, for our
improvement, a part of the Fifty-eighth Psalm:

"The wicked are estranged from
     the womb, they goe astray
as soon as ever they are borne,
     uttering lyes are they.
Their poyson's like serpents' poyson,
     they like deafe Aspe her eare
that stops. Though Charmer wisely charm,
     his voice she will not heare.
Within their mouth, doe thou their teeth,
     break out, O God most strong,
doe thou Jehovah, the great teeth
     break of the lions young."

It is small wonder that Anne Bradstreet's poems struck the unhappy
New Englanders who had been limited to verse of this description
as the work of one who could be nothing less than the "Tenth
Muse." When the first edition of her poems appeared, really in
1650, though the date is usually given as 1642, a younger
generation had come upon the scene. The worst hardships were
over. Wealth had accumulated, and the comfort which is the
distinguishing characteristic of New England homes to-day, was
well established. Harvard College was filled with bright young
scholars, in whom her work awakened the keenest enthusiasm; who
had insight enough to recognize her as the one shining example of
poetic power in that generation, and who wrote innumerable elegies
and threnodies on her life and work.

The elegy seems to have appealed more strongly to the Puritan mind
than any other poetical form, and they exhausted every verbal
device in perpetuating the memory of friends who scarcely needed
this new terror added to a death already surrounded by a gloom that
even their strongest faith hardly dispelled.

"Let groans inspire my quill," one clerical twister of language
began, and another wrote with the painful and elephantine
lightness which was the Puritan idea of humor, an epitaph which

may serve as sufficient illustration of the whole
unutterably dreary mass of verse:

"Gospel and law in's heart had each its column;
His head an index to the sacred volume;
His very name a title page and next
His life a commentary on the text.
Oh, what a monument of glorious worth,
When in a new edition he comes forth
Without _erratas_ may we think he'll be,
In leaves and covers of eternity."

Better examples were before them, for books were imported freely,
but minds had settled into the mould which they kept for more than
one generation, unaffected in slightest measure by the steady
progress of thought in the old home.

The younger writers were influenced to a certain degree by the new
school, but lacked power to pass beyond it. Pope was now in full
tide of success, and, with Thomson, Watts and Young, found hosts
of sympathetic and admiring readers who would have turned in
horror from the pages of Shakespeare or the early dramatists. The
measure adopted by Pope charmed the popular mind, and while it
helped to smooth the asperities of Puritan verse, became also the
easy vehicle of the commonplace. There were hints here and there
of something better to come, and in the many examples of verse
remaining it is easy to discern a coming era of free thought and
more musical expression. Peter Folger had sent out from the fogs
of Nantucket a defiant and rollicking voice; John Rogers and Urian
Oakes, both poets and both Harvard presidents, had done something
better than mere rhyme, but it remained for another pastor,
teacher and physician to sound a note that roused all New England.
Michael Wigglesworth might have been immortal, could the genius
born in him have been fed and trained by any of the "sane and
mighty masters of English song"; but, born to the inheritance of a
narrow and ferocious creed, with no power left to even admit the
existence of the beautiful, he was "forever incapable of giving
utterance to his genius--except in a dialect unworthy of it," and
became simply "the explicit and unshrinking rhymer of the five
points of Calvinism."

Cotton Mather describes him as "a feeble little shadow of a man."
He was "the embodiment of what was great, earnest and sad in
colonial New England." He was tenderly sympathetic, and his own
life, made up mostly of sorrow and pain, filled him with longing
to help others. "A sensitive, firm, wide-ranging, unresting
spirit, he looks out mournfully over the throngs of men that fill
the world, all of them totally depraved, all of them caught,
from
farthest eternity, in the adamantine meshes of God's decrees; the
most of them also being doomed in advance by those decrees to an
endless existence of ineffable torment; and upon this situation of
affairs the excellent Michael Wigglesworth proposes to make
poetry." His "Day of Doom," a horribly realistic description of
every terror of the expected judgment, was written in a swinging
ballad measure that took instant hold of the popular mind. No book
ever printed in America has met with a proportionate commercial
success. "The eighteen hundred copies of the first edition were sold
within a single year; which implies the purchase of a copy of
'The Day of Doom' by at least every thirty-fifth person in New

England.... Since that time the book has been repeatedly
published, at least once in England and at least eight times in
America, the last time being in 1867."

It penetrated finally all parts of the country where Puritan faith
or manners prevailed. It was an intellectual influence far beyond
anything we can now imagine. It was learned by heart along with
the catechism, and for a hundred years was found on every bookshelf, no matter how sparsely furnished otherwise. Even after the
Revolution, which produced the usual effect of all war in bringing
in unrestrained thought, it was still a source of terror, and
thrilled and prepared all readers for the equally fearful pictures
drawn by Edwards and his successors.

It is fortunate, perhaps, that Anne Bradstreet did not live to
read and be influenced by this poem, as simply candid in its form and
conception as the "Last Judgements" of the early masters, and like
them, portraying devils with much more apparent satisfaction than
saints. There is one passage that deserves record as evidence of what
the Puritan faith had done toward paralyzing common sense, though
there are still corners in the United States where it would
be read without the least sense of its grotesque horror. The
various classes of sinners have all been attended to, and now,
awaiting the last relay of offenders--

> "With dismal chains, and strongest reins
> Like prisoners of hell,
> They're held in place before Christ's face,
> Till he their doom shall tell.
> These void of tears, but filled with fears,
> And dreadful expectation
> Of endless pains and scalding flames,
> Stand waiting for damnation."

The saints have received their place and look with an ineffable
and satisfied smirk on the despair of the sinners, all turning at
last to gaze upon the battalion of "reprobate infants," described
in the same brisk measure:

> "Then to the bar all they drew near
> Who died in infancy,
> And never had, or good or bad,
> Effected personally.
> But from the womb unto the tomb
> Were straightway carried,
> Or, at the least, ere they transgressed--
> Who thus began to plead."

These infants, appalled at what lies before them, begin to first
argue with true Puritanic subtlety, and finding this useless,
resort to pitiful pleadings, which result in a slight concession,
though the unflinching Michael gives no hint of what either
the Judge or his victims would regard as "the easiest room."
The infants receive their sentence with no further remark.

> "You sinners are; and such a share
> As sinners may expect;
> Such you shall have, for I do save
> None but mine own elect.

Yet to compare your sin with their
    Who lived a longer time,
I do confess yours is much less,
    Though every sin's a crime.

A crime it is; therefore in bliss
    You may not hope to dwell;
But unto you I shall allow
    The easiest room in hell."

In such faith the little Bradstreets were brought up, and the
oldest, who became a minister, undoubtedly preached it with the
gusto of the time, and quoted the final description of the
sufferings of the lost, as an efficient argument with sinners:

"Then might you hear them rend and tear
    The air with their outcries;
The hideous noise of their sad voice,
    Ascendeth to the skies.
They wring their hands, their cartiff-
    hands, And gnash their teeth for terror;
They cry, they roar, for anguish sore,
    And gnaw their tongue for horror.
But get away without delay;
    Christ pities not your cry;
Depart to hell, there may you yell
    And roar eternally.

             *   *   *   *
                    *

"Die fain they would, if die they
    could, But death will not be had;
God's direful wrath their bodies hath
    Forever immortal made.
They live to lie in misery
    And bear eternal woe;
And live they must whilst God is just
    That he may plague them so."

Of the various literary children who may be said to have been
nurtured on Anne Bradstreet's verses, three became leaders of New
England thought, and all wrote elegies on her death, one of them

of marked beauty and power. It remained for a son of the
sulphurous Wigglesworth, to leave the purest fragment of poetry
the epoch produced, the one flower of a life, which at once buried
itself in the cares of a country pastorate and gave no further
sign of gift or wish to speak in verse. The poem records the fate of
a gifted classmate, who graduated with him at Harvard, sailed for
England, and dying on the return voyage, was buried at sea. It is a
passionate lamentation, an appeal to Death, and at last a quiet
resignation to the inevitable, the final lines having a
music and a pathos seldom found in the crabbed New England verse:

"Add one kind drop unto his watery
    tomb; Weep, ye relenting eyes and ears;
See, Death himself could not refrain,
    But buried him in tears."

With him the eighteenth century opens, beyond which we have no present interest, such literary development as made part of Anne Bradstreet's knowledge ending with the seventeenth.

CHAPTER VIII.

SOME PHASES OF EARLY COLONIAL LIFE.

Much of the depression evident in Anne Bradstreet's earlier verses came from the circumstances of her family life. No woman could have been less fitted to bear absence from those nearest to her, and though her adhesive nature had made her take as deep root in Ipswich, as if further change could not come, she welcomed anything that diminished the long separations, and made her husband's life center more at home. One solace seems to have been always open to her, her longest poem, the "Four Monarchies," showing her devotion to Ancient history and the thoroughness with which she had made it her own. Anatomy seems to have been studied also, the "Four Humours in Man's Constitution," showing an intimate acquaintance with the anatomical knowledge of the day; but in both cases it was not, as one might infer from her references to Greek and Latin authors, from original sources. Sir Walter Raleigh's "History of the World," Archbishop Usher's "Annals of the World," and Pemble's "Period of the Persian Monarchy," were all found in Puritan libraries, though she may have had access to others while still in England. Pemble was in high favor as an authority in Biblical exposition, the title of his book being a stimulant to every student of the prophecies: "The Period of the Persian Monarchy, wherein sundry places of Ezra, Nehemiah and Daniel are cleared, Extracted, contracted and Englished, (much of it out of Dr. Raynolds) by the late learned and godly man, Mr. William Pemble, of Magdalen Hall, in Oxford."

This she read over and over again, and many passages in her poem on the "Four Monarchies" are merely paraphrases of this and Raleigh's work, though before a second edition was printed she had read Plutarch, and altered here and there as she saw fit to introduce his rendering. Galen and Hippocrates, whom she mentions familiarly, were known to her through the work of the "curious learned Crooke," his "Description of the Body of Man, Collected and Translated out of all the best Authors on Anatomy, especially out of Gasper, Banchinus, and A. Sourentius," being familiar to all students of the day.

If her muse could but have roused to a sense of what was going on about her, and recorded some episodes which Winthrop dismisses with a few words, we should be under obligations that time could only deepen. Why, for instance, could she not have given her woman's view of that indomitable "virgin mother of Taunton," profanely described by Governor Winthrop as "an ancient maid, one Mrs. Poole. She went late thither, and endured much hardships, and lost much cattle. Called, after, Taunton."

Precisely why Mrs. Poole chose Tecticutt, afterward Titicut, for

her venture is not known, but the facts of her rash experiment must
have been discussed at length, and moved less progressive maids
and matrons to envy or pity as the chance might be. But not a hint
of this surprising departure can be found in any of
Mistress Bradstreet's remains, and it stands, with no comment save
that of the diligent governor's faithful pen, as the first example
of an action, to be repeated in these later days in prairie farms
and Western ranches by women who share the same spirit, though
more often young than "ancient" maids. But ancient, though in her
case a just enough characterization, was a term of reproach for
any who at sixteen or eighteen at the utmost, remained unmarried,
and our present custom of calling every maiden under forty,
"girl" would have struck the Puritan mothers with a sense of
preposterousness fully equal to ours at some of their doings.

A hundred years passed, and then an appreciative kinsman, who had
long enjoyed the fruit of her labors, set up "a faire slab," still
to be seen in the old burying ground.

HERE RESTS THE

REMAINS OF

MRS. ELIZABETH POOL,

A NATIVE OF OLD ENGLAND,

Of good family, friends and prospects,
all which she left in the prime of her life, to enjoy
the religion of her conscience in this distant
wilderness;

A great proprietor of the township of Taunton,

A chief promoter of its settlement and its incorporation
1639-40,

about which time she settled near this spot; and,

having employed the opportunity

of her virgin state in piety, liberality and sanctity of

manners, Died May 21st A.D. 1654, aged 65.

to whose memory

this monument is gratefully erected by her next of kin,

JOHN BORLAND, ESQUIRE,

A.D. 1771.

Undoubtedly every detail of this eccentric settlement was talked
over at length, as everything was talked over. Gossip never had
more forcible reason for existence, for the church covenant
compelled each member to a practical oversight of his neighbor's
concerns, the special clause reading: "We agree to keep mutual
watch and ward over one another."

At first, united by a common peril, the dangers of this were less perceptible. The early years held their own necessities for discussion, and the records of the time are full of matter that Anne Bradstreet might have used had she known her opportunity. She was weighed down like every conscientious Puritan of the day not only by a sense of the infinitely great, but quite as strenuously by the infinitely little. It is plain that she saw more clearly than many of her time, and there are no indications in her works of the small superstitions held by all. Superstition had changed its name to Providence, and every item of daily action was believed to be under the constant supervision and interference of the Almighty. The common people had ceased to believe in fairies and brownies, but their places had been filled by Satan's imps and messengers, watchful for some chance to confound the elect.

The faith in dreams and omens of every sort was not lessened by the transference of the responsibility for them to the Lord, and the superstition of the day, ended later in a credulity that accepted the Salem Witchcraft delusion with all its horrors, believing always, that diligent search would discover, if not the Lord's, then the devil's hand, working for the edification or confounding of the elect. Even Winthrop does not escape, and in the midst of wise suggestions for the management of affairs sandwiches such a record as the following: "At Watertown there was (in the view of divers witnesses) a great combat between a mouse and a snake; and after a long fight, the mouse prevailed and killed the snake. The pastor of Boston, Mr. Wilson, a very sincere, holy man, hearing of it, gave this interpretation: That the snake was the devil; the mouse was a poor, contemptible, people, which God had brought hither, which should overcome Satan here, and dispossess him of his kingdom. Upon the same occasion, he told the governor that, before he was resolved to come into this country, he dreamed he was here, and that he saw a church arise out of the earth, which grew up and became a marvelously goodly church."

They had absolute faith that prayer would accomplish all things, even to strengthening a defective memory. Thomas Shepard, whose autobiography is given in Young's "Chronicles of Massachusetts Bay," gave this incident in his life when a student and "ambitious of learning and being a scholar; and hence, when I could not take notes of the sermon I remember I was troubled at it, and prayed the Lord earnestly that he would help me to note sermons; and I see some cause of wondering at the Lord's providence therein; for as soon as ever I had prayed (after my best fashion) Him for it, I presently, the next Sabbath, was able to take notes, who the precedent Sabbath, could do nothing at all that way."

Anthony Thacher, whose story may have been told in person to Governor Dudley's family, and whose written description of his shipwreck, included in Young's "Chronicles," is one of the most picturesque pieces of writing the time affords, wrote, with a faith that knew no question: "As I was sliding off the rock into the sea the Lord directed my toes into a joint in the rock's side, as also the tops of some of my fingers, with my right hand, by means whereof, the wave leaving me, I remained so, hanging on the rock, only my head above water."

When individual prayer failed to accomplish a desired end, a fast

and the united storming of heaven, never failed to bring victory
to the besiegers. Thus Winthrop writes: "Great harm was done in
corn, (especially wheat and barley) in this month, by a
caterpillar, like a black worm about an inch and a half long. They
eat up first the blades of the stalk, then they eat up the
tassels, whereupon the ear withered. It was believed by divers
good observers, that they fell in a great thunder shower, for
divers yards and other places, where not one of them was to be
seen an hour before, were immediately after the shower almost
covered with them, besides grass places where they were not so
easily discerned. They did the most harm in the southern
parts.... In divers places the churches kept a day of humiliation,
and presently after, the caterpillars vanished away."

Still another instance, the fame of which spread through the whole
Colony and confounded any possible doubter, found record in the
"Magnalia", that storehouse of fact so judiciously combined with
fable that the author himself could probably never tell what he
had himself seen, and what had been gleaned from others. Mr. John
Wilson, the minister of the church at Boston until the arrival of
Cotton, was journeying with a certain Mr. Adams, when tidings came
to the latter of the probably fatal illness of his daughter. "Mr.
Wilson, looking up to heaven, began mightily to wrestle with
God for the life of the young woman ... then, turning himself
about unto Mr. Adams, 'Brother,' said he, 'I trust your daughter
shall
live; I believe in God she shall recover of this sickness.' And so
it marvelously came to pass, and she is now the fruitful mother of
several desirable children."

Among the books brought over by John Winthrop the younger, was a
volume containing the Greek testament, the Psalms, and the English
Common Prayer, bound together, to which happened an accident,
which was gravely described by the Governor in his daily history
of events:

"Decem 15. About this time there fell out a thing worthy of
observation. Mr. Winthrop the younger, one of the magistrates,
having many books in a chamber where there was corn of divers
sorts, had among them one, wherein the Greek testament, the psalms
and the common prayer were bound together. He found the common
prayer eaten with mice, every leaf of it, and not any of the two
other touched, nor any other of his books, though there were above
a thousand. Not a Puritan of them all, unless it may be the
governor himself, but believed that the mice were agents of
the Almighty sent to testify His dissatisfaction with the
objectionable form of prayer, and not a fact in daily life but
became more and more the working of Providence. Thus, as the good
governor records later:

"A godly woman of the church of Boston, dwelling sometimes
in London, brought with her a parcel of very fine linen of great
value, which she set her heart too much upon, and had been at
charge to have it all newly washed, and curiously folded and
pressed, and so left it in press in her parlor over night. She had
a negro maid went into the room very late, and let fall some snuff of
the candle upon the linen, so as by morning all the linen was burned
to tinder, and the boards underneath, and some stools and a part of
the wainscot burned and never perceived by any in the
house, though some lodged in the chamber overhead, and no ceiling

between. But it pleased God that the loss of this linen did her much good, both in taking off her heart from worldly comforts, and in preparing her for a far greater affliction by the untimely death of her husband, who was slain not long after at Isle of Providence."

The thrifty housewife's heart goes out to this sister, whose "curiously folded and pressed linen," lavender-scented and fair, was the one reminder of the abounding and generous life from which she had come. It may have been a comfort to consider its loss a direct dispensation for her improvement, and by this time, natural causes were allowed to have no existence save as they became tools of this "Wonder-working Providence." It was the day of small things more literally than they knew, and in this perpetual consideration of small things, the largeness of their first purpose dwindled and contracted, and inconceivable pettiness came at last to be the seal upon much of their action. Mr. Johnson, a minister whose course is commented upon by Bradford, excommunicated his brother and own father, for disagreement from him in certain points of doctrine, though the same zeal weakened when called upon to act against his wife, who doubtless had means of influencing his judgment unknown to the grave elders who remonstrated. But the interest was as strong in the cut of a woman's sleeve as in the founding of a new Plantation. They mourned over their own degeneracy. "The former times were better than these," the croakers sighed, and Governor Bradford wrote of this special case; "In our time his wife was a grave matron, and very modest both in her apparel and all her demeanor, ready to any good works in her place, and helpful to many, especially the poor, and an ornament to his calling. She was a young widow when he married her, and had been a merchant's wife by whom he had a good estate, and was a godly woman; and because she wore such apparel as she had been formerly used to, which were neither excessive nor immodest, for their chiefest exception were against her wearing of some whalebone in the bodice and sleeves of her gown, corked shoes and other such like things as the citizens of her rank then used to wear. And although, for offence sake, she and he were willing to reform the fashions of them, so far as might be, without spoiling of their garments, yet it would not content them except they came full up to their size. Such was the strictness or rigidness (as now the term goes) of some in those times, as we can by experience and of our own knowledge, show in other instances."

Governor Bradford, who evidently leans in his own mind toward the side of Mistress Johnson, proceeds to show the undue severity of some of the brethren in Holland. "We were in the company of a godly man that had been a long time prisoner at Norwich for this cause, and was by Judge Cooke set at liberty. After going into the country he visited his friends, and returning that way again to go into the Low Countries by ship at Yarmouth, and so desired some of us to turn in with him to the house of an ancient woman in the city, who had been very kind and helpful to him in his sufferings. She knowing his voice, made him very welcome, and those with him. But after some time of their entertainment, being ready to depart, she came up to him and felt of his hand (for her eyes were dim with age) and perceiving it was something stiffened with starch, she was much displeased and reproved him very sharply, fearing God would not prosper his journey. Yet the man was a plain country man, clad in gray russet, without either welt or guard (as the proverb is) and the band he wore, scarce worth three-pence, made of their own home-spinning; and he was godly and humble as he was plain. What would such professors, if they were now living, say to the excess of our times?"

Women spoke their minds much more freely in the early days than later they were allowed to, this same "ancient woman" of Amsterdam, having a sister worker of equally uncompromising tongue and tendencies, who was, for her various virtues chosen as deaconess, "and did them service for many years, though she was sixty years of age when she was chosen. She honored her place and was an ornament to the congregation. She usually sat in a convenient place in the congregation, with a little birchen rod in her hand, and kept little children in great awe from disturbing the congregation. She did frequently visit the sick and weak, especially women, and, as there was need, called out maids and young women to watch and do them other helps as their necessity did require; and if they were poor, she would gather relief for them of those that were able, or acquaint the deacons; and she was obeyed as a mother in Israel and an officer of Christ."

Whether this dame had the same objection to starch as the more "ancient" one, is not recorded, but in any case she was not alone. Men and women alike, forswore the desired stiffness, retaining it only in their opinions. By the time that Anne Bradstreet had settled in Andover, bodily indulgence so far as adornment or the gratification of appetite went, had become a matter for courts to decide upon. Whether Simon Bradstreet gave up the curling locks which, while not flowing to his shoulders as in Colonel Hutchinson's case, still fell in thick rings about his neck, we have no means of knowing. His wife would naturally protest against the cropping, brought about by the more extreme, "who put their own cropped heads together in order to devise some scheme for compelling all other heads to be as well shorn as theirs were."

One of the first acts of John Endecott when again appointed governor of Massachusetts Bay, was "to institute a solemn association against long hair," but his success was indifferent, as evidenced in many a moan from reverend ministers and deacons. John Eliot, one of the sweetest and most saintly spirits among them, wrote that it was a "luxurious feminine prolixity for men to wear their hair long and to ... ruffle their heads in excesses of this kind," but in later years, with many another wearied antagonist of this abomination, added hopelessly--"the lust is insuperable." Tobacco was fulminated against with equal energy, but no decree of court could stamp out the beloved vice. Winthrop yielded to it, but afterward renounced it, and the ministers compared its smoke to the smoke ascending from the bottomless pit, but no denunciation could effectually bar it out, and tobacco and starch in the end asserted their right to existence and came into constant use. A miraculous amount of energy had been expended upon the heinousness of their use, and the very fury of protest brought a reaction equally strong. Radical even in her conservatism, New England sought to bind in one, two hopelessly incompatible conditions: intellectual freedom and spiritual slavery. Absolute obedience to an accepted formula of faith was hardly likely to remain a fact for a community where thought was stimulated not only by education and training but every circumstance of their daily lives. A people who had lived on intimate terms with the innermost counsels of the Almighty, and who listened for hours on Sunday to speculations on the component elements not only of the Almighty, but of all His works were, while apparently most reverential, losing all capacity for reverence in any ancient sense. Undoubtedly this very speculation did much to give breadth and largeness, too much belief preparing the way, first, for no belief, and, at last, for a return to the best in the old and a combination of certain features of the new, which seems destined to make something better for practical as well as spiritual life than the world has ever known.

The misfortune of the early Puritan was in too rigid a creed, too settled an assurance that all the revelation needed had been given. Unlike the Dunkard elders, who refused to formulate a creed, lest it should put them in a mental attitude that would hinder further glimpses of truth, they hastened to bind themselves and all generations to come in chains, which began to rattle before the last link was forged. Not a Baptist, or Quaker, or Antinomian but gave himself to the work of protestation, and the determined effort to throw off the tyranny and presumption of men no wiser than he. Whippings, imprisonments and banishments silenced these spirits temporarily, but the vibration of particles never ceased, and we know the final result of such action. No wonder that the silent work of disintegration, when it showed itself in the final apparent collapse of all creeds, was looked upon with horrified amazement, and a hasty gathering up of all the old particles with a conviction that fusing and forging again was as easy of accomplishment now as in the beginning. The attempt has proved their error.

Up to nearly the opening of the eighteenth century New England life kept pace with the advances in England. There was constant coming and going and a sense of common interests and common needs. But even before emigration practically ceased, the changes in modes of speech were less marked than in the old home. English speech altered in many points during the seventeenth century. Words dropped out of use, their places filled by a crowd of claimants, sometimes admitted after sharp scrutiny, as often denied, but ending in admitting themselves, as words have a trick of doing even when most thoroughly outlawed. But in New England the old methods saw no reason for change.

Forms of speech current in the England of the seventeenth century crystallized here and are heard to-day. "Yankeeisms" is their popular title, but the student of old English knows them rather as "Anglicisms." "Since the year 1640 the New England race has not received any notable addition to its original stock, and to-day their Anglican blood is as genuine and unmixed as that of any county in England."

Dr. Edward Freeman, in his "Impressions of America," says of New England particularly, the remark applying in part also to all the older states: "When anything that seems strange to a British visitor in American speech or American manners is not quite modern on the face of it, it is pretty certain to be something which was once common to the older and the newer England, but which the newer England has kept, while the older England has cast it aside." Such literature as had birth in New England adhered chiefly to the elder models, and has thus an archaic element that broader life and intercourse would have eliminated. The provincial stage, of feeble and uncertain, or stilled but equally uncertain expression was at hand, but for the first generation or so the

colonists had small time to consider forms of speech. Their passion
for knowledge, however, took on all the vitality that had forsaken
English ground, and that from that day to this, has made the first
thought of every New England community, East or West, a school.
Their corner-stone "rested upon a book." It has been calculated that
there was one Cambridge graduate for every two- hundred and
fifty inhabitants, and within six years from the
landing of John Winthrop and his party, Harvard College had begun
its work of baffling "that old deluder, Sathan," whose business in
part it was "to keep men from the knowledge of the Scriptures." To
secular learning they were indifferent, but every man must be able
to give reason for the faith that was in him, and the more tongues
in which such statement could be made the more confusion for this
often embarrassed but still undismayed Sathan. Orders of nobility
among them had passed. Very rarely were they joined by even a
simple "Sir," and as years went on, nobility came to be synonymous
with tyranny, and there was less and less love for every owner of
a title. To them the highest earthly distinction came to be found
in the highest learning. The earnest student deserved and obtained
all the honors that man could give him, and his epitaph even
recorded the same solemn and deep-seated admiration. "The ashes of
an hard student, a good scholar, and a great Christian."

Anne Bradstreet shared this feeling to the full, and might easily
have been the mother of whom Mather writes as saying to her little
boy: "Child, if God make thee a good Christian and a good scholar,
thou hast all that thy mother ever asked for thee." Simon
Bradstreet became both, and in due time pleased his mother by
turning sundry of her "Meditations" into Latin prose, in which
stately dress they are incorporated in her works. The New England
woman kept up as far as possible the same pursuits in which she
had been trained, and among others the concoction of innumerable
tinctures and waters, learned in the 'still-room' of every
substantial English home. Room might have given place to a mere
corner, but the work went on with undiminished interest and
enthusiasm. There were few doctors, and each family had its own
special formulas--infallible remedies for all ordinary diseases
and used indiscriminately and in combination where a case seemed
to demand active treatment. They believed in their own medicines
absolutely, and required equal faith in all upon whom they
bestowed them.

Sturdy English stock as were all these New England dames, and
blessed with a power of endurance which it required more than one
generation to lessen, they were as given to medicine-taking as
their descendants of to-day, and fully as certain that their own
particular prescription was more efficacious than all the rest put
together. Anne Bradstreet had always been delicate, and as time
went on grew more and more so. The long voyage and confinement to
salt food had developed certain tendencies that never afterward
left her, and there is more than a suspicion that scurvy had attacked
her among the rest. Every precaution was taken by Governor
Winthrop to prevent such danger for those who came later, and he
writes to his wife, directing her preparations for the
voyage: "Be sure to be warme clothed & to have store of fresh
provisions, meale, eggs putt up in salt or ground mault, butter,
ote meal, pease & fruits, & a large strong chest or 2, well
locked, to keep these provisions in; & be sure they be bestowed in
the shippe where they may be readyly come by.... Be sure to have

ready at sea 2 or 3 skilletts of several syzes, a large fryinge panne, a small stewinge panne, & a case to boyle a pudding in; store of linnen for use at sea, & sacke to bestow among the saylors: some drinking vessells & peuter & other vessells."

Dr. Nathaniel Wright, a famous physician of Hereford, and private physician to Oliver Cromwell for a time, had given Winthrop various useful prescriptions, and his medicines were in general use, Winthrop adding in this letter: "For physick you shall need no other but a pound of Doctor Wright's _Electuariu lenitivu_, & his direction to use it, a gallon of scirvy grasse, to drink a litle 5 or 6 morninges together, with some saltpeter dissolved in it, & a little grated or sliced nutmeg."

Dr. Wright's prescriptions were supplemented by a collection prepared for him by Dr. Edward Stafford of London, all of which were used with great effect, the governor's enthusiasm for medical receipts and amateur practice, passing on through several generations. A letter to his son John at Ispwich contains some of his views and a prescription for pills which were undoubtedly taken faithfully by Mistress Anne and administered as faithfully to the unwilling Simon, who like herself suffered from one or two attacks of fever. The colonists were, like all breakers of new ground, especially susceptible to fevers of every variety, and Governor Winthrop writes anxiously: "You must be very careful of taking cold about the loins; & when the ground is open, I will send you some pepper-wort roots. For the flux, there is no better medicine than the cup used two or three times, &, in case of sudden torments, a clyster of a quart of water boiled to a pint, which, with the quantity of two or three nutmegs of saltpetre boiled in it, will give present ease.

"For the pills, they are made of grated pepper, made up with turpentine, very stiff, and some flour withal; and four or five taken fasting, & fast two hours after. But if there be any fever with the flux, this must not be used till the fever is removed by the cup."

Each remedy bears the internal warrant of an immediate need for a fresh one, and it is easy to see from what source the national love of patent medicines has been derived. Another prescription faithfully tried by both giver and receiver, and which Anne Bradstreet may have tested in her various fevers, was sent to John Winthrop, Jr., by Sir Kenelm Digby and may be found with various other singularities in the collections of the Massachusetts Historical Society. "For all sorts of agues, I have of late tried the following magnetical experiment with infallible success. Pare the patient's nails when the fit is coming on, and put the parings into a little bag of fine linen or sarsenet, and tie that about a live eel's neck in a tub of water. The eel will die and the patient will recover. And if a dog or hog eat that eel, they will also die. I have known one that cured all deliriums and frenzies whatsoever, and at once taking, with an elixer made of dew, nothing but dew purified & nipped up in a glass & digested 15 months till all of it was become a gray powder, not one drop of humidity remaining. This I know to be true, & that first it was as black as ink, then green, then gray, & at 22 month's end it was as white & lustrous as any oriental pearl. But it cured manias at 15 months' end."

The mania for taking it or anything else sufficiently mysterious and unpleasant to give a value to its possession remains to this day. But the prescriptions made up by the chief magistrate had a double efficacy for a time that believed a king's touch held instant cure for the king's evil, and that the ordinary marks known to every physician familiar with the many phases of hysteria, were the sign-manual of witches. The good governor's list of remedies had been made up from the Stafford prescriptions, the diseases he arranged to deal with being "plague, smallpox, fevers, king's evil, insanity, and falling sickness," besides broken bones and all ordinary injuries.

Simples and mineral drugs are used indiscriminately, and there is one remedy on which Dr. Holmes comments, in an essay on "The Medical Profession in Massachusetts," "made by putting live toads into an earthern pot so as to half fill it, and baking and burning them 'in the open ayre, not in a house'--concerning which latter possibility I suspect Madam Winthrop would have had something to say--until they could be reduced by pounding, first into a brown and then into a black, powder." This powder was the infallible remedy "against the plague, small-pox; purples, all sorts of feavers; Poyson; either by way of Prevention or after Infection." Consumption found a cure in a squirrel, baked alive and also reduced to a Powder, and a horrible witches' broth of earth-worms and other abominations served the same purpose. The governor makes no mention of this, but he gives full details of an electuary of millipedes, otherwise sowbugs, which seems to have been used with distinguished success. Coral and amber were both powdered and used in special cases, and antimony and nitre were handled freely, with rhubarb and the whole series of ancient remedies. The Winthrop papers hold numberless letters from friends and patients testifying to the good he had done them or begging for further benefactions, one of these from the agitator, Samuel Gostun, who at eighty-two had ceased to trouble himself over anything but his own infirmities, holding a wonder how "a thing so little in quantity, so little in sent, so little in taste, and so little to sence in operation, should beget and bring forth such efects."

These prescriptions were handed down through four generations of Winthrops, who seem to have united law and medicine, a union less common than that of divinity and medicine.

Michael Wigglesworth, whom we know best through his "Day of Doom," visited and prescribed for the sick, "not only as a Pastor but as a Physician too, and this not only in his own town, but also in all those of the vicinity." But this was in later days, when John Eliot's desire had been accomplished, written to the Rev. Mr. Shepard in 1647: "I have thought in my heart that it were a very singular good work, if the Lord would stirre up the hearts of some or other of his people in England, to give some maintenance toward some Schoole or Collegiate exercise this way, wherein there should be Anatomies and other instructions that way, and where there might be some recompense given to any that should bring in any vegetable or other thing that is vertuous in the way of Physick. There is another reason which moves my thought and desires this way, namely, that our young students in Physick may be trained up better than they yet bee, who have onely theoreticall knowledge, and are forced to fall to practice before ever they saw an Anatomy made, or duely trained up in making experiments, for we never had but one Anatomy in the countrey."

This anatomy had been made by Giles Firmin, who was the friend of Winthrop and of the Bradstreet's, and who found the practice of medicine so little profitable that he wrote to the former: "I am strongly set upon to studye divinity; my studyes else must be lost, for physick is but a meene helpe." A "meene helpe" it proved for many years, during which the Puritan dames steeped herbs and made ointments and lotions after formulas learned in the still-room at home. The little Bradstreet's doubtless swallowed their full share, though fortunately blessed for the most part with the sturdy constitution of their father, who, save for a fever or two, escaped most of the sicknesses common to the colonists and lived through many serene and untroubled years of physical and mental health, finding life enjoyable even at four-score and ten.

CHAPTER

IX.

ANDOVER.

What causes may have led to the final change of location we have no means of knowing definitely, save that every Puritan desired to increase the number of churches as much as possible; a tendency inherited to its fullest by their descendants. On the 4th of March, 1634-5, "It is ordered that the land aboute Cochichowicke, shall be reserved for an inland plantacon, & that whosoever will goe to inhabite there, shall have three yeares imunity from all taxes, levyes, publique charges & services whatsoever, (millitary dissipline onely excepted), etc."

Here is the first suggestion of what was afterward to become Andover, but no action was taken by Bradstreet until 1638, when in late September, "Mr. Bradstreet, Mr. Dudley, Junior, Captain Dennison, Mr. Woodbridge and eight others, are allowed (upon their petition) to begin a plantation at Merrimack."

This plantation grew slowly. The Bradstreets lingered at Ipswich, and the formal removal, the last of many changes, did not take place until September, 1644. Simon Bradstreet, the second son, afterward minister at New London, Conn., whose manuscript diary is a curious picture of the time, gives one or two details which aid in fixing the date.

"1640. I was borne N. England, at Ipswitch, Septem. 28 being Munday 1640.

"1651. I had my Education in the same Town at the free School, the master of w'ch was my ever respected ffreind Mr. Ezekiell Cheevers. My Father was removed from Ipsw. to Andover, before I was putt to school, so yt my schooling was more chargeable."

The thrifty spirit of his grandfather Dudley is shown in the final line, but Simon Bradstreet the elder never grudged the cost of anything his family needed or could within reasonable bounds desire, and stands to-day as one of the most signal early examples of that New England woman's ideal, "a good provider."

Other threads were weaving themselves into the "sad-colored" web of daily life, the pattern taking on new aspects as the days went on. Four years after the landing of the Arbella and her consorts, one of the many bands of Separatists, who followed their lead, came over, the celebrated Thomas Parker, one of the chief among them, and his nephew, John Woodbridge, an equally important though less distinguished member of the party. They took up land at Newbury, and settled to their work of building up a new home, as if no other occupation had ever been desired.

The story of John Woodbridge is that of hundreds of young Puritans who swelled the tide of emigration that between 1630 and 1640 literally poured into the country, "thronging every ship that pointed its prow thitherward." Like the majority of them, he was of good family and of strong individuality, as must needs be where a perpetual defiance is waged against law and order as it showed itself to the Prelatical party. He had been at Oxford and would have graduated, but for his own and his father's unwillingness that he should take the oath of conformity required, and in the midst of his daily labor, he still hoped privately to become one of that ministry, who were to New England what the House of Lords represented to the old. Prepossessing in appearance, with a singularly mild and gentle manner, he made friends on all sides, and in a short time came to be in great favor with Governor Dudley, whose daughter Mercy was then nearly the marriagable age of the time, sixteen. The natural result followed, and Mercy Dudley, in 1641, became Mercy Woodbridge, owning that name for fifty years, and bearing, like most Puritan matrons, many children, with the well marked traits that were also part of the time.

The young couple settled quietly at Newbury, but his aspiration was well known and often discussed by the many who desired to see the churches increased with greater speed. Dudley was one of the most earnest workers in this direction, but there is a suggestion that the new son-in-law's capacity for making a good bargain had influenced his feelings, and challenged the admiration all good New Englanders have felt from the beginning for any "fore handed" member of their community. This, however, was only a weakness among many substantial virtues which gave him a firm place in the memory of his parishioners. But the fact that after he resigned his ministry he was recorded as "remarkably blest in private estate," shows some slight foundation for the suggestion, and gives solid ground for Dudley's special interest in him.

A letter is still in existence which shows this, as well as Dudley's entire willingness to take trouble where a benefit to anyone was involved. Its contents had evidently been the subject of very serious consideration, before he wrote:

SON WOODBRIDGE:

On your last going from Rocksbury, I thought you would have returned again before your departure hence, and therefore neither bade you farewell, nor sent any remembrance to your wife. Since which time I have often thought of you, and of the course of your life, doubting you are not in the way wherein you may do God best service. Every man ought (as I take it) to serve God in such a way whereto he had best filled him by nature, education or gifts, or graces acquired. Now in all these respects I concieve you to be better fitted for the ministry, or teaching a school, than for husbandry. And I have been lately stirred up the rather to think thereof by occasion of Mr. Carter's calling to be pastor at Woburn the last week, and Mr. Parker's calling to preach at Pascattaway, whose abilities and piety (for aught I know) surmount not yours. There is a want of school-masters hereabouts, and ministers are, or in likelihood will be, wanting ere long. I desire that you would seriously consider of what I say, and take advise of your uncle, Mr. Nayse, or whom you think meetest about it; withal considering that no man's opinion in a case wherein he is interested by reason of your departure from your present habitation is absolutely to be allowed without comparing his reason with others. And if you find encouragement, I think you were best redeem what time you may without hurt of your estate, in perfecting your former studies. Above all, commend the case in prayer to God, that you may look before you with a sincere eye upon his service, not upon filthy lucre, which I speak not so much for any doubt I have of you, but to clear myself from that suspicion in respect of the interest I have in you. I need say no more. The Lord direct and bless you, your wife and children, whom I would fain see, and have again some thoughts of it, if I live till next summer.

> Your very loving father,
> THOMAS
> DUDLEY.
Rocksbury, November 28, 1642.
To my very loving son, Mr. John Woodbridge, at his house in Newbury.

As an illustration of Dudley's strong family affection the letter is worth attention, and its advice was carried out at once. The celebrated Thomas Parker, his uncle, became his instructor, and for a time the young man taught the school in Boston, until fixed upon as minister for the church in Andover, which in some senses owes its existence to his good offices. The thrifty habits which had made it evident in the beginning to the London Company that Separatists were the only colonists who could be trusted to manage finances properly, had not lessened with years, and had seldom had more thorough gratification than in the purchase of Andover, owned then by Cutshamache "Sagamore of ye Massachusetts."

If he repented afterward of his bargain, as most of them did, there is no record, but for the time being he was satisfied with "ye sume of L6 & a coate," which the Rev. John Woodbridge duly paid over, the town being incorporated under the name of Andover in 1646, as may still be seen in the Massachusetts Colony Records, which read: "At a general Court at Boston 6th of 3d month, 1646, Cutshamache, Sagamore of Massachusetts, came into the court and acknowledged that, for the sum of L6 and a coat which he had already received, he had sold to Mr. John Woodbridge, in behalf of the inhabitants of Cochichewick, now called Andover, all the right, interest and privilege in the land six miles southward from the town, two miles eastward to Rowley bounds, be the same more or less; northward to Merrimack river, provided that the Indian called Roger, and his company, may have liberty to take alewives in Cochichewick river for their own eating; but if they either

spoil or steal any corn or other fruit to any considerable value
of the inhabitants, the liberty of taking fish shall forever
cease, and the said Roger is still to enjoy four acres of ground
where now he plants."

Punctuation and other minor matters are defied here, as in many
other records of the time, but it is plain that Cutshamache
considered that he had made a good bargain, and that the Rev. John
Woodbridge, on his side was equally satisfied.

The first settlements were made about Cochichewick Brook, a "fair
springe of sweet water." The delight in the cold, clear New
England water comes up at every stage of exploration in the early
records. In the first hours of landing, as Bradford afterward
wrote, they "found springs of fresh water of which we were
heartily glad, and sat us down and drunk our first New England
water, with as much delight as ever we drunk drink in all our
lives."

"The waters are most pure, proceeding from the entrails of rocky
mountains," wrote John Smith in his enthusiastic description, and
Francis Higginson was no less moved. "The country is full of
dainty springs," he wrote, "and a sup of New England's air is
better than a whole draught of old England's ale." The "New
English Canaan" recorded: "And for the water it excelleth Canaan
by much; for the land is so apt for fountains, a man cannot dig
amiss. Therefore if the Abrahams and Lots of our time come
thither, there needs be no contention for wells. In the delicacy
of waters, and the conveniency of them, Canaan came not near this
country." Boston owed its first settlement to its "sweet and
pleasant springs," and Wood made it a large inducement to
emigration, in his "New England's Prospect." "The country is as
well watered as any land under the sun; every family or every two
families, having a spring of sweet water betwixt them. It is
thought there can be no better water in the world." New Englanders
still hold to this belief, and the soldier recalls yet the vision
of the old well, or the bubbling spring in the meadow that
tantalized and mocked his longing in the long marches, or in the
hospital wards of war time.

The settlement gathered naturally about the brook, and building
began vigorously, the houses being less hastily constructed than
in the first pressure of the early days, and the meeting-house
taking precedence of all.

Even, however, with the reverence inwrought in the very name of
minister we must doubt if Anne Bradstreet found the Rev. John
Woodbridge equal to the demand born in her, by intercourse with
such men as Nathaniel Ward or Nathaniel Rogers, or that he could
ever have become full equivalent for what she had lost. With her
intense family affection, she had, however, adopted him at once,
and we have very positive proof of his deep interest in her,
which showed itself at a later date. This change from simple
"husbandman" to minister had pleased her pride, and like all
ministers he had shared the hardships of his congregation and
known often sharp privation. It is said that he was the second one
ordained in New England, and like most others his salary for years
was paid half in wheat and half in coin, and his life divided
itself between the study and the farm, which formed the chief

support of all the colonists. His old record mentions how he endeared himself to all by his quiet composure and patience and his forgiving temper. He seems to have yearned for England, and this desire was probably increased by his connection with the Dudley family. Anne Bradstreet's sympathies, in spite of all her theories and her determined acceptance of the Puritan creed, were still monarchical, and Mercy would naturally share them. Dudley himself never looked back, but the "gentlewoman of fortune" whom he married, was less content, and her own hidden longing showed itself in her children. Friends urged the young preacher to return, which he did in 1647, leaving wife and children behind him, his pastorate having lasted but a year. There is a letter of Dudley's, written in 1648, addressed to him as "preacher of the word of God at Andover in Wiltshire," and advising him of what means should be followed to send his wife and children, but our chief interest in him lies in the fact, that he carried with him the manuscript of Anne Bradstreet's poems, which after great delay, were published at London in 1650. He left her a quiet, practically unknown woman, and returned in 1662, to find her as widely praised as she is now forgotton; the "Tenth Muse, Lately sprung up in America."

What part of them were written in Andover there is no means of knowing, but probably only a few of the later ones, not included in the first edition. The loneliness and craving of her Ipswich life, had forced her to composition as a relief, and the major part of her poems were written before she was thirty years old, and while she was still hampered by the methods of the few she knew as masters. With the settling at Andover and the satisfying companionship of her husband, the need of expression gradually died out, and only occasional verses for special occasions, seem to have been written. The quiet, busy life, her own ill-health, and her absorption in her children, all silenced her, and thus, the work that her ripened thought and experience might have made of some value to the world, remained undone. The religious life became more and more the only one of any value to her, and she may have avoided indulgence in favorite pursuits, as a measure against the Adversary whose temptations she recorded. Our interest at present is in these first Andover years, and the course of life into which the little community settled, the routine holding its own interpretation of the silence that ensued. The first sharp bereavement had come, a year or so before the move was absolutely determined upon, Mrs. Dudley dying late in December of 1643, at Roxbury, to which they had moved in 1639, and her epitaph as written by her daughter Anne, shows what her simple virtues had meant for husband and children.

AN EPITAPH

ON MY DEAR AND EVER-HONORED

MOTHER, MRS. DOROTHY DUDLEY,

WHO DECEASED DECEMB 27 1643, AND OF HER AGE 61.

Here lyes
A worthy Matron of unspotted life,
A loving Mother and obedient
wife, A friendly Neighbor pitiful to
poor,

Whom oft she fed and clothed with her store,
To Servants wisely aweful but yet kind,
And as they did so they reward did find;
A true Instructer of her Family,
The which she ordered with dexterity.
The publick meetings ever did frequent,
And in her Closet constant hours she spent;
Religious in all her words and wayes
Preparing still for death till end of dayes;
Of all her Children, Children lived to
see, Then dying, left a blessed memory."

There is a singular aptitude for marriage in these old Puritans. They
"married early, and if opportunity presented, married often." Even
Governor Winthrop, whose third marriage lasted for thirty years,
and whose love was as deep and fervent at the end as in the
beginning, made small tarrying, but as his biographer delicately
puts it, "he could not live alone, and needed the support and
comfort which another marriage could alone afford him." He did
mourn the faithful Margaret a full year, but Governor Dudley
had fewer scruples and tarried only until the following April,
marrying then Catherine, widow of Samuel Hackburne, the first son
of this marriage, Joseph Dudley, becoming even more distinguished
than his father, being successively before his death, Governor of
Massachusetts, Lieutenant Governor of the Isle of Wight, and first
Chief Justice of New York, while thirteen children handed on the
name. The first son, Samuel, who married a daughter of Governor
Winthrop, and thus healed all the breaches that misunderstanding
had made, was the father of eighteen children, and all through the
old records are pictures of these exuberant Puritan families.
Benjamin Franklin was one of seventeen. Sir William Phipps, the
son of a poor gunsmith at Pemaquid, and one of the first and most
notable instances of our rather tiresome "self-made men," was one
of twenty-six, twenty-one being sons, while Roger Clapp of
Dorchester, handed down names that are in themselves the story of
Puritanism, his nine, being Experience, Waitstill, Preserved,
Hopestill, Wait, Thanks, Desire, Unite and Supply. The last name
typifies the New England need, and Tyler, whose witty yet
sympathetic estimate of the early Puritans is yet to be surpassed,
writes: "It hardly needs to be mentioned after this, that the
conditions of life there were not at all those for which Malthus
subsequently invented his theory of inhospitality to infants.
Population was sparce; work was plentiful; food was plentiful;
and the arrival in the household of a new child was not the arrival
of
a new appetite among a brood of children already half-fed--it was
rather the arrival of a new helper where help was scarcer than
food; it was, in fact, a fresh installment from heaven of what
they called, on Biblical authority, the very 'heritage of the
Lord.' The typical household of New England was one of patriarchal
populousness. Of all the sayings of the Hebrew Psalmist--except,
perhaps, the damnatory ones--it is likely that they rejoiced most
in those which expressed the Davidic appreciation of multitudinous
children: 'As arrows are in the hand of a mighty man, so are
children of the youth. Happy is the man that hath his quiver full
of them; they shall not be ashamed, but they shall speak with the
enemies in the gate.' The New Englanders had for many years quite
a number of enemies in the gate, whom they wished to be able to
speak with, in the unabashed manner intimated by the devout
warrior of Israel."

Hardly a town in New England holds stronger reminders of the past, or has a more intensely New England atmosphere than Andover, wherein the same decorous and long-winded discussions of fate, fore-knowledge and all things past and to come, still goes on, as steadily as if the Puritan debaters had merely transmigrated, not passed over, to a land which even the most resigned and submissive soul would never have wished to think of as a "Silent Land." All that Cambridge has failed to preserve of the ancient spirit lives here in fullest force, and it stands to-day as one of the few representatives remaining of the original Puritan faith and purpose. Its foundation saw instant and vigorous protest, at a small encroachment, which shows strongly the spirit of the time. A temporary church at Rowley was suggested, while the future one was building, and Hubbard writes: "They had given notice thereof to the magistrates and ministers of the neighboring churches, as the manner is with them in New England. The meeting of the assembly was to be at that time at Rowley; the forementioned plantations being but newly erected, were not capable to entertain them that were likely to be gathered together on that occasion. But when they were assembled, most of those who were to join together in church fellowship, at that time, refused to make confession of their faith and repentance, because, as was said, they declared it openly before in other churches upon their admission into them. Whereupon the messengers of the churches not being satisfied, the assembly broke up, before they had accomplished what they intended."

English reticence and English obstinacy were both at work, the one having no mind to make a private and purely personal experience too common; the other, resenting the least encroachment on the Christian liberty they had sought and proposed to hold. By October, the messengers had decided to compromise, some form of temporary church was decided upon, and the permanent one went up swiftly as hands could work. It had a bell, though nobody knows from whence obtained, and it owned two galleries, one above another, the whole standing till 1711, when a new and larger one became necessary, the town records describing, what must have been a building of some pretension, "50 feet long, 45 feet wide, and 24 feet between joints"; and undoubtedly a source of great pride to builders and congregation. No trace of it at present remains, save the old graveyard at the side, "an irregular lot, sparsely covered with ancient moss-grown stones, in all positions, straggling, broken and neglected, and overrun with tall grass and weeds." But in May, as the writer stood within the crumbling wall, the ground was thick with violets and "innocents," the grass sprung green and soft and thick, and the blue sky bent over it, as full of hope and promise as it seemed to the eyes that two hundred years before, had looked through tears, upon its beauty. From her window Mistress Bradstreet could count every slab, for the home she came to is directly opposite, and when detained there by the many illnesses she suffered in later days, she could, with opened windows, hear the psalm lined out, and even, perhaps, follow the argument of the preacher. But before this ample and generous home rose among the elms, there was the usual period of discomfort and even hardship. Simon Bradstreet was the only member of the little settlement who possessed any considerable property, but it is evident that he shared the same discomforts in the beginning. In 1658 there is record of a house which he had owned, being sold to another proprieter, Richard Sutton, and this was probably the log-house built before their coming, and lived in until the larger one had slowly been made ready.

The town had been laid out on the principle followed in all the early settlements, and described in one of the early volumes of the Massachusetts Historical Society Collections. Four, or at the utmost, eight acres, constituted a homestead, but wood-lots and common grazing lands, brought the amount at the disposal of each settler to a sufficient degree for all practical needs. It is often a matter of surprise in studying New England methods to find estates which may have been owned by the same family from the beginning, divided in the most unaccountable fashion, a meadow from three to five miles from the house, and wood-lots and pasture at equally eccentric distances. But this arose from the necessities of the situation. Homes must be as nearly side by side as possible, that Indians and wild beasts might thus be less dangerous and that business be more easily transacted. Thus the arrangement of a town was made always to follow this general plan:

"Suppose ye towne square 6 miles every waye. The houses orderly placed about ye midst especially ye meeting house, the which we will suppose to be ye center of ye wholl circumference. The greatest difficulty is for the employment of ye parts most remote, which (if better direction doe not arise) may be this: the whole being 6 miles, the extent from ye meeting-house in ye center, will be unto every side 3 miles; the one half whereof being 2500 paces round about & next unto ye said center, in what condition soever it lyeth, may well be distributed & employed unto ye house within ye compass of ye same orderly placed to enjoye comfortable conveniance. Then for that ground lying without, ye neerest circumference may be thought fittest to be imployed in farmes into which may be placed skillful bred husbandmen, many or fewe as they may be attayned unto to become farmers, unto such portions as each of them may well and in convenient time improve according to the portion of stocke each of them may be intrusted with."

House-lots would thus be first assigned, and then in proportion to each of them, the farm lands, called variously, ox-ground, meadow-land, ploughing ground, or mowing land, double the amount being given to the owner of an eight-acre house-lot, and such lands being held an essential part of the property. A portion of each township was reserved as "common or undivided land," not in the sense in which "common" is used in the New England village of to-day, but simply for general pasturage. With Andover, as with many other of the first settlements, these lands were granted or sold from time to time up to the year 1800, when a final sale was made, and the money appropriated for the use of free schools.

As the settlement became more secure, many built houses on the farm lands, and removed from the town, but this was at first peremptorily forbidden, and for many years after could not be done without express permission. Mr. Bradstreet, as magistrate, naturally remained in the town, and the new house, the admiration of all and the envy of a few discontented spirits, was watched as it grew, by its mistress, who must have rejoiced that at last some prospect of permanence lay before her. The log house in which she waited, probably had not more than four rooms, at most, and forced them to a crowding which her ample English life had made doubly distasteful. She had a terror of fire and with reason, for while still at Cambridge her father's family had had in 1632 the narrowest of escapes, recorded by Winthrop in his Journal: "About this time Mr. Dudley, his house, at Newtown, was preserved from burning down, and all his family from being destroyed by gunpowder, by a marvellous deliverance--the hearth of the hall chimney burning all night upon a principal beam, and store of powder being near, and not discovered till they arose in the morning, and then it began to flame out."

The thatch of the early house, which were of logs rilled in with clay, was always liable to take fire, the chimneys being of logs and often not clayed at the top. Dudley had warned against this carelessness in the first year of their coming, writing: "In our new town, intended this summer to be builded, we have ordered, that no man there shall build his chimney with wood, nor cover his house with thatch, which was readily assented unto; for that divers houses since our arrival (the fire always beginning in the wooden chimneys), and some English wigwams, which have taken fire in the roofs covered with thatch or boughs." With every precaution, there was still constant dread of fire, and Anne must have rejoiced in the enormous chimney of the new house, heavily buttressed, running up through the centre and showing in the garret like a fortification. This may have been an enlargement on the plan of the first, for the house now standing, took the place of the one burned to the ground in July, 1666, but duplicated as exactly as possible, at a very short time thereafter. Doubts have been expressed as to whether she ever lived in it, but they have small ground for existence. It is certain that Dudley Bradstreet occupied it, and it has been known from the beginning as the "Governor's house." Its size fitted it for the large hospitality to which she had been brought up and which was one of the necessities of their position, and its location is a conspicuous and important one.

Whatever temptation there may have been to set houses in the midst of grounds, and make their surroundings hold some reminder of the fair English homes they had left, was never yielded to. To be near the street, and within hailing distance of one another, was a necessity born of their circumstances. Dread of Indians, and need of mutual help, massed them closely together, and the town ordinances forbade scattering. So the great house, as it must have been for long, stood but a few feet from the old Haverhill and Boston road, surrounded by mighty elms, one of which measured, twenty-five years ago, "sixteen and a half feet in circumference, at one foot above the ground, well deserving of mention in the 'Autocrat's' list of famous trees." The house faces the south, and has a peculiar effect, from being two full stories high in front, and sloping to one, and that a very low one, at the back. The distance between caves and ground is here so slight, that one may fancy a venturous boy in some winter when the snow had drifted high, sliding from ridge pole to ground, and even tempting a small and ambitious sister to the same feat. Massive old timbers form the frame of the house, and the enormous chimney heavily buttressed on the four sides is exactly in the center, the fireplaces being rooms in themselves. The rooms at present are high studded, the floor having been sunk some time ago, but the doors are small and low, indicating the former proportions and making a tall man's progress a series of bows. Some of the walls are wainscotted and some papered, modern taste, the taste of twenty-five years ago, having probably chosen to remove wainscotting, as despised then as it is now desired. At the east is a deep hollow through which flows a little brook, skirted by alders, "green in summer, white in winter," where the Bradstreet children waded, and fished for shiners with a crooked pin, and made dams, and conducted themselves in all points like the children of to-day. Beyond the brook rises the hill, on the slope of which the meeting-house once stood, and where wild strawberries grew as they grow to-day.

A dense and unbroken circle of woods must have surrounded the settlement, and cut off many glimpses of river and hill that to-day make the drives about Andover full of surprise and charm. Slight changes came in the first hundred years. The great mills at Lawrence were undreamed of and the Merrimack flowed silently to the sea, untroubled by any of mans' uses.

Today the hillsides are green and smooth. Scattered farms are seen, and houses outside the town proper are few, and the quiet country gives small hint of the active, eager life so near it. In 1810, Dr. Timothy Dwight, whose travels in America were read with the same interest that we bestow now upon the "Merv Oasis," or the "Land of the White Elephant," wrote of North Andover, which then held many of its original features:

"North Andover is a very beautiful piece of ground. Its surface is elegantly undulating, and its soil in an eminent degree, fertile. The meadows are numerous, large and of the first quality. The groves, charmingly interspersed, are tall and thrifty. The landscape, everywhere varied, neat and cheerful, is also everywhere rich.

"The Parish is a mere collection of plantations, without anything like a village. The houses are generally good, some are large and elegant The barns are large and well-built and indicate a fertile and well-cultivated soil.

"Upon the whole, Andover is one of the best farming towns in Eastern Massachusetts."

Andover roads were of incredible crookedness, though the Rev. Timothy makes no mention of this fact: "They were at first designed to accommodate individuals, and laid out from house to house," and thus the traveller found himself quite as often landed in a farm-yard, as at the point aimed for. All about are traces of disused and forgotten path-ways--

"Old roads winding, as old roads
will, Some to a river and some to a
mill,"

and even now, though the inhabitant is sure of his ground, the stranger will swear that there is not a street, called, or deserving to be called, straight, in all its borders. But this was of even less consequence then than now. The New England woman has never walked when she could ride, and so long as the church stood within easy distance, demanded nothing more. One walk of Anne Bradstreets' is recorded in a poem, and it is perhaps because it was her first, that it made so profound an impression, calling

out, as we shall presently see, some of the most natural and
melodious verse which her serious and didactic Muse ever allowed
her, and being still a faithful picture of the landscape it
describes. But up to the beginning of the Andover life, Nature had
had small chance of being either seen or heard, for an increasing
family, the engrossing cares of a new settlement, and the Puritan
belief that "women folk were best indoors," shut her off from
influences that would have made her work mean something to the
present day. She had her recreations as well as her cares, and we
need now to discover just what sort of life she and the Puritan
sisterhood in general led in the first years, whose "new manners
and customs," so disturbed her conservative spirit.

CHAPTER X.

VILLAGE LIFE IN 1650.

Of the eight children that came to Simon and Anne Bradstreet, but
one was born in the "great house" at Andover, making his
appearance in 1652, when life had settled into the routine that
thereafter knew little change, save in the one disastrous experience
of 1666. This son, John, who like all the rest, lived
to marry and leave behind him a plenteous family of children, was
a baby of one year old, when the first son, Samuel, "stayed for
many years," was graduated at Harvard College, taking high honor
in his class, and presently settling as a physician in Boston,
sufficiently near to be called upon in any emergency in the
Andover home, and visited often by the younger brothers, each of
whom became a Harvard graduate. Samuel probably had no share in
the removal, but Dorothy and Sarah, Simon and Hannah, were all old
enough to rejoice in the upheaval, and regard the whole episode as
a prolonged picnic made for their especial benefit. Simon was
then six years old, quite ready for Latin grammar and other
responsibilities of life, and according to the Puritan standard,
an accountable being from whom too much trifling could by no means
be allowed, and who undoubtedly had a careful eye to the small
Hannah, aged four, also old enough to knit a stocking and sew a seam,
and read her chapter in the Bible with the best. Dorothy and Sarah
could take even more active part, yet even the mature ages
of eight and ten did not hinder surreptitious tumbles into heaped
up feather beds, and a scurry through many a once forbidden corner
of the Ipswich home. For them there was small hardship in the log
house that received them, and unending delight in watching the
progress of the new. And one or another must often have ridden
before the father, who loved them with more demonstration than the
Puritan habit allowed, and who in his frequent rides to the new
mill built on the Cochichewick in 1644, found a petitioner
always urging to be taken, too. The building of the mill probably
preceded that of the house, as Bradstreet thought always of public
interests before his own, though in this case the two were nearly
identical, a saw and grist-mill being one of the first necessities
of any new settlement, and of equal profit to owner and users.

Anne Bradstreet was now a little over thirty, five children
absorbing much of her thought and time, three more being added

during the first six years at Andover. When five had passed out
into the world and homes of their own, she wrote, in 1656, half
regretfully, yet triumphantly, too, a poem which is really a
family biography, though the reference to her fifth child as a
son, Mr. Ellis regards as a slip of the pen:

"I had eight birds hatcht in one nest,
Four Cocks there were, and Hens the rest; I
nurst them up with pain and care,
Nor cost, nor labour did I spare, Till at
the last they felt their wing, Mounted
the Trees, and learn'd to sing; Chief of
the Brood then took his flight
To Regions far, and left me quite;
My mournful chirps I after send,
Till he return, or I do end;
Leave not thy nest, thy Dam and Sire,
Fly back and sing amidst this Quire.
My second bird did take her flight,
And with her mate flew out of sight;
Southward they both their course did bend,
And Seasons twain they there did spend;
Till after blown by Southern gales,
They Norward steer'd with filled
Sayles. A prettier bird was no where
seen,
Along the beach among the treen.

I have a third of colour white
On whom I plac'd no small delight;
Coupled with mate loving and true,
Hath also bid her Dam adieu;
And where Aurora first appears,
She now hath percht, to spend her years;
One to the Academy flew
To chat among that learned crew;
Ambition moves still in his breast
That he might chant above the rest,
Striving for more than to do well,
That nightingales he might excell.
My fifth, whose down is yet scarce gone
Is 'mongst the shrubs and bushes flown,
And as his wings increase in strength,
On higher boughs he'l pearch at length.
My other three, still with me nest,
Untill they'r grown, then as the rest,
Or here or there, they'l take their flight,
As is ordain'd, so shall they light.
If birds could weep, then would my tears
Let others know what are my fears
Lest this my brood some harm should catch,
And be surpriz'd for want of watch,
Whilst pecking corn, and void of care
They fish un'wares in Fowler's snare;
Or whilst on trees they sit and sing,
Some untoward boy at them do fling;
Or whilst allur'd with bell and glass,
The net be spread, and caught, alas.
Or least by Lime-twigs they be foyl'd,
Or by some greedy hawks be spoyl'd.

O, would my young, ye saw my breast,
And knew what thoughts there sadly rest,
Great was my pain when I you bred,
Great was my care when I you fed,
Long did I keep you soft and warm,
And with my wings kept off all
harm;
My cares are more, and fears then ever,
My throbs such now, as 'fore were never;
Alas, my birds, you wisdome want,
Of perils you are ignorant;
Oft times in grass, on trees, in flight,
Sore accidents on you may light.
O, to your safety have an eye,
So happy may you live and die;
Mean while my dayes in tunes I'll spend,
Till my weak layes with me shall end.

In shady woods I'll sit and sing,
And things that past, to mind I'll bring.
Once young and pleasant, as are you,
But former boyes (no joyes) adieu.
My age I will not once lament,
But sing, my time so near is spent.
And from the top bough take my
flight, Into a country beyond sight,
Where old ones, instantly grow young,
And there with Seraphims set song;
No seasons cold, nor storms they see,
But spring lasts to eternity;
When each of you shall in your nest
Among your young ones take your rest,
In chirping language, oft them tell,
You had a Dam that lov'd you well,
That did what could be done for young,
And nurst you up till you were strong,
And 'fore she once would let you fly,
She shew'd you joy and misery;
Taught what was good, and what was ill,
What would save life, and what would
kill? Thus gone, amongst you I may live,
And dead, yet speak, and counsel give;
Farewel, my birds, farewel, adieu,
I happy am, if well with you.
    A. B."

The Bradstreets and Woodbridges carried with them to Andover, more
valuable worldly possessions than all the rest put together, yet
even for them the list was a very short one. An inventory of the
estate of Joseph Osgood, the most influential citizen after Mr.
Bradstreet, shows that only bare necessities had gone with him.
His oxen and cattle and the grain stored in his barn are given
first, with the value of the house and land and then follow the
list of household belongings, interesting now as showing with how
little a reputable and honored citizen had found it possible to
bring up a family.

A feather bed and furniture.
A flock bed, (being half feathers) &
furniture. A flock bed & furniture.

Five payre of sheets & an odd one.
Table linen.
Fower payre of pillow-beeres.
Twenty-two pieces of pewter.
For Iron pott, tongs, cottrell & pot-
hooks. Two muskets & a fowling-piece.
Sword, cutlass & bandaleeres.
Barrels, tubbs, trays, cheese-moates and pailes.
A Stand.
Bedsteads, cords & chayers.
Chests and wheels.

Various yards of stuffs and English cloth are also included, but
nothing could well be more meager than this outfit, though
doubtless it filled the narrow quarters of the early years.
Whatever may have come over afterward, there were none of the
heirlooms to be seen to-day, in the shape of family portraits, and
plate, china or heavily carved mahogany or oak furniture. For the
poorer houses, only panes of oiled paper admitted the light, and
this want of sunshine was one cause of the terrible loss of life
in fevers and various epidemics from which the first settlers
suffered. Leaden sashes held the small panes of glass used by the
better class, but for both the huge chimneys with their roaring
fires did the chief work of ventilation and purification, while
the family life centered about them in a fashion often described
and long ago lost.

There is a theory that our grandmothers in these first days of the
settlement worked with their own hands, with an energy never since
equalled, and more and more departed from as the years go on. But
all investigation of early records shows that, as far as
practicable, all English habits remained in full force, and among
such habits was that of ample service.

It is true that mistress and maid worked side by side, but the tasks
performed now by any farmer's wife are as hard and more continuous
than any labor of the early days, where many hands made light work.
If spinning and weaving have passed out of the hands
of women, the girls who once shared in the labor, and helped to
make up the patriarchal households of early times, have followed,
preferring the monotonous and wearing routine of mill-life, to the
stigma resting upon all who consent to be classed as "help". If
social divisions were actually sharper and more stringent in the
beginning, there was a better relation between mistress and maid,
for which we look in vain to-day.

In many cases, men and women secured their passage to America by
selling their time for a certain number of years, and others whose
fortunes were slightly better, found it well, until some means of
living was secured, to enter the families of the more wealthy
colonists, many of whom had taken their English households with
them. So long as families centered in one spot, there was little
difficulty in securing servants, but as new settlements were
formed servants held back, naturally preferring the towns to the
chances of Indian raids and the dangers from wild beasts.
Necessity brought about a plan which has lasted until within a
generation or so, and must come again, as the best solution of the
servant problem. Roger Williams writes of his daughter that "she
desires to spend some time in service & liked much Mrs. Brenton

who wanted help." This word "help" applied itself to such cases, distinguishing them from those of the ordinary servant, and girls of the good families put themselves under notable housekeepers to learn the secrets of the profession--a form of cooking and household economy school, that we sigh for vainly to-day. The Bradstreets took their servants from Ipswich, but others in the new town were reduced to sore straits, in some cases being forced to depend on the Indian woman, who, fresh from the wigwam, looked in amazement on the superfluities of civilized life. Hugh Peters, the dogmatic and most unpleasant minister of Salem, wrote to a Boston friend: "Sir, Mr Endecott & myself salute you in the Lord Jesus, &c. Wee have heard of a dividence of woman & children in the bay & would be glad of a share, viz: a young woman or girle & a boy if you thinke good." This was accomplished but failed to satisfy, for two years later Peters again writes: "My wife desires my daughter to send to Hanna that was her mayd, now at Charltowne, to know if shee would dwell with us, for truly wee are so destitute (having now but an Indian) that wee know not what to do." This was a desperate state of things, on which Lowell comments: "Let any housewife of our day, who does not find the Keltic element in domestic life so refreshing as to Mr. Arnold in literature, imagine a household with one wild Pequot woman, communicated with by signs, for its maid of all work, and take courage. Those were serious times indeed, when your cook might give warning by taking your scalp, or chignon, as the case might be, and making off with it, into the woods."

Negro slavery was the first solution of these difficulties and one hard-headed member of the Colony, Emanual Downing, as early as 1645, saw in the Indian wars and the prisoners that were taken, a convenient means of securing the coveted negro, and wrote to Winthrop: "A war with the Narragansett is very considerable to this plantation, ffor I doubt whither it be not synne in us, having power in our hands, to suffer them to maynteine the worship of the devill which their paw-wawes often doe; 2 lie, If upon a just warre the Lord should deliver them into our hands, wee might easily have men, woemen and children enough to exchange for Moores, which wilbe more gaynefull pillage for us than wee conceive, for I do not see how we can thrive untill wee gett into a stock of slaves, sufficient to doe all our buisenes, for our children's children will hardly see this great Continent filled with people, soe that our servants will still desire freedome to plant for themselves, and not stay but for verie great wages. And I suppose you know verie well how wee shall maynteine 20 Moores cheaper than one English servant."

The canny Puritan considered that Indian "devil-worship" fully balanced any slight wrong in exchanging them for, "Moores", and writes of it as calmly as he does of sundry other events, somewhat shocking to the modern mind. But, while slaves increased English servants became harder and harder to secure, and often revolted from the masters to whom their time had been sold. There is a certain relish in Winthrop's record of two disaffected ones, which is perhaps not unnatural even from him, and is in full harmony with the Puritan tendency to see a special Providence in any event according to their minds:

"Two men servants to one Moodye, of Roxbury, returning in a boat from the windmill, struck upon the oyster bank. They went out to

gather oysters, and not making fast their boat, when the float came, it floated away and they were both drowned, although they might have waded out on either side, but it was an evident judgement of God upon them, for they were wicked persons. One of them, a little before, being reproved for his lewdness, and put in mind of hell, answered that if hell were ten times hotter, he had rather be there than he would serve his master, &c. The occasion was because he had bound himself for divers years, and saw that,
if he had been at liberty, he might have had greater wages, though otherwise his master used him very well."

From whatever source the "Moores" were obtained, they were bought and sold during the first hundred years that Andover had existence. "Pomps' Pond" still preserves the memory of Pompey Lovejoy, servant to Captain William Lovejoy. Pompey's cabin stood there, and as election day approached, great store of election-cake and beer was manufactured for the hungry and thirsty voters, to whom it proved less demoralizing than the whiskey of to-day. There is a record of the death in 1683, of Jack, a negro servant of Captain Dudley Bradstreet's, who lost also, in 1693, by drowning, "Stacy, ye servant of Major Dudley Bradstreet, a mullatoe born in his house." Mistress Bradstreet had several, whose families grew up about her, their concerns being of quite as deep interest as those of her neighbors, and the Andover records hold many suggestions of the tragedies and comedies of slave life. Strong as attachments might sometimes be, the minister himself sold Candace, a negro girl who had grown up in his house, and five year old Dinah was sent from home and mother at Dunstable, to a new master in Andover, as witness the bill of sale, which has a curious flavor for a Massachusetts document:

"Received of Mr. John Abbott of Andover Fourteen pounds, thirteen shillings and seven pence, it being the full value of a negrow garl named Dinah about five years of age of a Healthy sound Constution, free from any Disease of Body and do hereby Deliver the same Girl to the said Abbott and promise to Defend him in the Improvement of her as his servant forever.

ROBERT BLOOD."

Undoubtedly Dinah and all her contemporaries proved infinitely better servants than the second generation of those brought from England; who even as early as 1656, had learned to prefer independence, the Rev. Zechariah Symmes writing feelingly: "Much ado I have with my own family, hard to get a servant glad of catechising or family duties. I had a rare blessing of servants in Yorkshire and those I brought over were a blessing, but the young brood doth much afflict me."

An enthusiastic cook, even of most deeply Puritanic spirit, had been known to steal out during some long drawn prayer, to rescue a favorite dish from impending ruin, and the offence had been condoned or allowed to pass unnoticed. But the "young brood" revolted altogether at times from the interminable catechisings and "family duties", or submitted in a sulky silence, at which the spirit of the master girded in vain.

There seems to have been revolt of many sorts. Nature asserted itself, and boys and girls smiled furtively upon one another, and young men and maidens planned means of outwitting stern masters and mistresses, and securing a dance in some secluded barn, or the semblance of a merry making in picnic or ride. But stocks, pillory and whipping-post awaited all offenders, who still found that the secret pleasure outweighed the public pain, and were brought up again and again, till years subdued the fleshly instincts, and they in turn wondered at their children's pertinacity in the same evil ways. Holidays were no part of the Puritan system, and the little Bradstreets took theirs on the way to and from school, doing their wading and fishing and bird's-nesting in this stolen time. There was always Saturday afternoon, and Anne Bradstreet was also, so far as her painful conscientiousness allowed, an indulgent mother, and gave her children such pleasure as the rigid life allowed.

Andover from the beginning had excellent schools, Mr. Dane and Mr. Woodbridge, the ministers, each keeping one, while "dame schools" also flourished, taking the place of the present Kindergarten, though the suppressed and dominated babies of three and four, who swung their unhappy feet far from the floor, and whose only reader was a catechism, could never in their wildest dreams have imagined anything so fascinating as the Kindergarten or primary school of to-day. Horn books were still in use and with reason, the often-flagellated little Puritans giving much time to tears, which would have utterly destroyed anything less enduring than horn. Until
1647, the teaching of all younger children had been done chiefly at home, and Anne Bradstreet's older children learned their letters at her knee, and probably, like all the children of the day, owned their little Bibles, and by the time they were three or four years of age, followed the expounding at family prayers with only a glance now and then toward the kitten, or the family dog, stretched out before the fire, and watching for any look of interest and recognition.

After 1647, and the order of the General Court, "that every township in this jurisdiction, after the Lord hath increased them to fifty house-holders, shall then forthwith appoint one within their towns to teach all such children as shall resort to him, to read and write." The district school-house waited till Indian raids had ceased to be dreaded, but though the walk to the small, square building which in due time was set in some piece of woods or at a point where four roads meet, was denied them, it was something to come together at all, and the children found delight in berrying or nutting, or the crackle of the crisp snow-crust, over which they ran.

They waked in those early days, often with the snow lying lightly on their beds under the roof, through the cracks of which it sifted, and through which they saw stars shine or the morning sunlight flicker. Even when this stage passed, and the "great house" received them, there was still the same need for rushing down to the fire in kitchen or living-room, before which they dressed, running out, perhaps, in the interludes of strings and buttons, to watch the incoming of the fresh logs which Caesar or Cato could never bear alone.

In the Bradstreet mansion, with its many servants, there was less need of utilizing every child as far as possible, but that all should labor was part of the Puritan creed, and the boys shared the work of foddering the cattle, bringing in wood and water, and gaining the appetite which presently found satisfaction, usually in one of two forms of porridge, which for the first hundred and fifty years was the Puritan breakfast. Boiled milk, lightly thickened with Indian meal, and for the elders made more desirable by "a goode piece of butter," was the first, while for winter use, beans or peas were used, a small piece of pork or salted beef giving them flavor, and making the savory bean porridge still to be found here and there. Wheaten bread was then in general use; much more so than at a later date, when "rye and Indian" took its place, a fortunate choice for a people who, as time went on, ate more and more salt pork and fish.

Game and fresh fish were plentiful in the beginning and poultry used with a freedom that would seem to the farmer of to-day, the maddest extravagance. The English love of good cheer was still strong, and Johnson wrote in his "Wonder-Working Providence": "Apples, pears and quince tarts, instead of their former pumpkin-pies. Poultry they have plenty and great rarity, and in their feasts have not forgotten the English fashion of stirring up their appetites with variety of cooking their food."

Certain New England dishes borrowed from the natives, or invented to meet some emergency, had already become firmly established. Hasty-pudding, made chiefly then as now, from Indian meal, was a favorite supper dish, rye often being used instead, and both being eaten with molasses, and butter or milk. Samp and hominy, or the whole grain, as "hulled corn", had also been borrowed from the Indians, with "succotash", a fascinating combination of young beans and green corn. Codfish made Saturday as sacred as Friday had once been, and baked beans on Sunday morning became an equally inflexible law. Every family brewed its own beer, and when the orchards had grown, made its own cider. Wine and spirits were imported, but rum was made at home, and in the early records of Andover, the town distiller has honorable mention. Butcher's meat was altogether too precious to be often eaten, flocks and herds bearing the highest money value for many years, and game and poultry took the place of it. But it was generous living, far more so than at the present day, abundance being the first essential where all worked and all brought keen appetites to the board, and every householder counted hospitality one of the cardinal virtues.

Pewter was the only family plate, save in rarest instances. Forks had not yet appeared, their use hardly beginning in England before 1650, save among a few who had travelled and adopted the custom. Winthrop owned one, sent him in 1633, and the Bradstreets may have had one or more, but rather as a curiosity than for daily use. Fingers still did much service, and this obliged the affluence of napkins, which appears in early inventories. The children ate from wooden bowls and trenchers, and their elders from pewter. Governor Bradford owned "fourteen dishes of that material, thirteen platters, three large and two small plates, a candlestick and a bottle," and many hours were spent in polishing the rather refractory metal. He also owned "four large silver spoons" and nine smaller ones. But spoons, too, were chiefly pewter, though often merely wood, and table service was thus reduced as nearly to first principles as possible. Very speedily, however, as the Colony prospered, store of silver and china was accumulated, used only on state occasions, and then carefully put away.

The servant question had other phases than that of mere inadequacy, and there are countless small difficulties recorded; petty thefts, insolent speeches, and the whole familiar list which we are apt to consider the portion only of the nineteenth century. But there is nothing more certain than that, in spite of creeds, human nature remains much the same, and that the Puritan matron fretted as energetically against the pricks in her daily life, as any sinner of to-day. Mistress Bradstreet, at least, had one experience in which we hear of her as "very angry at the mayde", and which gave food for gossips for many a day.

Probably one of the profoundest excitements that ever entered the children's lives, was in the discovery of certain iniquities perpetrated by a hired servant John--whose surname, if he ever had one, is lost to this generation, and who succeeded in hiding his evil doings so thoroughly, that there were suspicions of every one but himself. He was a hard worker, but afflicted with an inordinate appetite, the result of which is found in this order:

"To the Constable of Andover. You are hereby required to attach the body of John----, to answer such compt as shall be brought against him, for stealing severall things, as pigges, capons, mault, bacon, butter, eggs &c, & for breaking open a seller-doore in the night several times &c. 7th 3d month 1661."

John, suddenly brought to trial, first affirmed that his appetite was never over large, but that the food provided the Bradstreet servants "was not fit for any man to eate," the bread especially being "black & heavy & soure," and that he had only occasionally taken a mere bite here and there to allay the painful cravings such emptiness produced. But hereupon appeared Goodwife Russ, in terror lest she should be accused of sharing the spoils, and testifying that John had often brought chickens, butter, malt and other things to her house and shared them with Goodman Russ, who had no scruples. The "mayde had missed the things" and confided her trouble to Goodwife Russ, who had gone up to the great house, and who, pitying the girl, knowing that "her mistress would blame her and be very angry," brought them all back, and then told her husband and John what she had done. Another comrade made full confession, testifying in court that at one time they killed and roasted a "great fatt pigg" in the lot, giving what remained "to the dogges," John seasoning the repast with stories of former thefts. It was in court that Master Jackson learned what had been the fate of "a great fatt Turkey ... fatted against his daughter's marriage" and hung for keeping in a locked room, down the chimney of which, "2 or 3 fellowes" let the enterprising John by a rope who, being pulled up with his prize, "roasted it in the wood and ate it," every whit. Down the same chimney he went for "strong beare," and anyone who has once looked upon and into an ancient Andover chimney will know that not only John, but the "2 or 3 fellowes," as well, could have descended side by side.

Then came a scene in which little John Bradstreet, aged nine, had part, seeing the end if not the beginning, of which Hannah Barnard "did testifye that being in my father's lott near Mr. Bradstreet's barn, did see John run after Mr. Bradstreet's fouls & throughing sticks and stones at them & into the Barne."

Looking through a crack to find out the result she "saw him throw out a capon which he had killed, and heard him call to Sam Martin to come; but when he saw that John Bradstreet was with Martin, he ran and picked up the capon and hid it under a pear tree."

This pear tree, climbed by every Bradstreet child, stood at the east of the old house, and held its own till well into the present century, and little John may have been on his way for a windfall, when the capon flew toward him. To stealing was added offences much more malicious, several discreet Puritan lads, sons of the foremost land holders having been induced by sudden temptation, to join him in running Mr. Bradstreet's wheels down hill into a swamp, while at a later date they watched him recreating himself in the same manner alone, testifying that he "took a wheele off Mr. Bradstreet's tumbril and ran it down hill, and got an old wheel from Goodman Barnard's land, & sett it on the tumbril."

John received the usual punishment, but mended his ways only for a season, his appetite rather increasing with age, and his appearance before the Court being certain in any town to which he went. No other servant seems to have given special trouble, and probably all had laid to heart the "Twelve Good Rules," printed and hung in every colonial kitchen:

Profane no Divine ordinance.
Touch no state matters.
Urge no healths. Pick
no quarrels. Encourage
no vice. Repeat no
grievances. Reveal no
secrets. Mantain no ill
opinions. Make no
comparisons. Keep no
bad company. Make no
long meals. Lay no
wagers.

The problem of work and wages weighed heavily on the young Colony. There were grasping men enough to take advantage of the straits into which many came through the scarcity of labor, and Winthrop, as early as 1633, had found it necessary to interfere. Wages had risen to an excessive rate, "so as a carpenter would have three shillings a day, a labourer two shillings and sixpence &c.; and accordingly those that had commodities to sell, advanced their prices sometime double to that they cost in England, so as it grew to a general complaint, which the court taking knowledge of, as also of some further evils, which were springing out of the excessive rates of wages, they made an order, that carpenters, masons, &c., should take but two shillings the day, and labourers but eighteen pence, and that no commodity should be sold at above fourpence in the shilling more than it cost for ready money in England; oil, wine, &c., and cheese, in regard of the hazard of bringing, &c., excepted. The evils which were springing, &c., were: 1. Many spent much time idly, &c., because they could get as much in four days as would keep them a week. 2. They spent much in tobacco and strong waters, &c., which was a great waste to the Commonwealth, which by reason of so many commodities expended, could not have subsisted to this time, but that it was supplied by the cattle and corn which were sold to new comers at very dear

rates." This bit of extortion on the part of the Colony as a
government, does not seem to weigh on Winthrop's mind with by any
means as great force as that of the defeated workmen, and he gives
the colonial tariff of prices with even a certain pride: "Corn at
six shillings the bushel, a cow at L20--yea, some at L24, some
L26--a mare at L35, an ewe goat at 3 or L4; and yet many cattle
were every year brought out of England, and some from
Virginia." At last the new arrivals revolted, and one order ruled
for all,
the rate of profit charged, being long fixed at four pence in the
shilling. Andover adopted this scale, being from the beginning of
a thrifty turn of mind, which is exemplified in one of the first
ordinances passed. Many boys and girls had been employed by the
owners of cattle to watch and keep them within bounds, countless
troubles arising from their roaming over the unfenced lands. To
prevent the forming of idle habits the Court at once, did
"hereupon order and decree that in every towne the chosen men are
to take care of such as are sett to keep cattle, that they be sett
to some other employment withall, as spinning upon the rock,
knitting & weaving tape, &c., that boyes and girls be not
suffered to converse together."

Such conversations as did take place had a double zest from the
fact that the sharp-eyed herdsman was outwitted, but as a rule the
small Puritans obeyed orders and the spinners and knitters in the
sun, helped to fill the family chests which did duty as bureaus,
and three varieties of which are still to be seen in old houses on
the Cape, as well as in the Museum at Plymouth. The plain sea-
chest, like the sailor's chest of to-day, was the property of all
alike, and usually of solid oak. A grade above this, came another
form, with turned and applied ornaments and two drawers at the
bottom, a fine specimen of which is still in the old Phillips
house at North Andover, opposite the Bradstreet house. The last
variety had more drawers, but still retained the lid on top, which
being finally permanently fastened down, made the modern bureau.
High-backed wooden chairs and an immense oaken table with folding
ladder legs, furnished the living-room, settles being on either
side of the wide chimney, where, as the children roasted apples or
chestnuts, they listened to stories of the wolves, whose howl even
then might still be heard about the village. There are various
references to "wolf-hooks" in Governor Bradstreet's accounts,
these being described by Josselyn as follows:

"Four mackerel hooks are bound with brown thread and wool wrapped
around them, and they are dipped into melted tallow till they be
as big and round as an egg. This thing thus prepared is laid by some
dead carcase which toles the wolves. It is swallowed by them and is
the means of their being taken."

Every settler believed that "the fangs of a wolf hung about
children's necks keep them from frightning, and are very good to
rub their gums with when they are breeding of teeth." It was not
at all out of character to look on complacently while dogs
worried
an unhappy wolf, the same Josselyn writing of one taken in a trap:
"A great mastiff held the wolf . . . Tying him to a stake we bated
him with smaller doggs and had excellent sport; but his hinder leg
being broken, they knocked out his brains."

To these hunts every man and boy turned out, welcoming the break
in the monotonous life, and foxes and wolves were shot by the

dozen, their method being to "lay a sledg-load of cods-heads on the other side of a paled fence when the moon shines, and about nine or ten of the clock, the foxes come to it; sometimes two or three or half a dozen and more; these they shoot, and by that time they have cased them there will be as many more; so they continue shooting and killing of foxes as long as the moon shineth."

Road-making became another means of bringing them together for something besides religious services, and as baskets of provisions were taken with the workers, and the younger boys were allowed to share in the lighter part of the work, a suggestion of merry-making was there also. These roads were often changed, being at no time much more than paths marked by the blazing of trees and the clearing away of timber and undergrowth. There were no bridges save over the narrower streams, fording being the custom, till ferries were established at various points. Roads and town boundaries were alike undetermined and shifting. "Preambulators," otherwise surveyors, found their work more and more complicated. "Marked trees, stakes and stones," were not sufficient to prevent endless discussions between selectmen and surveyors, and there is a document still on file which shows the straits to which the unhappy "preambulators" were sometimes reduced.

"To Ye Selectmen of Billerica: Loving friends and neighbors, we have bine of late under such surcomstances that wee could not tell whether wee had any bounds or no between our towne, but now we begine to think we have--this therefore are to desier you to send some men to meet with ours upon the third Munday of ye next month by nine a'clock in ye morning, if it be a faire day, if not the next drie day, and so to run one both side of the river and to meet at the vesil place and the west side of ye river."

There were heart burnings from another source than this, and one which could never be altered by selectmen, whether at home or abroad. For generations, no person was allowed to choose a seat in church, a committee, usually the magistrates, settling the places of all. In the beginning, after the building of any meeting-house, the seats were all examined and ranked according to their desirability, this process being called, "dignifying the pews."
All who held the highest social or ecclesiastical positions were then placed; and the rest as seemed good, the men on one side, the women on another, and the children, often on a low bench outside the pews, where they were kept in order by the tithing man, who, at the first symptom of wandering attention, rapped them over the head with his hare's foot mounted on a stick, and if necessary, withdrew them from the scene long enough for the administration of a more thorough discipline.

There are perpetual complaints of partiality--even hints that bribery had been at work in this "seating the meeting-house," and the committee chosen found it so disagreeable a task that Dudley Bradstreet, when in due time his turn came to serve, protested against being compelled to it, and at last revolted altogether.

At Boston a cage had been set up for Sabbath-breakers, but Andover found easier measures sufficient, though there are constant offences recorded. A smile in meeting brought admonishment, and a whisper, the stocks, and when the boys were massed in the galleries the tithing man had active occupation during the entire service, and could have had small benefit of the means of grace. Two were necessary at last, the records reading: "We have ordered Thomas Osgood and John Bridges to have inspection over the boys in the galleries on the Sabbath, that they might be contained in order in the time of publick exercise."

Later, even worse trouble arose. The boys would not be "contained," and the anxious selectmen wrote: "And whereas there is grevious complaints of great prophaneness of ye Sabbath, both in y time of exercise, at noon time, to ye great dishonor of God, scandall of religion, & ye grief of many serious Christians, by young persons, we order & require ye tything-men & constables to tak care to p'vent such great and shamefull miscarriages, which are soe much observed and complained of."

The little Bradstreets, chilled to the bone by sitting for hours in the fireless church, could rush home to the warm hearth and the generous buttery across the street, but many who had ridden miles, and who ate a frosty lunch between services may be pardoned for indulging in the "great and shameful miscarriages," which were, undoubtedly, a rush across the pews or a wrestle on the meeting-house steps. Even their lawlessness held more circumspectness than is known to the most decorous boy of to-day, and it gained with every generation, till neither tithing-men nor constables had further power to restrain it, the Puritans of the eighteenth century wailing over the godlessness and degeneracy of the age as strenuously as the pessimists of the nineteenth. Even for the seventeenth there are countless infractions of law, and a study of court records would leave the impression of a reckless and utterly defiant community, did not one recall the fact that life was so hedged about with minute detail, that the most orderly citizen of this day would have been the disorderly one of that.

One resource, of entertainment, was always open to Puritan households. Hospitality was on a scale almost of magnificence, and every opportunity seized for making a great dinner or supper, the abundant good cheer of which was their strongest reminder of England. The early privations were ended, but to recall them gave an added zest, and we may fancy Roger Clap repeating the experience found in his memoir, with a devout thankfulness that such misery was far behind them.

"Bread was so scarce, that frequently I thought the very crusts of my father's table would have been very sweet unto me. And when I could have meal and water and salt boiled together who could wish better. It was not accounted a strange thing in those days to drink water, and to eat samp or hominy without butter or milk. Indeed it would have been strange to see a piece of roast beef, mutton or veal, though it was not long before there was roast goat."

Generous living had become the colonial characteristic. Even in the first years, while pressure was still upon them, and supplies chiefly from England, one of them wrote:

"Sometimes we used bacon and buttered pease, sometimes buttered bag pudding, made with currants and raisins, sometimes drinked pottage of beer and oatmeal, and sometimes water pottage well buttered."

Health had come to many who had been sickly from childhood. In fact, in spite of the theory we are all inclined to hold, that "the former days were better than these," and our ancestors men and women of a soundness and vigor long since lost, there is every proof that the standard of health has progressed with all other standards, and that the best blood of this generation is purer and less open to disorder than the best blood of that. Francis Higginson may stand as the representative of many who might have written with him:

"Whereas I have for divers years past been very sickly and ready to cast up whatsoever I have eaten, . . . He hath made my coming to be a method to cure me of a wonderful weak stomach and continual pain of melancholy mind from the spleen."

His children seem to have been in equally melancholy case, but he was able after a year or two of New England life to write:

"Here is an extraordinary clear and dry air, that is of a most healing nature to all such as are of a cold, melancholy, phlegmatic, rheumatic temper of body."

The Puritans, as life settled into a less rasping routine than that of the early years, grew rotund and comfortable in expression, and though the festivities of training days, and the more solemn one of ordination or Thanksgiving day, meant sermon and prayers of doubled length, found this only an added element of enjoyment. Judge Sewall's diary records many good dinners; sometimes as "a sumptuous feast," sometimes as merely "a fine dinner," but always with impressive unction. At one of these occasions he mentions Governor Bradstreet as being present and adds that he "drank a glass or two of wine, eat some fruit, took a pipe of tobacco in the New Hall, wished me joy of the house and desired our prayers."

At Andover he was equally ready for any of these diversions, though never intemperate in either meat or drink, but, like every magistrate, he kept open house, and enjoyed it more than some whose austerity was greater, and there are many hints that Mistress Bradstreet provided good cheer with a freedom born of her early training, and made stronger by her husband's tastes and wishes. The Andover dames patterned after her, and spent many of the long hours, in as close following of honored formulas as the new conditions allowed, laying then the foundation for that reputation still held by Andover housewives, and derided by one of her best known daughters, as "the cup-cake tendencies of the town."

CHAPTER XI.

A FIRST EDITION.

Though the manuscript of the first edition of Anne Bradstreet's poems was nearly if not entirely complete before the removal to

Andover, some years were still to pass before it left her hands
entirely, though her brother-in-law, knowing her self-distrustful
nature, may have refused to give it up when possession had once
been obtained. But no event in her life save her marriage, could
have had quite the same significance to the shy and shrinking
woman, who doubted herself and her work alike, considering any
real satisfaction in it a temptation of the adversary. Authorship
even to-day has its excitements and agitations, for the maker of
the book if not for its readers. And it is hardly possible to
measure the interest, the profound absorption in the book, which
had been written chiefly in secret in hours stolen from sleep, to
ensure no trenching on daylight duties. We are helpless to form
just judgment of what the little volume meant to the generation in
which it appeared, simply because the growth of the critical
faculty has developed to an abnormal degree, and we demand in the
lightest work, qualities that would have made an earlier poet
immortal.

This is an age of versification. The old times--when a successful
couplet had the same prominence and discussion as a walking match
to-day; when one poet thought his two lines a satisfactory
morning's work, and another said of him that when such labor
ended, straw was laid before the door and the knocker tied up--are
over, once for all. Now and then a poet stops to polish, but for
the most part spontaneity, fluency, gush, are the qualities
demanded, and whatever finish may be given, must be dominated by
these more apparent facts. Delicate fancies still abound, and are more
and more the portion of the many; but Fancy fills the place
once held for Imagination, a statelier and nobler dame, deaf to
common voices and disdaining common paths. Every country paper,
every petty periodical, holds verse that in the Queen Anne period
in literature would have given the author permanent place and
name. All can rhyme, and many can rhyme melodiously. The power of
words fitly set has made itself known, and a word has come to be
judged like a note in music--as a potential element of harmony--a
sound that in its own place may mean any emotion of joy or sorrow,
hate or love. Whether a thought is behind these alluring rhythms,
with their sensuous swing or their rush of sound, is immaterial so
long as the ear has satisfaction; thus Swinburne and his school
fill the place of Spenser and the elder poets, and many an "idle
singer of an empty day" jostles aside the masters, who can wait,
knowing that sooner or later, return to them is certain.

Schools have their power for a time, and expression held in their
moulds forgets that any other form is possible. But the throng who
copied Herrick are forgotten, their involved absurdities and
conceits having died with the time that gave them birth. The
romantic school had its day, and its power and charm are
uncomprehended by the reader of this generation. And the Lake
poets, firmly as they held the popular mind, have no place now,
save in the pages where a school was forgotten and nature and
stronger forces asserted their power.

No poet has enduring place whose work has not been the voice of
the national thought and life in which he has had part. Theology,
politics, great questions of right, all the problems of human life
in any age may have, in turn, moulded the epic of the period; but,
from Homer down, the poet has spoken the deepest thought of the
time, and where he failed in this has failed to be heard beyond

his time. With American poets, it has taken long for anything
distinctively American to be born. With the early singers,
there
was simply a reproduction of the mannerisms and limitations of the
school for which Pope had set all the copies. Why not, when it was
simply a case of unchangeable identity, the Englishman being no less
an Englishman because he had suddenly been put down on the
American side of the Atlantic? Then, for a generation or so, he
was too busy contending with natural forces, and asserting his
claims to life and place on the new continent, to have much
leisure for verse-making, though here and there, in the stress of
grinding days, a weak and uncertain voice sounded at times. Anne
Bradstreet's, as we know, was the first, and half assured, half
dismayed at her own presumption, she waited long, till convinced
as other authors have since been, by the "urgency of friends,"
that her words must have wider spread than manuscript could give
them. Now and again it is asserted that the manuscript for the
first edition was taken to London without her knowledge and
printed in the same way, but there is hardly the slightest ground
for such conclusion, while the elaborate dedication and the many
friendly tributes included, indicate the fullest knowledge and
preparation. All those whose opinion she most valued are
represented in the opening pages of the volume.

Evidently they felt it necessary to justify this extraordinary
departure from the proper sphere of woman, a sphere as sharply
defined and limited by every father, husband and brother, as their
own was left uncriticised and unrestrained. Nathaniel Ward forgot
his phillipics against the "squirrel's brains" of women, and
hastened to speak his delight in the little book, and Woodbridge
and John Rogers and sundry others whose initials alone are affixed
to their prose or poetical tributes and endorsements, all banded
together to sustain this first venture. The title page follows the
fashion of the time, and is practically an abstract of what
follows.

        *   *   *   *

* THE TENTH MUSE,

LATELY SPRUNG UP IN

AMERICA, OR

_Severall Poems, compiled with great variety of Wit and
Learning, full of Delight, wherein especially is contained
a Compleat discourse, and Description of_

      (ELEMENTS,
      (CONSTITUTIONS,
THE FOUR--(AGES OF
MAN,
      (SEASONS OF THE YEAR.

_Together with an Exact Epitomie of the Four
  Monarchies, viz.:_
     (ASSYRIAN,
THE (
    PERSIAN, (
    GRECIAN,
    (ROMAN.

Also, a Dialogue between Old England and New, concerning the Late Troubles; with divers other pleasant and serious Poems.

BY A GENTLEWOMAN IN THOSE PARTS.

Printed at London for Stephen Bowtell at the signe of the Bible in Popes Head-Alley, 1650.

*   *   *   *   *

Whether Anne herself wrote the preface is uncertain. It is apologetic enough for one of her supporters, but has some indications that she chose the first word should be her own.

KIND READER:

Had I opportunity but to borrow some of the Author's wit, 'tis possible I might so trim this curious work with such quaint expressions, as that the Preface might bespeak thy further Perusal; but I fear 'twill be a shame for a Man that can speak so little, to be seen in the title-page of this Woman's Book, lest by comparing the one with the other, the Reader should pass his sentence that it is the gift of women not only to speak most, but to speak best; I shall leave therefore to commend that, which with any ingenious Reader will too much commend the Author, unless men turn more peevish than women, to envy the excellency of the inferiour Sex. I doubt not but the Reader will quickly find more than I can say, and the worst effect of his reading will be unbelief, which will make him question whether it be a woman's work and aske, "Is it possible?"

If any do, take this as an answer from him that dares avow it: It is the Work of a Woman, honoured, and esteemed where she lives, for her gracious demeanour, her eminent parts, her pious conversation, her courteous disposition, her exact diligence in her place, and discreet managing of her Family occasions, and more than so, these Poems are the fruit but of some few houres, curtailed from her sleep and other refreshments. I dare adde but little lest I keep thee too long; if thou wilt not believe the worth of these things (in their kind) when a man sayes it, yet believe it from a woman when thou seest it. This only I shall annex, I fear the displeasure of no person in the publishing of these Poems but the Author, without whose knowledg, and contrary to her expectation, I have presumed to bring to publick view, what she resolved in such a manner should never see the Sun; but I found that diverse had gotten some Scattered Papers, and affected them well, were likely to have sent forth broken pieces, to the Authors predjudice, which I thought to prevent, as well as to pleasure those that earnestly desired the view of the whole.

Nathaniel Ward speaks next and with his usual conviction that his word is all that is necessary to stamp a thing as precisely what he considers it to be.

Mercury shew'd Appollo, Bartas Book,
Minerva this, and wish't him well to
look, And tell uprightly which did which
excell,

He view'd and view'd, and vow'd he could not tel.
They bid him Hemisphear his mouldy nose,
With's crack't leering glasses, for it would pose
The best brains he had in's old pudding-pan,
Sex weigh'd, which best, the Woman or the Man?
He peer'd and por'd & glar'd, & said for wore,
I'me even as wise now, as I was before;
They both 'gan laugh, and said it was no mar'l
The Auth'ress was a right Du Bartas Girle,
Good sooth quoth the old Don, tell ye me so,
I muse whither at length these Girls will
go; It half revives my chil frost-bitten
blood,
To see a Woman once, do aught that's good;
And chode by Chaucer's Book, and Homer's Furrs,
Let Men look to't, least Women wear the Spurrs.
                    N. Ward.

John Woodbridge takes up the strain in lines of much easier verse,
in which he pays her brotherly tribute, and is followed by his
brother, Benjamin, who had been her neighbor in Andover.

UPON THE AUTHOR; BY A KNOWN

FRIEND. Now I believe Tradition, which doth

call
The Muses, Virtues, Graces, Females all;
Only they are not nine, eleven nor three; Our
Auth'ress proves them but one unity.
Mankind take up some blushes on the score;
Monopolize perfection no more;
In your own Arts confess yourself out-done,
The Moon hath totally eclips'd the Sun,
Not with her Sable Mantle muffling him;
But her bright silver makes his gold look dim;
Just as his beams force our pale lamps to wink,
And earthly Fires, within their ashes shrink.
                    _B. W._

IN PRAISE OF THE AUTHOR, MISTRESS
ANNE BRADSTREET,

Virtues true and lively Pattern, Wife of the
Worshipfull Simon Bradstreet Esq: At present
residing in the Occidental
parts of the World in America,
Alias Nov-Anglia.

What golden splendent Star is this so bright,
One thousand Miles twice told, both day and night,
(From the Orient first sprung) now from the West
That shines; swift-winged Phoebus, and the rest
Of all Jove's fiery flames surmounting far
As doth each Planet, every falling Star;
By whose divine and lucid light most clear,
Nature's dark secret mysteryes appear;
Heavens, Earths, admired wonders, noble acts
Of Kings and Princes most heroick facts,
And what e're else in darkness seemed to dye,
Revives all things so obvious now to th' eye,
That he who these its glittering rayes views o're,

Shall see what's done in all the world before.
                    _N. H._

Three other friends add their testimony before we come to the
dedication.

UPON THE AUTHOR.

'Twere extream folly should I dare attempt,
To praise this Author's worth with complement;
None but herself must dare commend her parts,
Whose sublime brain's the Synopsis of Arts.
Nature and Skill, here both in one agree,
To frame this Master-piece of Poetry:
False Fame, belye their Sex no more, it can
Surpass, or parrallel the best of Man.
                    _C. B._

ANOTHER TO MRS. ANNE

BRADSTREET, Author of this Poem.

I've read your Poem (Lady) and admire,
Your Sex to such a pitch should e're aspire;
Go on to write, continue to relate,
New Historyes, of Monarchy and State:
And what the Romans to their Poets gave,
Be sure such honour, and esteem you'l have.
                    _H. S._

AN ANAGRAM.

ANNA BRADSTREET. DEER NEAT AN

BARTAS. So Bartas like thy fine spun Poems

been,
That Bartas name will prove an Epicene.

ANOTHER.

ANNA BRADSTREET. ARTES BRED NEAT AN.

There follows, what can only be defined as a gushing tribute from
John Rogers, also metrical, though this was not included until the
second edition.

"Twice I have drunk the nectar of your lines," he informs her,
adding that, left "thus weltring in delight," he is scarcely
capable of doing justice either to his own feelings, or the work
which has excited them, and with this we come at last to the
dedication in which Anne herself bears witness to her obligations
to her father.

_To her most Honoured Father, Thomas Dudley, Esq;
these humbly presented,_

Dear Sir of late delighted with the sight
Of your four Sisters cloth'd in black and
white. Of fairer Dames the Sun n'er Saw the
face, Though made a pedestal for Adams
Race;

Their worth so shines in these rich lines you show
Their paralels to finde I scarely know
To climbe their Climes, I have nor strength nor skill
To mount so high requires an Eagle's quill;
Yet view thereof did cause my thoughts to soar,
My lowly pen might wait upon these four
I bring my four times four, now meanly
clad To do their homage, unto yours, full
glad; Who for their Age, their worth and
quality Might seem of yours to claim
precedency; But by my humble hand, thus
rudely pen'd
They are, your bounden handmaids to attend
These same are they, from whom we being have
These are of all, the Life, the Muse, the Grave;
These are the hot, the cold, the moist, the dry,
That sink, that swim, that fill, that upwards fly,
Of these consists our bodies, Clothes and Food,
The World, the useful, hurtful, and the good,
Sweet harmony they keep, yet jar oft times
Their discord doth appear, by these harsh rimes
Yours did contest for wealth, for Arts, for Age,
My first do shew their good, and then their rage.
My other foures do intermixed tell
Each others faults, and where themselves excel;
How hot and dry contend with moist and cold,
How Air and Earth no correspondence hold,
And yet in equal tempers, how they 'gree
How divers natures make one Unity
Something of all (though mean) I did intend
But fear'd you'ld judge Du Bartas was my friend.
I honour him, but dare not wear his wealth
My goods are true (though poor) I love no stealth
But if I did I durst not send them you
Who must reward a Thief, but with his due.
I shall not need, mine innocence to clear
These ragged lines will do 't when they appear;
On what they are, your mild aspect I crave
Accept my best, my worst vouchsafe a Grave.
From her that to your self, more duty owes
Then water in the boundess Ocean flows.
        Anne Bradstreet.
March 20, 1642.

The reference in the second line, to "your four Sisters, clothed
in black and white," is to a poem which the good governor is said
to have written in his later days, "on the Four Parts of the
World," but which a happy fate has spared us, the manuscript
having been lost or destroyed, after his death. His daughter's
verse is often as dreary, but both dedication and prologue admit
her obligations to du Bartas, and that her verse was modeled upon
his was very plain to Nathaniel Ward, who called her a "right du
Bartas girl," with the feeling that such imitation was infinitely
more creditable to her than any originality which she herself
carefully disclaims in the

PROLOGUE.

1

To sing of Wars, of Captains, and of Kings,
Of cities founded, Commonwealths begun,
For my mean pen are too superior things:
Or how they all, or each their dates have run
Let Poets and Historians set these forth,
My obscure Lines shall not so dim their worth.

2

But when my wondring eyes and envious heart
Great Bartas sugared lines, do but read o'er
Fool I do grudg the Muses did not part
'Twixt him and me that overfluent
store; A Bartas can do what a Bartas
will
But simple I according to my skill.

3

From school-boyes' tongues no rhet'rick we expect
Nor yet a sweet Consort from broken strings,
Nor perfect beauty, where's a main defect;
My foolish, broken, blemish'd Muse so sings
And this to mend, alas, no Art is able,
'Cause nature, made it so irreparable.

4

Nor can I, like that fluent sweet-tongu'd Greek,
Who lisp'd at first, in future times speak plain
By Art he gladly found what he did seek
A full requital of his, striving pain
Art can do much, but this maxima's most sure
A weak or wounded brain admits no cure.

5

I am obnoxious to each carping tongue
Who says my hand a needle better fits,
A Poet's pen all Scorn I should thus wrong,
For such despite they cast on Female wits;
If what I do prove well, it won't advance,
They'l say it's stolen, or else it was by chance.

6

But sure the Antique Greeks werc far more mild
Else of our Sexe, why feigned they those Nine
And poesy made, Calliope's own child;
So 'mongst the rest they placed the Arts' Divine,
But this weak knot, they will full soon untie,
The Greeks did nought, but play the fools & lye.

7

Let Greeks be Greeks, and women what they are
Men have precedency and still excel,
It is but vain unjustly to wage warre:
Men can do best, and women know it well
Preheminence in all and each is yours;

Yet grant some small acknowledgement of ours.

8

And oh ye high flown quills that soar the Skies,
And ever with your prey still catch your praise,
If e're you daigne these lowly lines your eyes
Give Thyme or Parsley wreath, I ask no bayes,
This mean and unrefined ure of mine
Will make you glistening gold, but more to shine.

With the most ambitious of the longer poems--"The Four Monarchies"-
- and one from which her readers of that day probably derived the most
satisfaction, we need not feel compelled to linger. To them its
charm lay in its usefulness. There were on sinful fancies; no trifling
waste of words, but a good, straightforward narrative of things it
was well to know, and Tyler's comment upon it will be echoed by
every one who turns the apallingly matter-of-fact pages: "Very
likely, they gave to her their choicest praise, and called
her, for this work, a painful poet; in which compliment every
modern reader will most cordially join."

Of much more attractive order is the comparatively short poem, one
of the series of quaternions in which she seems to have delighted.
"The Four Elements" is a wordy war, in which four personages,
Fire, Earth, Air and Water, contend for the precedence, glorifying
their own deeds and position and reproaching the others for their
shortcomings and general worthlessness with the fluency and fury
of seventeenth century theological debate. There are passages,
however, of real poetic strength and vividness, and the poem is
one of the most favorable specimens of her early work. The four
have met and at once begin the controversy.

The Fire, Air, Earth and Water did contest
Which was the strongest, noblest and the best,
Who was of greatest use and might'est force;
In placide Terms they thought now to discourse,
That in due order each her turn should speak;
But enmity this amity did break
All would be chief, and all scorn'd to be under
Whence issued winds & rains, lightning & thunder.
The quaking earth did groan, the Sky looked black,
The Fire, the forced Air, in sunder crack;
The sea did threat the heav'ns, the heavn's the earth,
All looked like a Chaos or new birth;
Fire broyled Earth, & scorched Earth it choaked
Both by their darings, water so provoked That
roaring in it came, and with its source Soon
made the Combatants abate their force;

The rumbling, hissing, puffing was so great
The worlds confusion, it did seem to threat
Till gentle Air, Contention so abated
That betwixt hot and cold, she arbitrated
The others difference, being less did cease
All storms now laid, and they in perfect peace
That Fire should first begin, the rest consent,
The noblest and most active Element.

Fire rises, with the warmth one would expect, and recounts her
services to mankind, ending with the triumphant assurance, that,
willing or not, all things must in the end be subject to her
power.

What is my worth (both ye) and all men
know, In little time I can but little show,
But what I am, let learned Grecians say
What I can do well skil'd Mechanicks
may; The benefit all living by me finde,
All sorts of Artists, here declare your mind,
What tool was ever fram'd, but by my might?
Ye Martilisk, what weapons for your fight
To try your valor by, but it must feel
My force? Your Sword, & Gun, your Lance of
steel Your Cannon's bootless and your powder too
Without mine aid, (alas) what can they do;
The adverse walls not shak'd, the Mines not blown
And in despight the City keeps her own;
But I with one Granado or Petard
Set ope those gates, that 'fore so strong were bar'd
Ye Husband-men, your Coulters made by me
Your Hooes your Mattocks, & what ere you see
Subdue the Earth, and fit it for your Grain
That so it might in time requite your pain;
Though strong-limb'd Vulcan forg'd it by his
skill I made it flexible unto his will;
Ye Cooks, your Kitchen implements I frame
Your Spits, Pots, Jacks, what else I need not name
Your dayly food I wholsome make, I warm
Your shrinking Limbs, which winter's cold doth harm
Ye Paracelsians too in vain's your skill
In Chymistry, unless I help you Still.

And you Philosophers, if e're you made
A transmutation it was through mine aid,
Ye silver Smiths, your Ure I do refine
What mingled lay with Earth I cause to shine,
But let me leave these things, my fame aspires
To match on high with the Celestial fires;
The Sun an Orb of fire was held of old,
Our Sages new another tale have told;
But be he what they will, yet his aspect
A burning fiery heat we find reflect
And of the self same nature is with mine
Cold sister Earth, no witness needs but thine;
How doth his warmth, refresh thy frozen back
And trim thee brave, in green, after thy black.
Both man and beast rejoyce at his approach,
And birds do sing, to see his glittering Coach
And though nought, but Salamanders live in fire
And fly Pyrausta call'd, all else expire,
Yet men and beasts Astronomers will tell
Fixed in heavenly Constellations dwell,
My Planets of both Sexes whose degree
Poor Heathen judg'd worthy a Diety;
There's Orion arm'd attended by his dog;
The Theban stout Alcides with his Club;
The valiant Persens, who Medusa slew,

The horse that kil'd Beleuphon, then flew.
My Crab, my Scorpion, fishes you may see
The Maid with ballance, twain with horses three,
The Ram, the Bull, the Lion, and the Beagle,
The Bear, the Goat, the Raven, and the Eagle,
The Crown, the Whale, the Archer, Bernice Hare
The Hidra, Dolphin, Boys that water bear,
Nay more, then these, Rivers 'mongst stars are found
Eridanus, where Phaeton was drown'd.
Their magnitude, and height, should I recount
My Story to a volume would amount;
Out of a multitude these few I touch,
Your wisdome out of little gather
much.

I'le here let pass, my choler, cause of wars
And influence of divers of those stars
When in Conjunction with the Sun do more
Augment his heat, which was too hot before.
The Summer ripening season I do claim,
And man from thirty unto fifty
framed, Of old when Sacrifices were
Divine,
I of acceptance was the holy Signe,
'Mong all thy wonders which I might recount,
There's none more strange then Aetna's Sulphry mount
The choaking flames, that from Vesuvius flew
The over curious second Pliny flew,
And with the Ashes that it sometimes shed
Apulia's 'jacent parts were covered. And
though I be a servant to each man Yet by
my force, master, my masters can.
What famous Towns, to Cinders have I turned?
What lasting forts my Kindled wrath hath burned?
The Stately Seats of mighty Kings by me
In confused heaps, of ashes may you see.
Where's Ninus great wall'd Town, & Troy of old
Carthage, and hundred more in stories told
Which when they could not be o'ercome by foes
The Army, thro'ugh my help victorious rose
And Stately London, our great Britian's
glory My raging flame did make a mournful
story, But maugre all, that I, or foes could do
That Phoenix from her Bed, is risen New.
Old sacred Zion, I demolished thee
Lo great Diana's Temple was by me,
And more than bruitish London, for her lust
With neighbouring Towns, I did consume to dust
What shall I say of Lightning and of Thunder
Which Kings & mighty ones amaze with
wonder,
Which make a Caesar, (Romes) the world's proud head,
Foolish Caligula creep under 's bed.
Of Meteors, Ignus fatuus and the rest,
But to leave those to th' wise, I judge it best.
The rich I oft made poor, the strong I maime,
Not sparing Life when I can take the same;
And in a word, the world I shall consume
And all therein, at that great day of Doom;
Not before then, shall cease, my raging ire
And then because no matter more for fire
Now Sisters pray proceed, each in your Course

As I, impart your usefulness and force.

Fully satisfied that nothing remains to be said, Fire takes her
place among the sisterhood and waits scornfully for such poor plea
as Earth may be able to make, surprised to find what power of
braggadocio still remains and hastens to display itself.

The next in place Earth judg'd to be her due,
Sister (quoth shee) I come not short of you,
In wealth and use I do surpass you all,
And mother earth of old men did me call
Such is my fruitfulness, an Epithite,
Which none ere gave, or you could claim of sight
Among my praises this I count not least,
I am th' original of man and beast,
To tell what Sundry fruits my fat soil yields
In Vineyards, Gardens, Orchards & Corn-fields,
Their kinds, their tasts, their Colors & their
smells Would so pass time I could say nothing
else.
The rich, the poor, wise, fool, and every sort
Of these so common things can make report.
To tell you of my countryes and my Regions,
Soon would they pass not hundreds but legions;
My cities famous, rich and populous,
Whose numbers now are grown innumerous,
I have not time to think of every part,
Yet let me name my Grecia, 'tis my heart.
For learning arms and arts I love it well,
But chiefly 'cause the Muses there did dwell.

Ile here skip ore my mountains reaching skyes,
Whether Pyrenean, or the Alpes, both lyes
On either side the country of the Gaules
Strong forts, from Spanish and Italian brawles,
And huge great Taurus longer then the rest,
Dividing great Armenia from the least;
And Hemus, whose steep sides none foot upon,
But farewell all for dear mount Helicon,
And wondrous high Olimpus, of such fame,
That heav'n itself was oft call'd by that name.
Parnapus sweet, I dote too much on thee,
Unless thou prove a better friend to me:
But Ile leap ore these hills, not touch a dale,
Nor will I stay, no not in Temple Vale,
He here let go my Lions of Numedia,
My Panthers and my Leopards of Libia,
The Behemoth and rare found Unicorn,
Poyson's sure antidote lyes in his horn,
And my Hiaena (imitates man's voice)
Out of great numbers I might pick my choice,
Thousands in woods & plains, both wild &
tame, But here or there, I list now none to name;
No, though the fawning Dog did urge me sore,
In his behalf to speak a word the more,
Whose trust and valour I might here commend;
But times too short and precious so to spend.
But hark you wealthy merchants, who for prize
Send forth your well man'd ships where sun doth rise,
After three years when men and meat is spent,

My rich Commodityes pay double rent.
Ye Galenists, my Drugs that come from thence,
Do cure your Patients, fill your purse with pence;
Besides the use of roots, of hearbs, and plants,
That with less cost near home supply your wants.
But Mariners where got your ships and Sails,
And Oars to row, when both my Sisters fails
Your Tackling, Anchor, compass too is mine,
Which guides when sun, nor moon, nor stars do shine.
Ye mighty Kings, who for your lasting fames
Built Cities, Monuments, call'd by your
names, Were those compiled heaps of massy
stones That your ambition laid, ought but my
bones? Ye greedy misers, who do dig for gold
For gemms, for silver, Treasures which I hold,
Will not my goodly face your rage suffice
But you will see, what in my bowels
lyes? And ye Artificers, all Trades and
forts
My bounty calls you forth to make reports,
If ought you have, to use, to wear, to eat,
But what I freely yield, upon your sweat?
And Cholerick Sister, thou for all thine ire
Well knowst my fuel, must maintain thy
fire.

As I ingenuously with thanks confess,
My cold thy fruitfull heat doth crave no
less; But how my cold dry temper works
upon The melancholy Constitution;
How the Autumnal season I do sway,
And how I force the gray-head to obey,
I should here make a short, yet true narration.
But that thy method is mine imitation
Now must I shew mine adverse quality,
And how I oft work man's mortality;
He sometimes finds, maugre his toiling pain
Thistles and thorns where he expected grain.
My sap to plants and trees I must not grant,
The vine, the olive, and the fig tree want:
The Corn and Hay do fall before the're mown,
And buds from fruitfull trees as soon as blown;
Then dearth prevails, that nature to suffice
The Mother on her tender infant flyes;
The husband knows no wife, nor father sons.
But to all outrages their hunger runs:
Dreadful examples soon I might produce,
But to such Auditors 'twere of no use,
Again when Delvers dare in hope of gold
To ope those veins of Mine, audacious bold;
While they thus in mine entrails love to
dive, Before they know, they are inter'd
alive.
Y' affrighted nights appal'd, how do ye shake,
When once you feel me your foundation quake?
Because in the Abysse of my dark womb
Your cities and yourselves I oft intomb:
O dreadful Sepulcher! that this is true
Dathan and all his company well knew,
So did that Roman far more stout than wise
Bur'ing himself alive for honours
prize. And since fair Italy full sadly
knowes

What she hath lost by these remed'less woes.
Again what veins of poyson in me lye,
Some kill outright, and some do stupifye:
Nay into herbs and plants it sometimes creeps,
In heats & colds & gripes & drowzy sleeps;
Thus I occasion death to man and beast
When food they seek, & harm mistrust the least,
Much might I say of the hot Libian sand
Which rise like tumbling Billows on the Land
Wherein Cambyses Armie was o'rethrown
(but winder Sister, 'twas when you have blown)
I'le say no more, but this thing add I must
Remember Sons, your mould is of my dust
And after death whether interr'd or burn'd
As Earth at first so into Earth returned.

Water, in no whit dismayed by pretensions which have left no room
for any future claimant, proceeds to prove her right to the
championship, by a tirade which shows her powers quite equal to
those of her sisters, considering that her work in the floods has
evidenced itself quite as potent as anything Fire may claim in the
future.

Scarce Earth had done, but th' angry water moved.
Sister (quoth she) it had full well behoved
Among your boastings to have praised me
Cause of your fruitfulness as you shall see:
This your neglect shews your ingratitude
And how your subtilty, would men delude
Not one of us (all knows) that's like to thee
Ever in craving from the other three;
But thou art bound to me above the rest,
Who am thy drink, thy blood, thy Sap, and best:

If I withhold what art thou? dead dry lump
Thou bearst nor grass or plant, nor tree nor stump,
Thy extream thirst is moistn'ed by my love
With springs below, and showres from above
Or else thy Sun-burnt face and gaping chops
Complain to th' heavens, if I withhold my
drops Thy Bear, thy Tiger and thy Lion stout,
When I am gone, their fierceness none needs doubt
Thy Camel hath no strength, thy Bull no force
Nor mettal's found in the courageous Horse
Hinds leave their calves, the Elephant the fens
The wolves and Savage beasts forsake their Dens
The lofty Eagle, and the stork fly low,
The Peacock and the Ostrich, share in woe,
The Pine, the Cedar, yea, and Daphne's Tree
Do cease to nourish in this misery,
Man wants his bread and wine, & pleasant fruits
He knows, such sweets, lies not in Earth's dry roots
Then seeks me out, in river and in well
His deadly malady I might expell:
If I supply, his heart and veins rejoyce,
If not, soon ends his life, as did his voyce;
That this is true, Earth thou can'st not deny
I call thine Egypt, this to verifie,
Which by my falling Nile, doth yield such store

That she can spare, when nations round are poor
When I run low, and not o'reflow her brinks
To meet with want, each woeful man bethinks;
And such I am in Rivers, showrs and springs
But what's the wealth, that my rich Ocean brings
Fishes so numberless, I there do hold
If thou should'st buy, it would exhaust thy gold:

There lives the oyly Whale, whom all men know
Such wealth but not such like, Earth thou maist show.
The Dolphin loving musick, Arians friend
The witty Barbel, whose craft doth her commend
With thousands more, which now I list not name
Thy silence of thy Beasts doth cause the same
My pearles that dangle at thy Darling's ears,
Not thou, but shel-fish yield, as Pliny clears,
Was ever gem so rich found in thy trunk
As Egypts wanton, Cleopatra drunk?
Or hast thou any colour can come nigh
The Roman purple, double Tirian dye?
Which Caesar's Consuls, Tribunes all adorn,
For it to search my waves they thought no Scorn,
Thy gallant rich perfuming Amber greece
I lightly cast ashore as frothy fleece:
With rowling grains of purest massie gold,
Which Spains Americans do gladly hold.

Earth thou hast not moe countrys vales & mounds
Then I have fountains, rivers lakes and ponds;
My sundry seas, black, white and Adriatique,
Ionian, Baltique, and the vast Atlantique,
Aegean, Caspian, golden rivers fire,
Asphaltis lake, where nought remains alive:
But I should go beyond thee in my boasts,
If I should name more seas than thou hast Coasts,
And be thy mountains ne'er so high and steep,
I soon can match them with my seas as deep.
To speak of kinds of waters I neglect,
My diverse fountains and their strange effect:
My wholsome bathes, together with their cures;
My water Syrens with their guilefull lures,
The uncertain cause of certain ebbs and flows,
Which wondring Aristotles wit n'er knows,
Nor will I speak of waters made by art,
Which can to life restore a fainting heart.
Nor fruitfull dews, nor drops distil'd from
eyes, Which pitty move, and oft deceive the
wise: Nor yet of salt and sugar, sweet and
smart, Both when we lift to water we convert.
Alas thy ships and oars could do no good
Did they but want my Ocean and my flood.

The wary merchant on his weary beast
Transfers his goods from south to north and east,
Unless I ease his toil, and do transport
The wealthy fraight unto his wished port,
These be my benefits, which may suffice:
I now must shew what ill there in me lies.
The flegmy Constitution I uphold,

All humours, tumours which are bred of
cold: O're childhood and ore winter I bear
sway, And Luna for my Regent I obey.
As I with showers oft times refresh the earth,
So oft in my excess I cause a dearth,
And with abundant wet so cool the ground,
By adding cold to cold no fruit proves
found. The Farmer and the Grasier do
complain
Of rotten sheep, lean kine, and mildew'd grain.
And with my wasting floods and roaring torrent,
Their cattel hay and corn I sweep down current.
Nay many times my Ocean breaks his bounds,
And with astonishment the world confounds,
And swallows Countryes up, ne'er seen again,
And that an island makes which once was main:
Thus Britian fair ('tis thought) was cut from
France Scicily from Italy by the like chance,
And but one land was Africa and Spain
Untill proud Gibraltar did make them
twain. Some say I swallow'd up (sure tis a
notion) A mighty country in th' Atlantique
Ocean.
I need not say much of my hail and Snow,
My ice and extream cold, which all men
know, Whereof the first so ominous I rain'd,
That Israel's enemies therewith were brain'd;
And of my chilling snows such plenty be,
That Caucasus high mounts are seldome free,
Mine ice doth glaze Europes great rivers o're,
Till sun release, their ships can sail no more,
All know that inundations I have made,
Wherein not men, but mountains seem'd to wade;
As when Achaia all under water stood,
That for two hundred years it n'er prov'd good.
Deucalions great Deluge with many moe,
But these are trifles to the flood of Noe,
Then wholly perish'd Earths ignoble race,
And to this day impairs her beauteous face,
That after times shall never feel like woe,
Her confirm'd sons behold my colour'd bow.
Much might I say of wracks, but that He spare,
And now give place unto our Sister Air.

There is a mild self-complacency, a sunny and contented assertion
about "sister Air," that must have proved singularly aggravating
to the others, who, however, make no sign as to the final results, the
implication being, that she is after all the one absolutely
indispensable agent. But to end nowhere, each side fully convinced
in its own mind that the point had been carried in its own favor,
was so eminently in the spirit of the time, that there be no
wonder at the silence as to the real victor, though it is
surprising that Mistress Bradstreet let slip so excellent an
opportunity for the moral so dear to the Puritan mind.

Content (quoth Air) to speak the last of you,
Yet am not ignorant first was my due:
I do suppose you'l yield without controul I
am the breath of every living soul. Mortals,
what one of you that loves not me
Abundantly more than my Sisters three?

And though you love fire, Earth and Water well
Yet Air beyond all these you know t' excell.
I ask the man condemn'd that's neer his death,
How gladly should his gold purchase his breath,
And all the wealth that ever earth did give,
How freely should it go so he might live:
No earth, thy witching trash were all but
vain, If my pure air thy sons did not sustain,
The famish'd thirsty man that craves supply,
His moving reason is, give least I dye,
So both he is to go though nature's spent
To bid adieu to his dear Element.

Nay what are words which do reveal the mind,
Speak who or what they will they are but wind.
Your drums your trumpets & your organs
found, What is't but forced air which doth
rebound,
And such are ecchoes and report of th' gun
That tells afar th' exploit which it hath done,
Your songs and pleasant tunes they are the same,
And so's the notes which Nightingales do frame.
Ye forging Smiths, if bellows once were gone
Your red hot work more coldly would go on.
Ye Mariners, tis I that fill your sails,
And speed you to your port with wished gales.
When burning heat doth cause you faint, I cool,
And when I smile, your ocean's like a pool.
I help to ripe the corn, I turn the
mill, And with myself I every
Vacuum fill.
The ruddy sweet sanguine is like to air,
And youth and spring, Sages to me compare,
My moist hot nature is so purely thin,
No place so subtilly made, but I get in.
I grow more pure and pure as I mount higher,
And when I'm thoroughly varifi'd turn fire:
So when I am condens'd, I turn to water,
Which may be done by holding down my vapour.

Thus I another body can assume,
And in a trice my own nature resume.
Some for this cause of late have been so bold
Me for no Element longer to hold,
Let such suspend their thoughts, and silent be,
For all Philosophers make one of me:
And what those Sages either spake or writ
Is more authentick then our modern wit.
Next of my fowles such multitudes there are,
Earths beasts and waters fish scarce can compare.
Th' Ostrich with her plumes th' Eagle with her eyn
The Phoenix too (if any be) are mine,
The Stork, the crane, the partridg, and the phesant
The Thrush, the wren, the lark a prey to th' pesant,
With thousands more which now I may omit
Without impeachment to my tale or wit.
As my fresh air preserves all things in life,
So when corrupt, mortality is rife;

Then Fevers, Pmples, Pox and Pestilence,
With divers more, work deadly consequence:

Whereof such multitudes have di'd and fled,
The living scarce had power to bury the dead;
Yea so contagious countryes have we known
That birds have not 'Scapt death as they have flown
Of murrain, cattle numberless did fall,
Men feared destruction epidemical.
Then of my tempests felt at sea and land,
Which neither ships nor houses could withstand,
What wofull wracks I've made may well appear,
If nought were known but that before Algere,
Where famous Charles the fifth more loss sustained
Then in his long hot war which Millain gain'd
Again what furious storms and Hurricanoes
Know western Isles, as Christophers Barbadoes;
Where neither houses, trees nor plants I spare,
But some fall down, and some fly up with air.
Earthquakes so hurtfull, and so fear'd of all,
Imprison'd I, am the original.
Then what prodigious sights I sometimes show,
As battles pitcht in th' air, as countryes know,
Their joyning fighting, forcing and retreat,
That earth appears in heaven, O wonder great!
Sometimes red flaming swords and blazing stars,
Portentous signs of famines, plagues and wars,
Which make the Monarchs fear their fates
By death or great mutation of their States.
I have said less than did my Sisters three,
But what's their wrath or force, the fame's in me.
To adde to all I've said was my intent,
But dare not go beyond my Element.

Here the contest ends, and though the second edition held slight
alterations here and there, no further attempt was made to add to
or take away from the verses, which are as a whole the best
examples of the early work, their composition doubtless beguiling
many weary hours of the first years in New England. "The four
Humours of Man" follows, but holds only a few passages of any
distinctive character, the poem, like her "Four Monarchies," being
only a paraphrase of her reading. In "The Four Seasons," there was
room for picturesque treatment of the new conditions that
surrounded her, but she seems to have been content, merely to touch
the conventional side of nature, and to leave her own impressions
and feelings quite out of the question. The verses should have held
New England as it showed itself to the colonists, with all the
capricious charges that moved their wonder in the
early days. There was everything, it would have seemed, to excite
such poetical power as she possessed, to the utmost, for even the
prose of more than one of her contemporaries gives hints of the
feeling that stirred within them as they faced the strange
conditions of the new home. Even when they were closely massed
together, the silent spaces of the great wilderness shut them in,
its mystery beguiling yet bewildering them, and the deep woods
with their unfamiliar trees, the dark pines on the hill-side, all
held the sense of banishment and even terror. There is small token
of her own thoughts or feelings, in any lines of hers, till late
in life, when she dropped once for all the methods that pleased her
early years, and in both prose and poetry spoke her real mind with
a force that fills one with regret at the waste of power in
the dreary pages of the "Four Monarchies." That she had keen

susceptibility to natural beauty this later poem abundantly
proves, but in most of them there is hardly a hint of what must
have impressed itself upon her, though probably it was the more
valued by her readers, for this very reason.

CHAPTER XII.

MISCELLANEOUS

POEMS.

Though the series of quaternions which form the major part of the
poems, have separate titles and were written at various times, they
are in fact a single poem, containing sixteen personified
characters, all of them giving their views with dreary facility
and all of them to the Puritan mind, eminently correct and respectable
personalities. The "Four Seasons" won especial commendations from
her most critical readers, but for all of them there seems to have been
a delighted acceptance of every word this phenomenal woman had
thought it good to pen. Even fifty years ago, a woman's work,
whether prose or verse, which came before the public, was hailed
with an enthusiastic appreciation, it is
difficult to-day to comprehend, Mrs. S. C. Hall emphasizing this
in a paragraph on Hannah More, who held much the relation to old
England that Anne Bradstreet did to the New. "In this age, when
female talent is so rife--when, indeed, it is not too much to say
women have fully sustained their right to equality with men in
reference to all the productions of the mind--it is difficult to
comprehend the popularity, almost amounting to adoration, with
which a woman writer was regarded little more than half a century
ago. Mediocrity was magnified into genius, and to have printed a
book, or to have written even a tolerable poem, was a passport
into the very highest society."

Even greater veneration was felt in days when many women, even of
good birth, could barely write their own names, and if Anne
Bradstreet had left behind her nothing but the quaternions, she would
long have ranked as a poet deserving of all the elegies and
anagrammatic tributes the Puritan divine loved to manufacture. The
"Four Seasons," which might have been written in Lincolnshire and
holds not one suggestion of the new life and methods the colonists
were fast learning, may have been enjoyed because of its reminders
of the old home. Certainly the "nightingale and thrush" did not
sing under Cambridge windows, nor did the "primrose pale," fill
the hands of the children who ran over the New England meadows. It
seems to have been her theory that certain well established forms
must be preserved, and so she wrote the conventional phrases of
the poet of the seventeenth century, only a line or two indicating
the real power of observation she failed to exercise.

THE FOUR SEASONS OF THE YEAR.

SPRING.

Another four I've left yet to bring on,
Of four times four the last Quarternion,
The Winter, Summer, Autumn & the Spring,

In season all these Seasons I shall bring;
Sweet Spring like man in his Minority,
At present claim'd, and had priority.
With Smiling face and garments somewhat green,
She trim'd her locks, which late had frosted been,
Nor hot nor cold, she spake, but with a breath,
Fit to revive, the nummed earth from death.
Three months (quoth she) are 'lotted to my share
March, April, May of all the rest most
fair. Tenth of the first, Sol into Aries
enters, And bids defiance to all tedious
winters,
Crosseth the Line, and equals night and day,
(Stil adds to th' last til after pleasant May)
And now makes glad the darkned nothern nights
Who for some months have seen but starry lights.
Now goes the Plow-man to his merry toyle,
He might unloose his winter locked soyle;
The Seeds-man too, doth lavish out his grain,
In hope the more he casts, the more to gain;
The Gardener now superfluous branches lops,
And poles erect for his young clambring hops.
Now digs then sowes his herbs, his flowers & roots
And carefully manures his trees of fruits.
The Pleiades their influence now give,
And all that seemed as dead afresh doth live.
The croaking frogs, whom nipping winter kil'd
Like birds now chirp, and hop about the field,
The Nightingale, the black-bird and the Thrush
Now tune their layes, on sprayes of every bush.

The wanton frisking Kid, and soft fleec'd Lambs
Do jump and play before their feeding Dams,
The tender tops of budding grass they crop,
They joy in what they have, but more in hope:
For though the frost hath lost his binding power,
Yet many a fleece of snow and stormy shower
Doth darken Sol's bright eye, makes us remember
The pinching North-west wind of cold December.
My Second month is April, green and fair,
Of longer dayes, and a more temperate Air:
The Sun in Taurus keeps his residence,
And with his warmer beams glareeth from thence
This is the month whose fruitful showers produces
All set and sown for all delights and uses:
The Pear, the Plum, and Apple-tree now flourish
The grass grows long the hungry beast to nourish
The Primrose pale, and azure violet
Among the virduous grass hath nature set,
That when the Sun on's Love (the earth) doth shine
These might as lace set out her garments fine.
The fearfull bird his little house now builds
In trees and walls, in Cities and in fields.
The outside strong, the inside warm and neat;
A natural Artificer compleat.
The clocking hen her chirping chickins leads
With wings & beak defends them from the gleads
My next and last is fruitfull pleasant
May, Wherein the earth is clad in rich
aray, The Sun now enters loving Gemini,

And heats us with the glances of his eye,
Our thicker rayment makes us lay aside
Lest by his fervor we be torrified.
All flowers the Sun now with his beams discloses,
Except the double pinks and matchless Roses.
Now swarms the busy, witty, honey-Bee,
Whose praise deserves a page from more than me
The cleanly Huswife's Dary's now in th'
prime, Her shelves and firkins fill'd for winter
time.
The meads with Cowslips, Honey-suckles dight,
One hangs his head, the other stands upright:
But both rejoice at th' heaven's clear smiling face,
More at her showers, which water them apace.
For fruits my Season yields the early Cherry,
The hasty Peas, and wholsome cool Strawberry.
More solid fruits require a longer time,
Each Season hath its fruit, so hath each Clime:
Each man his own peculiar excellence,
But none in all that hath preheminence.
Sweet fragrant Spring, with thy short pittance fly
Let some describe thee better than can I.
Yet above all this priviledg is thine,
Thy dayes still lengthen without least decline:

      SUMMER.

When Spring had done, the Summer did begin,
With melted tauny face, and garments thin,
Resembling Fire, Choler, and Middle age,
As Spring did Air, Blood, Youth in 's
equipage. Wiping the sweat from of her face
that ran, With hair all wet she pussing thus
began; Bright June, July and August hot are
mine,
In th' first Sol doth in crabbed Cancer shine.
His progress to the North now's fully done,
Then retrograde must be my burning Sun,
Who to his Southward Tropick still is bent,
Yet doth his parching heat but more augment
Though he decline, because his flames so fair,
Have throughly dry'd the earth, and heat the air.
Like as an Oven that long time hath been heat,
Whose vehemency at length doth grow so great,
That if you do withdraw her burning store,
'Tis for a time as fervent as before.
Now go those foolick Swains, the Shepherd Lads
To wash the thick cloth'd flocks with pipes full
glad In the cool streams they labour with delight
Rubbing their dirty coats till they look white;
Whose fleece when finely spun and deeply dy'd
With Robes thereof Kings have been dignified,
Blest rustick Swains, your pleasant quiet life,
Hath envy bred in Kings that were at strife,
Careless of worldly wealth you sing and pipe,
Whilst they'r imbroyl'd in wars & troubles
rife: Wich made great Bajazet cry out in 's
woes, Oh happy shepherd which hath not to
lose.

Orthobulus, nor yet Sebastia great,
But whist'leth to thy flock in cold and heat.

Viewing the Sun by day, the Moon by night
Endimions, Dianaes dear delight,
Upon the grass resting your healthy limbs,
By purling Brooks looking how fishes
swims, If pride within your lowly Cells ere
haunt,
Of him that was Shepherd then King go vaunt. This
moneth the Roses are distil'd in glasses, Whose
fragrant smel all made perfumes surpasses The
cherry, Gooseberry are now in th' prime,
And for all sorts of Pease, this is the time.
July my next, the hott'st in all the year,
The sun through Leo now takes his Career,
Whose flaming breath doth melt us from afar,
Increased by the star Ganicular,
This month from Julius Ceasar took its name,
By Romans celebrated to his fame.
Now go the Mowers to their flashing toyle,
The Meadowes of their riches to dispoyle,
With weary strokes, they take all in their
way, Bearing the burning heat of the long
day.
The forks and Rakes do follow them amain,
Wich makes the aged fields look young again,
The groaning Carts do bear away their prize,
To Stacks and Barns where it for Fodder lyes.
My next and last is August fiery hot
(For much, the Southward Sun abateth not)
This Moneth he keeps with Vigor for a space,
The dry'ed Earth is parched with his face.
August of great Augustus took its name,
Romes second Emperour of lasting fame,
With sickles now the bending Reapers goe
The rustling tress of terra down to mowe;
And bundles up in sheaves, the weighty wheat,
Which after Manchet makes for Kings to eat:
The Barly, Rye and Pease should first had place,
Although their bread have not so white a face.
The Carter leads all home with whistling voyce.
He plow'd with pain, but reaping doth rejoice,
His sweat, his toyle, his careful wakeful nights,
His fruitful Crop abundantly requites.
Now's ripe the Pear, Pear-plumb and Apricock,
The prince of plumbs, whose stone's as hard as Rock
The Summer seems but short, the Autumn hasts
To shake his fruits, of most delicious tasts
Like good old Age, whose younger juicy Roots
Hath still ascended, to bear goodly fruits. Until
his head be gray, and strength be gone. Yet
then appears the worthy deeds he'th done: To
feed his boughs exhausted hath his Sap, Then
drops his fruit into the eaters lap.

       _AUTUMN.

       —

Of Autumn moneths September is the prime,
Now day and night are equal in each Clime,
The twelfth of this Sol riseth in the Line,
And doth in poizing Libra this month shine.
The vintage now is ripe, the grapes are prest,
Whose lively liquor oft is curs'd and blest:

For nought so good, but it may be abused,
But its a precious juice when well its used.
The raisins now in clusters dryed be,
The Orange, Lemon dangle on the tree: The
Pomegranate, the Fig are ripe also, And
Apples now their yellow sides do show.
Of Almonds, Quinces, Wardens, and of Peach,
The season's now at hand of all and each,
Sure at this time, time first of all began,
And in this moneth was made apostate man:
For then in Eden was not only seen,
Boughs full of leaves, or fruits unripe or green,
Or withered stocks, which were all dry and dead,
But trees with goodly fruits replenished;
Which shows nor Summer, Winter nor the Spring
Our Grand-Sire was of Paradice made King:
Nor could that temp'rate Clime such difference make,
If cited as the most Judicious take.
October is my next, we hear in this
The Northern winter-blasts begin to hip,
In Scorpio resideth now the Sun,
And his declining heat is almost done.
The fruitless trees all withered now do stand,
Whose sapless yellow leavs, by winds are fan'd
Which notes when youth and strength have passed their prime
Decrepit age must also have its time.

The Sap doth slily creep toward the Earth
There rests, until the Sun give it a birth.
So doth old Age still tend until his grave,
Where also he his winter time must have;
But when the Sun of righteousness draws nigh,
His dead old stock, shall mount again on high.
November is my last, for Time doth haste,
We now of winters sharpness 'gins to taste
This moneth the Sun's in Sagitarius,
So farre remote, his glances warm not us.
Almost at shortest, is the shorten'd day,
The Northern pole beholdeth not one ray,
Nor Greenland, Groanland, Finland, Lapland, see
No Sun, to lighten their obscurity;
Poor wretches that in total darkness lye,
With minds more dark then is the dark'ned Sky.
Beaf, Brawn, and Pork are now in great request,
And solid meats our stomacks can digest.
This time warm cloaths, full diet, and good fires,
Our pinched flesh, and hungry marres requires;
Old cold, dry Age, and Earth Autumn resembles,
And Melancholy which most of all dissembles.
I must be short, and shorts the short'ned day,
What winter hath to tell, now let him say.

WINTER.

Cold, moist, young flegmy winter now doth lye
In swaddling Clouts, like new born Infancy
Bound up with frosts, and furr'd with hail &
snows, And like an Infant, still it taller grows;
December is my first, and now the Sun

To th' Southward Tropick, his swift race doth run:
This moneth he's hous'd in horned Capricorn,
From thence he 'gins to length the shortned morn,
Through Christendome with great Feastivity,
Now's held, (but ghest) for blest
Nativity, Cold frozen January next
comes in,
Chilling the blood and shrinking up the
skin; In Aquarius now keeps the long wisht
Sun,
And Northward his unwearied Course doth run:
The day much longer then it was before,
The cold not lessened, but augmented more.
Now Toes and Ears, and Fingers often freeze,
And Travellers their noses sometimes leese.

Moist snowie Feburary is my last,
I care not how the winter time doth haste,
In Pisces now the golden Sun doth shine,
And Northward still approaches to the Line,
The rivers 'gin to ope, the snows to melt,
And some warm glances from his face are felt;
Which is increased by the lengthen'd day,
Until by's heat, he drives all cold away,
And thus the year in Circle runneth round:
Where first it did begin, in th' end its
found.

With the final lines a rush of dissatisfaction came over the
writer, and she added certain couplets, addressed to her father,
for whom the whole set seems to have been originally written, and
who may be responsible in part for the bald and didactic quality
of most of her work.

My Subjects bare, my Brain is bad,
Or better Lines you should have had;
The first fell in so nat'rally,
I knew not how to pass it by;
The last, though bad I could not mend,
Accept therefore of what is pen'd,
And all the faults that you shall spy
Shall at your feet for pardon cry.

Mr. John Harvard Ellis has taken pains to compare various passages
in her "Four Monarchies" with the sources from which her
information was derived, showing a similarity as close as the
difference between prose and verse would admit. One illustration
of this will be sufficient. In the description of the murder of
the philosopher Callisthenes by Alexander the Great, which occurs
in her account of the Grecian Monarchy, she writes:

The next of worth that suffered after these,
Was learned, virtuous, wise Calisthenes,
Who loved his Master more than did the rest,
As did appear, in flattering him the least;
In his esteem a God he could not be,
Nor would adore him for a Deity.
For this alone and for no other cause,
Against his Sovereign, or against his Laws,
He on the Rack his Limbs in pieces rent,
Thus was he tortur'd till his life was spent
Of this unkingly act doth Seneca

This censure pass, and not unwisely say,
Of Alexander this the eternal crime,
Which shall not be obliterate by time.
Which virtue's fame can ne're redeem by far,
Nor all felicity of his in war.

When e're 'tis said he thousand thousands slew,
Yea, and Calisthenes to death he drew.
The mighty Persian King he over came,
Yea, and he killed Calisthenes of fame.
All countreyes, Kingdomes, Provinces he won,
From Hellespont, to the farthest Ocean.
All this he did, who knows not to be true?
But yet withal, Calisthenes he slew.
From Nacedon, his English did extend,
Unto the utmost bounds o' th' Orient,
All this he did, yea, and much more 'tis true,
But yet withal, Calisthenes he slew.

The quotation from Raleigh's "History of the World," which
follows, will be seen to hold in many lines the identical
words.

"Alexander stood behind a partition, and heard all that was
spoken, waiting but an opportunity to be revenged on Callisthenes,
who being a man of free speech, honest, learned, and a lover of
the king's honour, was yet soon after tormented to death, not for
that he had betrayed the king to others, but because he never
would condescend to betray the king to himself, as all his
detestable flatterers did. For in a conspiracy against the king,
made by one Hermolaus and others, (which they confessed,) he
caused Callisthenes, without confession, accusation or trial, to be
torn assunder upon the rack. This deed, unworthy of a king,
Seneca thus censureth. [He gives the Latin, and thus translates
it.] 'This is the eternal crime of Alexander, which no virtue nor
felicity of his in war shall ever be able to redeem. For as often
as any man shall say, He slew many thousand Persians, it shall be
replied, He did so, and he slew Callisthenes; when it shall be
said, He slew Darius, it shall be replied, And Callisthenes; when it
shall be said, He won all as far as to the very ocean, thereon also
he adventured with unusual navies, and extended his empire from
a corner of Thrace, to the utmost bounds of the orient; it
shall be said withal, But he killed Callisthenes. Let him have
outgone all the ancient examples of captains and kings, none of
all his acts makes so much to his glory, as Callisthenes to his
reproach'."

The school girl of the present day could furnish such arrangements
of her historical knowledge with almost as fluent a pen as that of
Mistress Bradstreet, who is, however, altogether innocent of any
intention to deceive any of her readers. The unlearned praised her
depth of learning, but she knew well that every student into whose
hands the book might fall, would recognize the source from which
she had drawn, and approve the method of its use. Evidently there
was nothing very vital to her in these records of dynasties and
wars, for not a line indicates any thrill of feeling at the tales
she chronicles. Yet the feeling was there, though reserved for a
later day. It is with her own time, or with the "glorious reign of
good Queen Bess," that she forgets to be didactic and allows
herself here and there, a natural and vigorous expression of

thought or feeling. There was capacity for hero-worship, in this
woman, who repressed as far as she had power, the feeling and
passion that sometimes had their way, though immediately subdued
and chastened, and sent back to the durance in which all feeling was
held. But her poem on Queen Elizabeth has here and there a quiet
sarcasm, and at one point at least rises into a fine scorn
of the normal attitude toward women:

> She hath wip'd off the aspersion of her Sex,
> That women wisdome lack to play the Rex.

Through the whole poem runs an evident, almost joyous delight in
what a woman has achieved, and as she passes from point to point,
gathering force with every period, she turns suddenly upon all
detractors with these ringing lines:

> Now say, have women worth or have they none?
> Or had they some, but with our Queen is't gone?
> Nay, masculines, you have thus taxed us long;
> But she, though dead, will vindicate our wrong.
> Let such as say our sex is void of reason,
> Know 'tis a slander now, but once was treason.

Sir Philip Sidney fills her with mixed feeling, her sense that
his "Arcadia" was of far too fleshly and soul-beguiling an
order of literature, battling with her admiration for his
character as a man, and making a diverting conflict between
reason and
inclination. As with Queen Elizabeth, she compromised by merely
hinting her opinion of certain irregularities, and hastened to
cover any damaging admission with a mantle of high and even
enthusiastic eulogy.

AN ELEGIE

upon that Honourable and renowned Knight
Sir Philip Sidney, who
was untimely slain at the Siege of Zutphen,
Anno, 1586.

> When England did enjoy her Halsion dayes,
> Her noble Sidney wore the Crown of Bayes;
> As well an honour to our British Land,
> As she that swayed the Scepter with her hand;
> Mars and Minerva did in one agree,
> Of Arms and Arts he should a pattern be,
> Calliope with Terpsichore did sing,
> Of poesie, and of musick, he was King;
> His Rhetorick struck Polimina dead,
> His Eloquence made Mercury wax red;
> His Logick from Euterpe won the
> Crown,
> More worth was his then Clio could set down.
> Thalia and Melpomene say truth,
> Witness Arcadia penned in his youth,
> Are not his tragick Comedies so acted,
> As if your ninefold wit had been compacted.
> To shew the world, they never saw before,
> That this one Volume should exhaust your store;
> His wiser dayes condemned his witty works,
> Who knows the spels that in his Rhetorick lurks,

But some infatuate fools soon caught therein,
Fond Cupids Dame had never such a gin,
Which makes severer eyes but slight that story,
And men of morose minds envy his glory:
But he's a Beetle-head that can't descry
A world of wealth within that rubbish lye,
And doth his name, his work, his honour wrong,
The brave refiner of our British tongue,
That sees not learning, valour and morality,
Justice, friendship, and kind hospitality,
Yea and Divinity within his book,
Such were prejudicate, and did not look.
In all Records his name I ever see
Put with an Epithite of dignity,
Which shows his worth was great, his honour such,
The love his Country ought him, was as much.
Then let none disallow of these my straines
Whilst English blood yet runs within my
veins, O brave Achilles, I wish some Homer
would Engrave in Marble, with Characters of
gold
The valiant feats thou didst on Flanders coast,
Which at this day fair Belgia may boast.
The more I say, the more thy worth I stain,
Thy fame and praise is far beyond my strain,
O Zutphen, Zutphen that most fatal City
Made famous by thy death, much more the pity:
Ah! in his blooming prime death pluckt this rose
E're he was ripe, his thread cut Atropos.
Thus man is born to dye, and dead is he,
Brave Hector, by the walls of Troy we see.
O who was near thee but did sore repine
He rescued not with life that life of thine;
But yet impartial Fates this boon did give,
Though Sidney di'd his valiant name should live:
And live it doth in spight of death through fame,
Thus being overcome, he overcame.
Where is that envious tongue, but can afford
Of this our noble Scipio some good word.

Great Bartas this unto thy praise adds more,
In sad sweet verse, thou didst his death deplore.
And Phoenix Spencer doth unto his life,
His death present in sable to his wife.
Stella the fair, whose streams from Conduits fell
For the sad loss of her Astrophel.
Fain would I show how he fame's paths did tread,
But now into such Lab'rinths I am lead,
With endless turnes, the way I find not out,
How to persist my Muse is more in doubt;
Wich makes me now with Silvester confess,
But Sidney's Muse can sing his worthiness.
The Muses aid I craved, they had no will
To give to their Detractor any quill,
With high disdain, they said they gave no more,
Since Sidney had exhausted all their store.
They took from me the Scribling pen I had,
I to be eas'd of such a task was glad
Then to reveng this wrong, themselves engage,
And drove me from Parnassus in a rage.

Then wonder not if I no better sped,
Since I the Muses thus have injured.
I pensive for my fault, sate down, and then
Errata through their leave, threw me my pen,
My Poem to conclude, two lines they deign
Which writ, she bad return't to them again;
So Sidneys fame I leave to Englands Rolls,
His bones do lie interr'd in stately Pauls.

HIS EPITAPH.

Here lies in fame under this stone,
Philip and Alexander both in one;
Heir to the Muses, the Son of Mars in Truth,
Learning, Valour, Wisdome, all in virtuous
youth, His praise is much, this shall suffice my
pen, That Sidney dy'd 'mong most renown'd of
men.

With Du Bartas, there is no hesitation or qualification. Steeped in
the spirit of his verse, she was unconscious how far he had
moulded both thought and expression, yet sufficiently aware of his
influence to feel it necessary to assert at many points her
freedom from it. But, as we have already seen, he was the Puritan
poet, and affected every rhymester of the time, to a degree which
it required generations to shake off. In New England, however,
even he, in time came to rank as light-minded, and the last shadow
of poetry fled before the metrical horrors of the Bay Psalm Book,
which must have lent a terror to rhyme, that one could wish might
be transferred to the present day. The elegy on Du Bartas is all
the proof needed to establish Anne Bradstreet as one of his most
loyal followers, and in spite of all protest to the contrary such
she was and will remain.

IN HONOUR OF DU BARTAS.

Among the happy wits this age hath shown
Great, dear, sweet Bartas thou art matchless known;
My ravished eyes and heart with faltering tongue,
In humble wise have vowed their service long
But knowing th' task so great & strength but small,
Gave o're the work before begun withal,
My dazled sight of late reviewed thy lines,
Where Art, and more than Art in nature shines,
Reflection from their beaming altitude
Did thaw my frozen hearts ingratitude
Which rayes darting upon some richer ground
Had caused flours and fruits soon to abound,
But barren I, my Dasey here do bring,
A homely flower in this my latter Spring, If
Summer, or my Autumm age do yield
Flours, fruits, in Garden Orchard, or in
Field, Volleyes of praises could I eccho then,
Had I an Angels voice, or Bartas pen;
But wishes can't accomplish my desire,
Pardon if I adore, when I admire.
O France thou did'st in him more glory gain
Then in St. Lewes, or thy last Henry Great,
Who tam'd his foes in warrs, in bloud and sweat,

Thy fame is spread as far, I dare be bold,
In all the Zones, the temp'rate, hot and cold,
Their Trophies were but heaps of wounded slain,
Shine the quintessence of an heroick brain.
The oaken Garland ought to deck their brows,
Immortal Bayes to thee all men allows,
Who in thy tryumphs never won by wrongs,
Lead'st millions chained by eyes, by ears, by tongues,
Oft have I wondred at the hand of heaven,
In giving one what would have served seven,
If e're this golden gift was show'd on any,
They shall be consecrated in my Verse,
And prostrate offered at great Bartas Herse;
My muse unto a child I may compare
Who sees the riches of some famous Fair, He
feeds his Eyes, but understanding lacks To
comprehend the worth of all those knacks
The glittering plate and Jewels he admires,
The Hats and Fans, the Plumes and Ladies tires,
And thousand times his mazed mind doth wish,
Some part (at least) of that great wealth was his,
But feeling empty wishes nought obtain,
At night turnes to his mothers cot again,
And tells her tales, (his full heart over glad)
Of all the glorious sights his Eyes have had;
But finds too soon his want of Eloquence,
The silly prattler speaks no word of sense;
But feeling utterance fail his great desires
Sits down in silence, deeply he admires,
Thus weak brained I, reading thy lofty stile,
Thy profound learning, viewing other while;
Thy Art in natural Philosophy,
Thy Saint like mind in grave
Divinity; Thy piercing skill in high
Astronomy, And curious insight in
anatomy;
Thy Physick, musick and state policy,
Valour in warr, in peace good husbandry,
Sure lib'ral Nature did with Art not small,
In all the arts make thee most liberal,
A thousand thousand times my senseless sences
Moveless stand charmed by thy sweet influences;
More senseless then the stones to Amphious Luto,
Mine eyes are sightless, and my tongue is mute,
My full astonish'd heart doth pant to break,
Through grief it wants a faculty to speak;
Thy double portion would have served many,
Unto each man his riches is assign'd
Of name, of State, of Body and of mind:

Thou had'st thy part of all, but of the last,
O pregnant brain, O comprehension vast;
Thy haughty Stile and rapted wit sublime
All ages wondring at, shall never climb,
Thy sacred works are not for imitation,
But monuments to future admiration,
Thus Bartas fame shall last while starrs do satnd,
And whilst there's Air or Fire, or Sea or Land.
But least my ignorance shall do thee wrong,
To celebrate thy merits in my Song.

He leave thy praise to those shall do thee right,
Good will, not skill, did cause me bring my
mite.

HIS EPITAPH.
Here lyes the Pearle of France, Parnassus glory;
The World rejoyc'd at's birth, at's death, was sorry,
Art and Nature joyn'd, by heavens high decree
Naw shew'd what once they ought, Humanity!
And Natures Law, had it been revocable
To rescue him from death, Art had been able,
But Nature vanquish'd Art, so Bartas dy'd;
But Fame out-living both, he is reviv'd.

Bare truth as every line surely appeared to the woman who wrote,
let us give thanks devoutly that the modern mind holds no capacity
for the reproduction of that

"Haughty Stile and rapted wit sublime
All ages wond'ring at shall never climb,"

and that more truly than she knew, his

"Sacred works are not for imitation
But Monuments to future Admiration."

Not the "future Admiration" she believed his portion, but
to the dead reputation which, fortunately for us, can have
no resurrection.

CHAPTER XIII.

CHANCES AND CHANGES.

With the appearance of the little volume and the passing of the
flutter of interest and excitement it had aroused, the Andover
life subsided into the channel through which, save for one or two
breaks, it was destined to run for many years. Until 1653, nothing
of note had taken place, but this year brought two events, one
full of the proud but quiet satisfaction the Puritan mother felt
in a son who had ended his college course with distinction, and
come home to renew the associations somewhat broken in his four
years absence; the other, a sorrow though hardly an unexpected
one. Samuel Bradstreet, who became a physician, living for many
years in Boston, which he finally left for the West Indies, was
about twenty at the time of his graduation from Harvard, the
success of which was very near Anne Bradstreet's heart and the
pride of his grandfather, Governor Dudley, who barely lived to see
the fruition of his wishes for this first child of his favorite
daughter. His death in July, 1653, softened the feeling that seems
slowly to have arisen against him in the minds of many who had
been his friends, not without reason, though many of them had
showed quite as thorough intolerance as he. With increasing years,
Dudley's spirit had hardened and embittered against all who
ventured to differ from the cast-iron theology his soul loved.
Bradstreet and Winthrop had both been a cross to him with the

toleration which seemed to him the child of Satan himself. His intense will had often drawn concessions from Winthrop at which his feelings revolted and he pursued every sort of sectary with a zeal that never flagged. Hutchinson wrote: "He was zealous beyond measure against all sorts of heretics," and Roger Williams said bitterly: "It is known who hindered but never promoted the liberty of other men's consciences."

Between the "vagaries of many sectaries," the persistent and irrepressible outbreaks from Roger Williams, the bewildering and confounding presumption of Anne Hutchinson, who seems to have been the forerunner of other Boston agitations of like nature, Governor Dudley's last days were full of astonishments, not the least being the steady though mild opposition of his son-in-law Bradstreet to all harsh measures. Toleration came to seem to him at last the crowning sin of all the ages, and his last recorded written words are a valiant testimony against it. There was a curious tendency to rhyme in the gravest of these decorous Fathers; a tendency carefully concealed by some, as in John Winthrop's case, who confined his "dropping into poetry" to the margins of his almanacs. Others were less distrustful, and printed their "painful verses" on broad sheets, for general circulation and oppression. Governor Dudley rhymed but once, but in the bald and unequal lines, found in his pocket after death, condensed his views of all who had disagreed from him, as well as the honest, sturdy conviction in which he lived and died. They were written evidently but a short time before his death, and are in the beginning much after the order of his daughter's first poem.

Dim Eyes, deaf Ears, cold Stomach, shew
My dissolution is in view,
Eleven times seven near liv'd have I.
And now God calls I willing Die,
My Shuttle's shot, my Race is run,
My Sun is set, my Day is done.
My span is measured, Tale is told,
My Flower is faded and grown old.
My Dream is vanish'd, Shadows fled,
My Soul with Christ, my Body Dead,
Farewel dear Wife, Children and Friends,
Hate Heresie, make Blessed Ends,
Bear Poverty, live with good
Men; So shall we live with Joy
agen.
Let men of God in Courts and Churches watch,
O're such as do a Toleration hatch,
Lest that ill Egg bring forth a Cockatrice
To poison all with Heresie and Vice.
If Men be left and otherwise Combine,
My epitaph's I DY'D NO
LIBERTINE.

To the old Puritan, scowling to the last at any shade of difference from the faith to which he would willingly have been a martyr, a "Libertine" included all blasphemous doubters and defiers of current beliefs--Quakers, Antinomians and other pestilent people who had already set the Colony by the ears and were soon to accomplish much more in this direction. The verses were at once creed and protest, and are a fair epitome of the Puritan mind in 1650. Other rhymes from other hands had expressed equally uncompromising opinions. He had survived the anagramatic

warning sent to him by an unknown hand in 1645, which still stands
on the files of the first Church in Roxbury, and which may have
been written by one of his opponents in the General Court.

THOMAS

DUDLEY. Ah! old must dye,
A death's head on your hand you need not weare;
A dying head you on your shoulders bear;
You need not one to mind you you must dye,
You in your name may spell mortalitye.
Young men may dye, but old men, these dye must,
'Twill not be long before you turn to dust.
Before you turn to dust! ah! must! old!
dye!
What shall young men doe, when old in dust do lye?
When old in dust lye, what New England doe?
When old in dust do lye it's best dye too.

Death condoned these offences, and left only the memory of his
impartial justice and his deep and earnest piety, and Morton wrote
of him, what expressed the feeling even of his enemies: "His love
to justice appeared at all times, and in special upon the
judgement seat, without respect of persons in judgement, and in
his own particular transactions with all men, he was exact and
exemplary. His zeal to order appeared in contriving good laws and
faithfully executing them upon criminal offenders, heretics and
underminers of true religion. He had a piercing judgement to
discover the wolf, though clothed with a sheepskin. His love to
the people was evident, in serving them in a public capacity many
years at his own cost, and that as a nursing father to the
churches of Christ. He loved the true Christian religion, and the
pure worship of God, and cherished as in his bosom, all godly
ministers and Christians. He was exact in the practice of piety,
in his person and family, all his life. In a word he lived
desired, and died lamented by all good men."

This was stronger language than the majority of his fellow-
colonists would have been inclined to use, his differences with
Governor Winthrop having embittered many of the latter's friends.
Winthrop's persistent gentleness went far toward quieting the
feeling against him, which seems to have taken deep root in
Dudley's breast, but the jealousy of his authority, and
questioning of his judgement, though perhaps natural from the
older man, brought about many uncomfortable complications. All
the towns about Boston had been ordered to send their quota to aid
in finishing the fort built in 1633, but Governor Dudley would not
allow any party from Newtown to be made up, nor would he give the
reason for such course to Governor Winthrop. There was cause, for
Salem and Saugus had failed to pay their share of money, and
Dudley's sense of justice would not allow his constituents to do
their share till all had paid the amount levied. Remonstrated
with, he wrote a most unpleasant letter, a habit of his when
offended, refusing to act till the reluctant Salem had paid. This
letter, brought to Winthrop by Mr. Hooker, he returned to him
at once. The rest of the story may be given in his own words.
The record stands in his journal given in the third person, and
as impartially as if told of another: "The governour told them it
should rest till the court, and withal gave the letter to Mr.
Hooker with this speech: I am not willing to keep such an occasion

of provocation by me. And soon after he wrote to the deputy (who had before desired to buy a fat hog or two of him, being somewhat short of provisions) to desire him to send for one, (which he would have sent him, if he had known when his occasion had been to have made use of it), and to accept it as a testimony of his good will; and lest he should make any scruple of it, he made Mr. Haynes and Mr. Hooker, (who both sojurned in his house) partakers with him. Upon this the deputy returned this answer: 'Your overcoming yourself hath overcome me. Mr. Haynes, Mr. Hooker, and myself, do most kindly accept your good will, but we desire, without offence, to refuse your offer, and that I may only trade with you for two hogs;' and so very lovingly concluded."

There was no word, however, of yielding the disputed point, which was settled for him a few days later. "The court being two days after, ordered, that Newtown should do their work as others had done, and then Salem, &c., should pay for three days at eighteen pence a man."

The records of that time hold instance after instance of the old man's obstinacy and Winthrop's gentle and most patient consideration. To Anne, however, who came in contact only with his milder side, it was an irreparable loss, and she never spoke of him save with grateful and tender remembrance, her elegy on his death, though conventional as the time made her, being full of the sorrow time soothed but never destroyed.

  To the Memory of my dear and ever honoured Father,
       Thomas Dudley Esq.

  Who deceased July 31, 1653, and of his Age, 77.

  By duty bound, and not by custome led
  To celebrate the praises of the dead,
  My mournfull mind, sore prest, in trembling verse
  Presents my Lamentations at his Herse,
  Who was my Father, Guide, Instructor too,
  To whom I ought whatever I could doe:
  Nor is't Relation near my hand shall tye;
  For who more cause to boast his worth than I?
  Who heard or saw, observed or knew him better?
  Or who alive then I, a greater debtor?
  Let malice bite, and envy knaw its fill,
  He was my Father, and Ile praise him still.
  Nor was his name, or life lead so obscure
  That pitty might some Trumpeters procure.
  Who after death might make him falsly seen
  Such as in life, no man could justly deem.
  Well known and lov'd where ere he liv'd, by most
  Both in his native, and in foreign coast,
  These to the world his merits could make known,
  So needs no Testimonial from his own;
  But now or never I must pay my Sum;
  While others tell his worth, Ile not be dumb:
  One of thy Founders, him New England know,
  Who staid thy feeble sides when thou wast low,
  Who spent his state, his strength & years with care
  That After-comers in them might have a share,
  True Patriot of this little Commonweal,

Who is't can tax thee ought, but for thy zeal?
Truths friend thou wert, to errors still a foe,
Which caus'd Apostates to maligne so.
Thy love to true Religion e're shall shine,
My Fathers God, be God of me and mine,
Upon the earth he did not build his nest,
But as a Pilgrim. what he had, possest,
High thoughts he gave no harbour in his heart,
Nor honours pufft him up, when he had part;
Those titles loathed, which some do too much love
For truly his ambition lay above.
His humble mind so lov'd
humility, He left it to his race for
Legacy;
And oft and oft, with speeches mild and wise,
Gave his in charge, that Jewel rich to prize.
No ostentation seen in all his wayes,
As in the mean ones of our foolish dayes. Which
all they have, and more still set to view, Their
greatness may be judg'd by what they shew. His
thoughts were more sublime, his actions wise,
Such vanityes he justly did despise.
Nor wonder 'twas, low things n'er much did move
For he a Mansion had, prepar'd above,
For which he sigh'd and pray'd & long'd full sore
He might be cloath'd upon, for evermore.
Oft spake of death, and with a smiling chear,
He did exult his end was drawing near,
Now fully ripe, as shock of wheat that's grown,
Death as a Sickle hath him timely mown,
And in celestial Barn hath hous'd him high,
Where storms, nor showrs, nor ought can damnifie.
His Generation serv'd, his labours cease;
And to his Fathers gathered is in peace.
Ah happy Soul, 'mongst Saints and Angels blest,
Who after all his toyle, is now at rest:
His hoary head in righteousness was found;
As joy in heaven on earth let praise resound.
Forgotten never be his memory,
His blessing rest on his posterity:
His pious Footsteps followed by his race,
At last will bring us to that happy place
Where we with joy each other's face shall see,
And parted more by death shall never be.

    HIS EPITAPH.

Within this Tomb a Patriot lyes
That was both pious, just and wise,
To Truth a shield, to right a Wall,
To Sectaryes a whip and Maul,
A Magazine of History,
A Prizer of good Company
In manners pleasant and severe
The Good him lov'd, the bad did fear,
And when his time with years was spent
If some rejoyc'd, more did lament.

Of the nine children, of whom Anne Bradstreet was the most
distinguished, the oldest son of his second wife took most

important part in the colonial life. Joseph Dudley, who was born
in 1647, became "Governor of Massachusetts, Lieutenant-Governor of
the Isle of Wight, and first Chief-Justice of New York. He had
thirteen children, one of whom, Paul, was also a distinguished man;
being Attorney-General and afterward Chief-Justice of
Massachusetts, Fellow of the Royal Society, and founder of the
Dudleian Lectures at Harvard College." His honors came to him
after the sister who prized them most had passed on to the Heaven
for which, even when happiest, she daily longed. None of the sons
possessed the strong characteristics of the father, but sons and
daughters alike seem to have inherited his love of books, as well
as of hospitality, and the name for every descendant has always
held honor, and often, more than fair ability. The preponderance
of ministers in every generation may, also, still gladden the
heart of the argumentative ancestor whose dearest pleasure was a
protracted tussle with the five points, and their infinitely
ramifying branches, aided and encouraged by the good wine and
generous cheer he set, with special relish, before all who could
meet him on his own ground.

It was fortunate for the daughter that many fresh interests were
springing up in her own family, which in 1654, received a new
member. One had already been added, in the person of the youngest
son John, who had been born in 1652, and was still a baby, and now
marriage gave another son, who valued her almost as heartily as
her own. Seaborn Cotton, whose name held always a reminder of the
stormy days on which his eyes opened, had grown into a decorous
youth, a course at Harvard, and an entering of his father's
profession, and though the old record holds no details, it is easy
to read between the lines, the story that told itself alike to
Puritan and Cavalier, and to which Mistress Dorothy listened with
a flutter beneath the gray gown that could not disguise the pretty
girlish outlines of her dainty figure. Dorothy, as well as the
other daughters, had been carefully trained in every housewifely
art, and though part of her mother's store of linen bleached in
Lincolnshire meadows, may have helped to swell her simple outfit,
it is probable that she spun and wove much of it herself. A
fulling mill, where the cloth made at home was finished and pressed,
had been built very early in the history of the town, and while there
were "spinsters" who went from house to house, much of the work
was done by mother and daughters. Seaborn Cotton, who must often
during his courtship have ridden over from Boston,
found Dorothy like the Priscilla she may have known, busy in the
graceful fashion of that older time, and--

... As he opened the door, he beheld the form of the maiden Seated
beside her wheel, and the carded wool like a snow-drift Piled at
her knee, her white hands feeding the ravenous spindle, While with
her foot on the treadle she guided the wheel in its motion.

Like Priscilla, too, she must have said--

... I knew it was you, when I heard your step in the passage, For
I was thinking of you as I sat there spinning and singing.

Dorothy had in full her mother's power of quiet devotion, and
became a model mother, as well as minister's wife, for the parish
at Hampton, N. H., where the young pastor began work in 1659, and
where after twenty-eight years of such labor as came to all

pioneers, she passed on, leaving nine children, whose name is still a familiar one in New England. Though the date of the next daughter's marriage is not quite as certain, it is given by some authorities as having taken place in the previous year, and in any case was within a few months of the same time. Contrary to the usual Puritan rule, which gave to most men from two to four wives, Sarah outlived her first husband, and married again, when a middle-aged but still young-hearted woman.

Marriage inevitably held some suggestion at least of merry-making, but the ceremony had been shorn of all possible resemblance to its English form. The Puritans were in terror lest any Prelatical superstitions or forms should cling to them in faintest degree, and Bradford wrote of the first marriage which took place in the Plymouth Colony: "The first marriage in this place, which, according to the laudable custom of the Low Countries, in which they had lived, was thought most requisite to be performed by the magistrate, as being a civil thing, ... and nowhere found in the Gospel to be laid on the ministers as a part of their office."

Winthrop, three of whose marriages had been in the parish church of his English home, shared the same feeling, and when preparations were made for "a great marriage to be solemnized at Boston," wrote: "The bridegroom being of Hingham, Mr. Hubbard's church, he was procured to preach, and came to Boston to that end. But the magistrates hearing of it, sent to him to forbear. We were not willing to bring in the English custom of ministers performing the solemnity of marriage, which sermons at such times might induce; but if any minister were present, and would bestow a word of exhortation, &c., it was permitted."

Fortunately for Dorothy and Sarah Bradstreet, their father was a magistrate, and his clear and gentle eyes the only ones they were obliged to face. Andover couples prefered him to any other and with reason, for while following the appointed method strictly, "giving the covenant unto the parties and also making the prayers proper for the occasion," he had no frowns for innocent enjoyment, and may even have allowed the dancing which was afterward forbidden.

In the beginning, as the largest in the township, his house had probably served as stopping-place for all travellers, where they were entertained merely as a matter of courtesy, though an "inholder" or "taverner" had been appointed and liscenced for Andover in 1648. Only an honored citizen could hold this office, and marriages were often celebrated in their houses, which naturally were enlarged at last to meet all necessities. But the strong liquors of the inn often circulated too freely, and quarrels and the stocks were at times the end of a day which it had been planned should hold all the merriment the Puritan temper would allow. Such misfortunes waited only on the humbler members of the community, who appear to have been sufficiently quarrelsome and excitable to furnish more occupiers of both pillory and stocks, than the religious character of the settlement would seem to admit, and who came to blows on the least provocation, using their fists with genuine English ardor, and submitting to punishment with composure, if only the adversary showed bruises enough for compensation. Wine and beer flowed freely at both the marriages, as they did at every entertainment, but Governor

Bradstreet, while having due liking for all good cheer, was
personally so abstinent that none would be likely in his presence
to forget proper bounds. Ministers and laymen alike drank an
amount impossible to these later days, and that if taken now would set
them down as hopeless reprobates; but custom sanctioned it, though
many had already found that the different climate rendered such
indulgence much more hazardous than the less exhilarating one of
England.

As the family lessened, the mother seems to have clung even more
closely to those that remained, and to have lost herself in work
for and with them. Whatever may have been written at this time,
appears to have been destroyed, nothing remaining but the poem
"Contemplations," which is more truly poetry than any of its more
labored predecessors, its descriptive passages holding much of the
charm of the lovely landscape through which she moved to the
river, flowing still through the Andover meadows.

CONTEMPLATIONS.

Some time now past in the Autumnal Tide
When Phoebus wanted but one hour to bed
The trees all richly clad, yet void of pride
Where gilded o're by his rich golden head.
Their leaves and fruits seemed painted but was true
Of green, of red, of yellow mixed hew,
Rapt were my sences at this delectable view.

I wist not what to wish, yet sure thought
I, If so much excellence abide below;
How excellent is he that dwells on high?
Whose power and beauty by his works we know.
Sure he is goodness, wisdome, glory, light,
That hath this under world so richly dight;
More Heaven than Earth was here, no winter & no night.

Then on a stately oak I cast mine Eye,
Whose ruffling top the Clouds seemed to aspire;
How long since thou wast in thine Infancy?
Thy strength and stature, more thy years admire.
Hath hundred winters past since thou wast born?
Or thousand since thou brakest thy shell of horn,
If so, all these as nought, Eternity doth scorn.

Then higher on the glistening Sun I gazed,
Whose beams was shaded by the leavie Tree,
The more I looked, the more I grew amazed,
And softly said, what glory's like to thee?
Soul of this world, this Universes Eye
Had I not, better known, (alas) the same had I.

Thou as a bridegroom from thy Chamber rushes
And as a strong man, joyes to run a race,
The morn doth usher thee with smiles and blushes
The Earth reflects her glances in thy face.
Birds, insects, Animals with Vegetive,
Thy heart from death and dulness doth revive:
And in the darksome womb of fruitful nature
dive.

Thy swift Annual and diurnal Course,
Thy daily streight and yearly oblique path.
Thy pleasing fervor and thy scorching force,
All mortals here the feeling knowledg hath.
Thy presence makes it day thy absence night,
Quaternal Seasons caused by thy might;
Hail Creature full of sweetness, beauty and delight.

Art them so full of glory, that no Eye
Hath strength, thy shining Rayes once to behold?
And is thy splendid throne erect so high?
As to approach it can no earthly mould.
How full of glory then must thy Creator
be? Who gave this bright light luster unto
thee, Admir'd, ador'd for ever, be that
Majesty.

Silent alone, where none or saw or heard,
In pathless paths I lead my wandering feet;
My humble eyes to lofty Skyes I rear'd,
To sing some song my mazed Muse thought meet.
My great Creator I would magnifie,
That nature had thus decked liberally;
But Ah, and Ah, again my imbecility.

The reader who may be disposed to echo this last line must bear in
mind always, that stilted as much of this may seem, it was in the
day in which it appeared a more purely natural voice than had been
heard at all, and as the poem proceeds it gains both in force and
beauty. As usual she reverts to the past for illustrations and
falls into a meditation aroused by the sights and sounds about
her. The path has led to the meadows not far from the river,
where--

I heard the merry grasshopper then sing, The
  black-clad Cricket, bear a second part,
They kept one tune and plaid on the same string,
  Seeming to glory in their little Art.
Shall Creatures abject, thus their voices raise? And
in their kind resound their makers praise, Whilst I
as mute, can warble forth no higher layes.

    *   *   *   *   *

When present times look back to Ages past,
  And men in being fancy those are dead,
It makes things gone perpetually to last,
  And calls back moneths and years that long since fled.
It makes a man more aged in conceit,
Then was Methuselah, or's grandsire great;
While of their persons & their acts his mind doth treat.

    *   *   *   *   *

Sometimes in Eden fair, he seems to be, Sees
glorious Adam there made Lord of all,
Fancyes the Apple, dangle on the Tree,
  That turn'd his Sovereign to a naked thral,
Who like a miscreant's driven from that place,
To get his bread with pain and sweat of face

A penalty impos'd on his backsliding Race.

    *   *   *   *   *

Here sits our Grandame in retired place,
And in her lap, her bloody Cain new-born,
The weeping Imp oft looks her in the face,
  Bewails his unknown hap and fate forlorn;
His Mother sighs to think of Paradise,
And how she lost her bliss to be more wise,
Beleiving him that was, and is Father of lyes.

    *   *   *   *   *

Here Cain and Abel came to sacrifice,
  Fruits of the Earth and Fallings each do bring,
On Abels gift the fire descends from Skies,
  But no such sign on false Cain's offering;
With sullen, hateful looks he goes his wayes;
Hath thousand thoughts to end his brothers dayes,
Upon whose blood his future good he hopes to raise.

    *   *   *   *   *

There Abel keeps his sheep no ill he thinks,
  His brother comes, then acts his fratracide
The Virgin Earth, of blood her first draught
  drinks, But since that time she often hath been
  clay'd;
The wretch with gastly face and dreadful mind,
Thinks each he sees will serve him in his kind,
Though none on Earth but kindred near, then could he find.

    *   *   *   *   *

Who fancyes not his looks now at the Barr,
  His face like death, his heart with horror fraught,
Nor Male-factor ever felt like warr,
  When deep dispair with wish of life hath
fought, Branded with guilt, and crusht with
treble woes,
A vagabond to Land of Nod he goes;
A City builds, that wals might him secure from foes.

    *   *   *   *   *

Who thinks not oft upon the Father's ages.
  Their long descent, how nephews sons they saw,
The starry observations of those Sages,
  And how their precepts to their sons were law,
How Adam sigh'd to see his Progeny,
Cloath'd all in his black sinful Livery,
Who neither guilt, nor yet the punishment could fly.

    *   *   *   *   *

Our Life compare we with their length of dayes
  Who to the tenth of theirs doth now arrive?
And though thus short, we shorten many wayes,
  Living so little while we are alive;
In eating, drinking, sleeping, vain delight,

So unawares comes on perpetual night,
And puts all pleasures vain unto eternal flight.

*   *   *   *   *

When I behold the heavens as in their prime,
  And then the earth, (though old) stil clad in green
The stones and trees insensible of time,
  Nor age nor wrinkle on their front are seen;
If winter come and greeness then do fade,
A Spring returns, and they more youthfull made;
But man grows old, lies down, remains where once he's laid.

*   *   *   *   *

By birth more noble then those creatures all,
Yet seems by nature and by custome curs'd,
No sooner born, but grief and care makes fall,
That state obliterate he had at first:
Nor youth, nor strength, nor wisdom spring again,
Nor habitations long their names retain,
But in oblivion to the final day remain.

*   *   *   *   *

Shall I then praise the heavens, the trees, the earth,
Because their beauty and their strength last longer
Shall I wish there, or never to have had birth,
Because they're bigger & their bodyes stronger?
Nay, they shall darken, perish, fade and dye,
And when unmade, so ever shall they lye,
But man was made for endless immortality.

Here at last she is released from the didactic. She can look at
the sun without feeling it necessary to particularize her
knowledge of its--

"... swift Annual and diurnal Course,
Thy daily streight and yearly oblique path."

Imagination has been weighted by the innumerable details, more and
more essential to the Puritan mind, but now she draws one long
free breath, and rises far beyond the petty limit of her usual
thought, the italicised lines in what follows holding a music
one may seek for in vain in any other verse of the period:

Under the cooling shadow of a stately Elm,
  Close sate I by a goodly Rivers side,
Where gliding streams the Rocks did overwhelm;
  A lonely place with pleasures dignifi'd,
I once that lov'd the shady woods so well,
Now thought the rivers did the trees excel,
And if the sun would ever shine there would I dwell.

*   *   *   *   *

While on the stealing stream I fixt mine eye,
  Which to the longed-for Ocean held its course,
I markt not crooks, nor rubs that there did lye

Could hinder ought but still augment its force,
_O happy Flood, quoth I, that holds thy race
Till thou arrive at thy beloved place,
Nor is it rocks or shoals that can obstruct thy pace_.

    *   *   *   *   *

Nor is't enough that thou alone may'st slide,
  But hundred brooks in thy cleer waves do meet,
So hand in hand along with thee they glide
  To Thetis house, where all embrace and greet:
Thou Emblem true of what I count the best,
O could I lead my Rivolets to rest,
So may we press to that vast mansion, ever blest.

    *   *   *   *   *

Ye fish which in this liquid Region 'bide,
  That for each season have your habitation,
Now salt, now fresh where you think best to glide,
  To unknown coasts to give a visitation,
In Lakes and ponds you leave your numerous fry,
So nature taught, and yet you know not why,
You watry folk that know not your felicity.

    *   *   *   *   *

Look how the wantons frisk to taste the air,
Then to the colder bottome streight they dive,
Eftsoon to Neptun's glassie Hall repair,
  To see what trade they great ones there do drive
Who forrage ore the spacious, sea-green field,
And take the trembling prey before it yield,
Whose armour is their scales, their spreading fins their shield.

    *   *   *   *   *

While musing thus with contemplation fed,
  And thousand fancies buzzing in my brain,
The sweet tongu'd Philomel percht ore my head,
And chanted forth a most melodious strain,
Which rapt me so with wonder and delight,
I judg'd my hearing better then my sight,
And wisht me wings with her awhile to take my flight.

    *   *   *   *   *

O merry Bird (said I) that fears no snares,
  That neither toyles nor hoards up in thy barn,
Feels no sad thoughts, no cruciating cares
  To gain more good, or shun what might thee harm.
Thy cloaths ne're wear, thy meat is everywhere,
Thy bed a bough, thy drink the water deer,
Reminds not what is past nor whats to come dost fear.

    *   *   *   *   *

_The dawning morn with songs thou dost prevent,
 Sets hundred notes unto thy feathered crew,

So each one tunes his pretty instrument,
  And warbling out the old, begin anew,
And thus they pass their youth in summer season,
Then follow thee into a better Region,
Where winter's never felt in that sweet airy legion_.

    *   *   *   *   *

Up to this point natural delight in the sights
  and sounds of a summer's day has had its way, and
undoubtedly struck her as far too much enjoyment
  for any sinful worm of the dust. She proceeds, therefore,
to chasten her too exuberant muse, presenting
for that sorely-tried damsel's inspection, the portrait
of man, as Calvin had taught her to view him.

    *   *   *   *   *

Man at the best a creature frail and vain,
  In knowledg ignorant, in strength but weak,
Subject to sorrows, losses, sickness, pain,
  Each storm his state, his mind, his body break,
From some of these he never finds cessation But
day or night, within, without, vexation, Troubles
from foes, from friends, from dearest
        nears't Relation.

    *   *   *   *   *

And yet this sinfull creature, frail and vain,
  This lump of wretchedness, of sin and sorrow,
This weather-beaten vessel wrackt with pain,
  Joyes not in hope of an eternal morrow;
Nor all his losses crosses and vexations
In weight and frequency and long duration,
Can make him deeply groan for that divine Translation.

    *   *   *   *   *

The Mariner that on smooth waves doth glide,
  Sings merrily and steers his Barque with ease,
As if he had command of wind and tide,
  And now become great Master of the seas;
But suddenly a storm spoiles all the sport,
And makes him long for a more quiet port,
Which 'gainst all adverse winds may serve for fort.

    *   *   *   *   *

So he that saileth in this world of pleasure,
  Feeding on sweets, that never bit of th' sowre,
That's full of friends, of honour and of treasure,
  Fond fool, he takes this earth even for heav'n's bower.
But sad affliction comes & makes him see,
Here's neither honour, wealth nor safety,
Only above is found all with security.

    *   *   *   *   *

O Time the fatal wrack
    of mortal things, That
  draws oblivion's curtain
            over Kings,
Their sumptuous monuments, men know them not,
   Their names without a Record are forgot,
Their parts, their ports, their pomp's all laid in th' dust,
Nor wit nor gold, nor buildings scape time's rust;
But he whose name is grav'd in the white stone
Shall last and shine when all of these are gone.

With this poem, Anne Bradstreet seems to have bidden a final
farewell to any attempt at sustained composition. A sense of
disgust at the poor result of long thought and labor appears to have
filled her, and this mood found expression in a deprecating little
poem in which humor struggles with this oppressive sense of
deficiency and incompleteness, the inclination on the whole,
however, as with most authors, being toward a lenient judgment of
her own inadequate accomplishment.

THE AUTHOR TO HER BOOK.

Thou ill-form'd offspring of my feeble
brain, Who after birth didst by my side
remain,
Till snatcht from thence by friends, less wise then true
Who thee abroad, expos'd to publick view,
Made thee in raggs, halting to th' press to trudg,
Where errors were not lessened (all may judg)
At thy return my blushing was not small,
My rambling brat (in print,) should mother
call, I cast thee by as one unfit for light,
Thy Visage was so irksome in my sight;
Yet being mine own, at length affection would
Thy blemishes amend, if so I could:
I wash'd thy face, but more defects I saw,
And rubbing off a spot, still made a flaw.
I stretcht thy joynts to make thee even feet,
Yet still thou run'st more hobling then is meet;
In better dress to trim thee was my mind,
But nought save home-spun Cloth, i' th' house I find
In this array, mong'st Vulgars mayst thou roam
In Critick's hands, beware thou dost not come;
And take thy way where yet thou art not known,
If for thy Father askt, say, thou hadst none;
And for thy Mother, she alas is poor.
Which caused her thus to turn thee out of door.

CHAPTER

XIV. THE

LEGACY.

Though it was only as a poet that Anne Bradstreet was known to her
own time, her real strength was in prose, and the "Meditations,
Divine and Morall," written at the request of her second son, the

Rev. Simon Bradstreet, to whom she dedicated them, March 20, 1664, show that life had taught her much, and in the ripened thought and shrewd observation of men and manners are the best testimony to

her real ability. For the reader of to-day they are of incomparably more interest than anything to be found in the poems. There is often the most condensed and telling expression; a swift turn that shows what power of description lay under all the fantastic turns of the style Du Bartas had created for her. That he underrated them was natural. The poems had brought her honor in the old home and the new. The meditations involved no anxious laboring after a rhyme, no straining a metaphor till it cracked. They were natural thought naturally expressed and therefore worthless for any literary purpose, and as she wrote, the wail of the Preacher repeated itself, and she smiled faintly as the words grew under her pen: "There is no new thing under the sun, there is nothing that can be sayd or done, but either that or something like it hath been done and sayd before."

Many of the paragraphs written in pain and weakness show how keenly she had watched the course of events, and what power of characterization she had to use, three of them especially holding the quiet sarcasm in which she occasionally indulged, though always with a tacit apology for the possession of such a quality. "Dimne eyes are the concomitants of old age; and short-sightednes in those that are eyes of a Republique, foretells a declineing state."

"Authority without wisdome, is like a heavy axe without an edge, fitter to bruise than polish."

"Ambitious men are like hops that never rest climbing so long as they have anything to stay upon; but take away their props, and they are of all, the most dejected."

The perpetual dissensions, religious and political, which threatened at times the absolute destruction of the Colony, were all familiar to her, and she draws upon them for illustrations of many points, others being afforded by her own experience with the eight children to whom she proved so devoted and tender a mother. Like other mothers, before and since, their differences in temperament and conduct, seem to have been a perpetual surprise, but that she had tact enough to meet each on his or her own ground, or gently draw them toward hers, seems evident at every point. That they loved her tenderly is equally evident, the diary of her second son mentioning her always as "my dear and honored mother," and all of them, though separated by early marriages for most of them, returning as often as practicable to the old roof, under which Thanksgiving Day had taken on the character it has held from that clay to this. The small blank-book which held these "Meditations" was copied carefully by Simon Bradstreet, and there is little doubt that each of the children did the same, considering it as much theirs as the brother's for whom it was originally intended. Whatever Anne Bradstreet did, she had her children always in view, and still another blank-book partially filled with religious reflections, and found among her papers after death, was dedicated, "To my dear children." The father probably kept the originals, but her words were too highly valued, not to have been eagerly desired by all. A special word to her son opens the series of "Meditations."

FOR MY DEARE SONNE SIMON BRADSTREET.

Parents perpetuate their lines in their posterity, and their maners in their imitation. Children do naturally rather follow the failings than the virtues of their predecessors, but I am persuaded better things of you. You once desired me to leave something for you in writing that you might look upon when you should see me no more. I could think of nothing more fit for you, nor of more ease to my selfe, than these short meditations following. Such as they are I bequeath to you: small legacys are accepted by true friends, much more by dutifull children. I have
avoyded incroaching upon others conceptions, because I would leave
you nothing but myne owne, though in value they fall short of all
in this kinde, yet I presume they will be better priz'd by you for
the Author's sake. The Lord blesse you with grace heer, and crown
you with glory heerafter, that I may meet you with rejoyceing at
that great day of appearing, which is the continuall prayer of

Your affectionate mother,

A. B.

March 20, 1664.

MEDITATIONS, DIVINE AND

MORALL. I.

There is no object that we see; no action that we doe; no good
that we injoy; no evill that we feele or feare, but we may make
some spiritu(a)ll, advantage of all: and he that makes such
improvement is wise as well as pious.

II.

Many can speak well, but few can do well. We are better Scholars
in the Theory then the practique part, but he is a true Christian
that is a proficient in both.

III.

Youth is the time of getting, middle age of improving, and old age
of spending; a negligent youth is usually attended by an ignorant
middle age, and both by an empty old age. He that hath nothing to
feed on but vanity and lyes must needs lye down in the Bed of
Sorrow.

IV.

A ship that beares much saile, and little or no ballast, is easily
overset; and that man, whose head hath great abilities, and his
heart little or no grace, is in danger of foundering.

V.

It is reported of the peakcock that, prideing himself in his gay
feathers, he ruffles them up; but, spying his black feet, he soon
lets fall his plumes, so he that glorys in his gifts and adornings
should look upon his Corruptions, and that will damp his high
thoughts.

VI.

The finest bread hath the least bran; the purest hony, the least
wax; and the sincerest Christian, the least self love.

VII.

The hireling that labors all the day, comforts himself that when
night comes he shall both take his rest and receive his reward;
the painfull Christian that hath wrought hard in God's vineyard,
and hath born the heat and drought of the day, when he perceives
his sun apace to decline, and the shadows of his evening to be
stretched out, lifts up his head with joy, knowing his refreshing
is at hand.

VIII.

Downny beds make drosey persons, but hard lodging keeps the eyes
open. A prosperous state makes a secure Christian, but adversity
makes him Consider.

IX.

Sweet words are like hony, a little may refresh, but too much
gluts the stomach.

X.

Diverse children have their different natures; some are like flesh
which nothing but salt will keep from putrefaction; some again
like tender fruits that are best preserved with sugar: those
parents are wise that can fit their nurture according to their
Nature.

XI.

That town which thousands of enemys without hath not been able to
take, hath been delivered up by one traytor within; and that man,
which all the temptations of Sathan without could not hurt, hath
been foild by one lust within.

XII.

Authority without wisdome is like a heavy axe without an
edge, fitter to bruise than polish.

XIII.

The reason why Christians are so both to exchange this world for a
better, is because they have more sence than faith: they se what they
injoy, they do but hope for that which is to come.

XIV.

If we had no winter, the spring would not be so pleasant; if we
did not sometimes tast of adversity, prosperity would not be so
welcome.

XV.

A low man can goe upright under that door wher a taller is glad to
stoop; so a man of weak faith, and mean abilities may undergo a
crosse more patiently than he that excells him, both in gifts and
graces.

XVI.

That house which is not often swept, makes the cleanly inhabitant
soone loath it, and that heart which is not continually purifieing
itself, is no fit temple for the spirit of God to dwell in.

XVII.

Few men are so humble as not to be proud of their abilitys; and
nothing will abase them more than this--What hast thou, but what
thou hast received? Come, give an account of thy stewardship.

XVIII.

He that will undertake to climb up a steep mountain with a great
burden on his back, will finde it a wearysome, if not an
impossible task; so he that thinks to mount to heaven clog'd with
the Cares and riches of this Life, 'tis no wonder if he faint by
the way.

XIX.

Corne, till it has passed through the Mill and been ground to
powder, is not fit for bread. God so deales with his servants: he
grindes them with grief and pain till they turn to dust, and then
are they fit manchet for his Mansion.

XX

God hath sutable comforts and supports for his children according
to their severall conditions if he will make his face to shine
upon them: he then makes them lye down in green pastures, and
leads them beside the still waters: if they stick in deepe mire
and clay, and all his waves and billows goe over their heads, He
then leads them to the Rock which is higher than they.

XXI.

He that walks among briars and thorns will be very carefull where
he sets his foot. And he that passes through the wilderness of
this world, had need ponder all his steps.

XXII.

Want of prudence, as well as piety, hath brought men into great
inconveniencys; but he that is well stored with both, seldom is so
insnared.

XXIII.

The skillfull fisher hath his severall baits for severall fish,
but there is a hooke under all; Satan, that great Angler, hath his
sundry bait for sundry tempers of men, which they all catch

gredily at, but few perceives the hook till it be too late.

XXIV.

There is no new thing under the sun, there is nothing that can be
sayd or done, but either that or something like it hath been both
done and sayd before.

XXV. An akeing head requires a soft pillow; and a drooping heart a
strong support.

XXVI.

A sore finger may disquiet the whole body, but an ulcer within
destroys it: so an enemy without may disturb a Commonwealth, but
dissentions within overthrow it.

XXVII.

It is a pleasant thing to behold the light, but sore eyes are not
able to look upon it; the pure in heart shall see God, but the
defiled in conscience shall rather choose to be buried under rocks
and mountains then to behold the presence of the Lamb.

XXVIII.

Wisedome with an inheritance is good, but wisedome without an
inheritance is better then an inheritance without wisedome.

XXIX.

Lightening doth generally preceed thunder, and stormes, raine; and
stroaks do not often fall till after threat'ning.

XXX.

Yellow leaves argue the want of Sap, and gray haires want of
moisture; so dry and saplesse performances are symptoms of little
spirituall vigor.

XXXI.

Iron till it be thoroughly heat is uncapable to be wrought; so God
sees good to cast some men into the furnace of affliction, and
then beats them on his anvile into what frame he pleases.

XXXII.

Ambitious men are like hops that never rest climbing soe long as
they have anything to stay upon; but take away their props and
they are, of all, the most dejected.

XXXIII.

Much Labour wearys the body, and many thoughts oppresse the minde:
man aimes at profit by the one, and content in the other; but
often misses of both, and findes nothing but vanity and vexation
of spirit.

XXXIV.

Dimne eyes are the concomitants of old age; and short-sightednes, in those that are eyes of a Republique, foretells a declineing State.

XXXV.

We read in Scripture of three sorts of Arrows--the arrow of an enemy, the arrow of pestilence, and the arrow of a slanderous tongue; the two first kill the body, the last the good name; the two former leave a man when he is once dead, but the last mangles him in his grave.

XXXVI.

Sore labourers have hard hands, and old sinners have brawnie consciences.

XXXVII.

Wickednes comes to its height by degrees. He that dares say of a lesse sin, is it not a little one? will ere long say of a greater, Tush, God regards it not!

XXXVIII.

Some Children are hardly weaned, although the breast be rub'd with wormwood or mustard, they will either wipe it off, or else suck down sweet and bitter together; so is it with some Christians, let God embitter all the sweets of this life, that so they might feed upon more substantiall food, yet they are so childishly sottish that they are still huging and sucking these empty brests, that God is forced to hedg up their way with thornes, or lay affliction on their loynes, that so they might shake hands with the world before it bid them farewell

XXXIX.

A Prudent mother will not clothe her little childe with a long and cumbersome garment; she easily forsees what events it is like to produce, at the best but falls and bruises, or perhaps somewhat worse, much more will the alwise God proportion his dispensations according to the Stature and Strength of the person he bestows them on. Larg indowments of honor, wealth, or a helthfull body would quite overthrow some weak Christian, therefore God cuts their garments short, to keep them in such trim that they might run the wayes of his Commandment.

XL.

The spring is a lively emblem of the resurrection. After a long winter we se the leavlesse trees and dry stocks (at the approach of the sun) to resume their former vigor and beauty in a more ample manner then what they lost in the Autumn; so shall it be at that great day after a long vacation, when the Sun of righteousness shall appear, those dry bones shall arise in far more glory then that which they lost at their creation, and in this transcends the spring, that their leafe shall never faile, nor their sap decline.

XLI.

A Wise father will not lay a burden on a child of seven yeares
old, which he knows is enough for one of twice his strength, much
less will our heavenly father (who knows our mould) lay such
afflictions upon his weak children as would crush them to the
dust, but according to the strength he will proportion the load,
as God hath his little children so he hath his strong men, such as
are come to a full stature in Christ; and many times he imposes
waighty burdens on their shoulders, and yet they go upright under
them, but it matters not whether the load be more or less if God
afford his help.

XLII.

I have seen an end of all perfection (sayd the royall prophet);
but he never sayd, I have seen an end of all sinning: what he did
say, may be easily sayd by many; but what he did not say, cannot
truly be uttered by any.

XLIII.

Fire hath its force abated by water, not by wind; and anger must
be alayed by cold words, and not by blustering threats.

XLIV.

A sharp appetite and a thorough concoction, is a signe of an
healthfull body; so a quick reception, and a deliberate
cogitation, argues a sound mind.

XLV.

We often se stones hang with drops, not from any innate moisture,
but from a thick ayer about them; so may we sometime se marble-
hearted sinners seem full of contrition; but it is not from any
dew of grace within, but from some black Clouds that impends them,
which produces these sweating effects.

XLVI.

The words of the wise, sath Solomon, are as nailes and as goads
both used for contrary ends--the one holds fast, the other puts
forward; such should be the precepts of the wise masters of
assemblys to their hearers, not only to bid them hold fast the
form of sound Doctrin, but also, so to run that they might obtain.

XLVII.

A shadow in the parching sun, and a shelter in the blustering
storme, are of all seasons the most welcome; so a faithfull friend
in time of adversity, is of all other most comfortable.

XLVIII.

There is nothing admits of more admiration, then God's various
dispensation of his gifts among the sons of men, betwixt whom he

hath put so vast a disproportion that they scarcely seem made of the same lump, or sprung out of the loynes of one Adam; some set in the highest dignity that mortality is capable of; and some again so base, that they are viler then the earth; some so wise and learned, that they seem like Angells among men; and some again so ignorant and Sotish, that they are more like beasts then men: some pious saints; some incarnate Devils; some exceeding beautyfull; and some extreamly deformed; some so strong and healthfull that their bones are full of marrow; and their breasts of milk; and some again so weak and feeble, that, while they live, they are accounted among the dead--and no other reason can be given of all this, but so it pleased him, whose will is the perfect rule of righteousness.

XLIX.

The treasures of this world may well be compared to huskes, for they have no kernell in them, and they that feed upon them, may soon stuffe their throats, but cannot fill their bellys; they may be choaked by them, but cannot be satisfied with them.

L.

Sometimes the sun is only shadowed by a cloud that wee cannot se his luster, although we may walk by his light, but when he is set we are in darkness till he arise again; so God doth sometime vaile his face but for a moment, that we cannot behold the light of his Countenance as at some other time, yet he affords so much light as may direct our way, that we may go forward to the Citty of habitation, but when he seems to set and be quite gone out of sight, then must we needs walk in darkness and se no light, yet then must we trust in the Lord, and stay upon our God, and when the morning (which is the appointed time) is come, the Sun of righteousness will arise with healing in his wings.

LI.

The eyes and the eares are the inlets or doores of the soule, through which innumerable objects enter, yet is not that spacious roome filled, neither doth it ever say it is enough, but like the daughters of the horsleach, crys, give, give! and which is most strang, the more it receives, the more empty it finds itself, and sees an impossibility, ever to be filled, but by Him in whom all fullness dwells.

LII.

Had not the wisest of men taught us this lesson, that all is vanity and vexation of spirit, yet our owne experience would soon have speld it out; for what do we obtain of all these things, but it is with labour and vexation? When we injoy them it is with vanity and vexation; and, if we loose them, then they are lesse then vanity and more then vexation.: so that we have good cause often to repeat that sentence, vanity of vanityes, vanity of vanityes, all is vanity.

LIII.

He that is to saile into a farre country, although the ship,

cabbin and provision, be all convenient and comfortable for him,
yet he hath no desire to make that his place of residence, but
longs to put in at that port where his bussines lyes; a Christian
is sailing through this world unto his heavenly country, and heere
he hath many conveniences and comforts; but he must beware of
desire(ing) to make this the place of his abode, lest he meet with
such tossings that may cause him to long for shore before he sees
land. We must, therefore, be beer as strangers and pilgrims, that we
may plainly declare that we seek a citty above, and wait all
the dayes of our appointed time till our chang shall come.

LIV.

He that never felt what it was to be sick or wounded, doth not
much care for the company of the physitian or chirurgian; but
if
he perceive a malady that threatens him with death, he will gladly
entertaine him, whom he slighted before: so he that never felt the
sicknes of sin, nor the wounds of a guilty conscience, cares not
how far he keeps from him that hath skill to cure it; but when he
findes his diseases to disrest him, and that he must needs perish
if he have no remedy, will unfeignedly bid him welcome that
brings a plaister for his sore, or a cordiall for his fainting.

LV.

We read of ten lepers that were cleansed, but of one that returned
thanks: we are more ready to receive mercys than we are to
acknowledg them: men can use great importunity when they are in
distresses, and show great ingratitude after their successes; but
he that ordereth his conversation aright, will glorifie him
that heard him in the day of his trouble.

LVI.

The remembrances of former deliverances is a great support in
present distresses: he that delivered me, sath David, from the paw
of the Lion and the paw of the Beare, will deliver mee from this
uncircumcised Philistin; and he that hath delivered mee, saith
Paul, will deliver mee: God is the same yesterday, to-day, and
forever; we are the same that stand in need of him, to-day as well
as yesterday, and so shall forever.

LVII.

Great receipts call for great returnes; the more that any man is
intrusted withall, the larger his accounts stands upon God's
score: it therefore behoves every man so to improve his talents,
that when his great Master shall call him to reckoning he may
receive his owne with advantage.

LVIII.

Sin and shame ever goe together. He that would be freed from the
last, must be sure to shun the company of the first.

LIX.

God doth many times both reward and punish for the same action: as
we see in Jehu, he is rewarded with a kingdome to the fourth

generation, for takeing veangence on the house of Ahab; and yet a
little while (saith God), and I will avenge the blood of Jezevel
upon the house of Jehu: he was rewarded for the matter, and yet
punished for the manner, which should warn him, that doth any
speciall service for God, to fixe his eye on the command, and not
on his own ends, lest he meet with Jehu's reward, which will end
in punishment.

LX.

He that would be content with a mean condition, must not cast his
eye upon one that is in a far better estate than himself, but let
him look upon him that is lower than he is, and, if he see that
such a one beares poverty comfortably, it will help to quiet him;
but if that will not do, let him look on his owne unworthynes,
and that will make him say with Jacob, I am lesse then the least
of thy mercys.

LXI.

Corne is produced with much labour, (as the husbandman well
knowes), and some land askes much more paines then some other doth to
be brought into tilth, yet all must be ploughed and harrowed;
some children (like sowre land) are of so tough and morose a
dispo(si)tion, that the plough of correction must make long
furrows on their back, and the Harrow of discipline goe often over
them, before they bee fit soile to sow the seed of morality, much
lesse of grace in them. But when by prudent nurture they are
brought into a fit capacity, let the seed of good instruction and
exhortation be sown in the spring of their youth, and a plentiful!
crop may be expected in the harvest of their yeares.

LXII.

As man is called the little world, so his heart may be cal'd the
little Commonwealth: his more fixed and resolved thoughts are like
to inhabitants, his slight and flitting thoughts are like
passengers that travell to and fro continually; here is also the
great Court of justice erected, which is always kept by conscience
who is both accuser, excuser, witness, and Judge, whom no bribes
can pervert, nor flattery cause to favour, but as he finds the
evidence, so he absolves or condemnes: yea, so Absolute is this
Court of Judicature, that there is no appeale from it--no, not to
the Court of heaven itself--for if our conscience condemn us, he,
also, who is greater than our conscience, will do it much more;
but he that would have boldness to go to the throne of grace to be
accepted there, must be sure to carry a certificate from the Court
of conscience, that he stands right there.

LXIII.

He that would keep a pure heart, and lead a blameless life, must
set himself alway in the awefull presence of God, the
consideration of his all-seeing eye will be a bridle to restrain
from evill, and a spur to quicken on to good duties: we certainly
dream of some remotenes betwixt God and us, or else we should not
so often faile in our whole Course of life as we doe; but he that
with David sets the Lord alway in his sight, will not
sinne against him.

LXIV.

We see in orchards some trees so fruitful, that the waight of their
Burden is the breaking of their limbs; some again are but meanly
loaden; and some among them are dry stocks: so it is in the church,
which is God's orchard, there are some eminent Christians that are
soe frequent in good dutys, that many times the waight thereof
impares both their bodys and estates; and there are some (and they
sincere ones too) who have not attained to that fruitfullness, altho
they aime at perfection: And again there are others that have nothing
to commend them but only a gay profession, and these are but leavie
Christians, which are in as much danger of being cut down as the
dry stock, for both cumber the ground.

LXV.

We see in the firmament there is but one Sun among a multitude
of starres, and those starres also to differ much one from the
other in regard of bignes and brightnes, yet all receive their
light from that one Sun: so is it in the church both militant and
triumphant, there is but one Christ, who is the Sun of righteousnes,
in the midst of an innumerable company of Saints and Angels; those
Saints have their degrees even in this life, Some
are Stars of the first magnitude, and some of a lesse degree; and
others (and they indeed the most in number), but small and
obscure, yet all receive their luster (be it more or less) from
that glorious Sun that inlightenes all in all; and, if some of
them shine so bright while they move on earth, how transcendently
splendid shall they be when they are fixt in their heavenly
spheres!

LXVI.

Men that have walked very extravagantly, and at last bethink
themselves of turning to God, the first thing which they eye, is
how to reform their ways rather than to beg forgivenes for their
sinnes; nature lookes more at a Compensation than at a pardon; but
he that will not come for mercy without mony and without price,
but bring his filthy raggs to barter for it, shall meet with
miserable disapointment, going away empty, beareing the reproach
of his pride and folly.

LXVII.

All the works and doings of God are wonderfull, but none more
awfull than his great worke of election and Reprobation; when we
consider how many good parents have had bad children, and againe
how many bad parents have had pious children, it should make us
adore the Soverainty of God who will not be tyed to time nor
place, nor yet to persons, but takes and chuses when and where and
whom he pleases: it should alsoe teach the children of godly
parents to walk with feare and trembling, lest they, through
unbeleif, fall short of a promise: it may also be a support to
such as have or had wicked parents, that, if they abide not in
unbeleif, God is able to grasse them in: the upshot of all should
make us, with the Apostle, to admire the justice and mercy of God,
and say, how unsearchable are his wayes, and his footsteps past

finding

out.

LXVIII.

The gifts that God bestows on the sons of men, are not only
abused, but most Commonly imployed for a Clean Contrary end, then
that which might be so many steps to draw men to God in
consideration of his bounty towards them, but have driven them the
further from him, that they are ready to say, we are lords, we
will come no more at thee. If outward blessings be not as wings to
help us mount upwards, they will Certainly prove Clogs and waights
that will pull us lower downward.

LXIX.

All the Comforts of this life may be compared to the gourd of
Jonah, that notwithstanding we take great delight for a season in
them, and find their Shadow very comfortable, yet their is some
worm or other of discontent, of feare, or greife that lyes at
root, which in great part withers the pleasure which else we
should take in them; and well it is that we perceive a decay in
their greennes, for were earthly comforts permanent, who would
look for heavenly?

LXX.

All men are truly sayd to be tenants at will, and it may as truly
be sayd, that all have a lease of their lives--some longer, some
shorter--as it pleases our great landlord to let. All have their
bounds set, over which they cannot passe, and till the expiration
of that time, no dangers, no sicknes, no paines nor troubles, shall
put a period to our dayes; the certainty that that time will
come, together with the uncertainty how, where, and when, should
make us so to number our days as to apply our hearts to wisedome,
that when wee are put out of these houses of clay, we may be sure of
an everlasting habitation that fades not away.

LXXI.

All weak and diseased bodys have hourly mementos of their
mortality. But the soundest of men have likewise their nightly
monitor by the embleam of death, which is their sleep (for so is
death often called), and not only their death, but their grave is
lively represented before their eyes, by beholding their bed; the
morning may mind them of the resurrection; and the sun approaching,
of the appearing of the sun of righteousnes, at whose comeing
they shall all rise out of their beds, the long night shall
fly away, and the day of eternity shall never end: seeing these
things must be, what manner of persons ought we to be, in all
good conversation?

LXXII.

As the brands of a fire, if once feverered, will of themselves goe
out, altho you use no other meanes to extinguish them, so distance
of place, together with length of time (if there be no intercourse)
will cool the affectiones of intimate friends, though tjere
should be no displeasance between them.

LXXIII.

A Good name is as a precious oyntment, and it is a great favor to have a
good repute among good men; yet it is not that which Commends us to
God, for by his ballance we must be weighed, and by his Judgment we
must be tryed, and, as he passes the sentence, So shall we stand.

LXXIV.

Well doth the Apostle call riches deceitfull riches, and they may
truely be compared to deceitfull friends who speake faire, and
promise much, but perform nothing, and so leave those in the lurch
that most relyed on them: so is it with the wealth, honours, and
plcasurcs of this world, which miserably delude men, and make them
put great confidence in them, but when death threatens, and
distresse lays hold upon them, they prove like the reeds of Egipt
that peirce instead of supporting, like empty wells in the time of
drought, that those that go to finde water in them, return with
their empty pitchers ashamed.

LXXV.

It is admirable to consider the power of faith, by which all
things are (almost) possible to be done; it can remove mountaines
(if need were) it hath stayd the course of the sun, raised the
dead, cast out divels, reversed the order of nature, quenched the
violence of the fire, made the water become firme footing for
Peter to walk on; nay more than all these, it hath overcome the
Omnipotent himself, as when Moses intercedes for the people, God
sath to him, let me alone that I may destroy them, as if Moses had
been able, by the hand of faith, to hold the everlasting arms of
the mighty God of Jacob; yea, Jacob himself, when he wrestled with
God face to face in Peniel: let me go! sath that Angell. I will
not let thee go, replys Jacob, till thou blesse me, faith is not
only thus potent, but it is so necessary that without faith there
is no salvation, therefore, with all our seekings and gettings,
let us above all seek to obtain this pearle of prise.

LXXVI.

Some Christians do by their lusts and Corruptions as the Isralits
did by the Canaanites, not destroy them, but put them under
tribute, for that they could do (as they thought) with lesse
hazard, and more profit; but what was the Issue? They became a
snare unto them, prickes in their eyes, and thornes in their
sides, and at last overcame them, and kept them under slavery; so it
is most certain that those that are disobedient to the Commandment
of God, and endeavour not to the utmost to drive out all their
accursed inmates, but make a league with them, they
shall at last fall into perpetuall bondage under them, unlesse the
great deliverer, Christ Jesus come to their rescue.

LXXVII.

God hath by his providence so ordered, that no one country hath
all Commoditys within itself, but what it wants, another shall
supply, that so there may be a mutuall Commerce through the world.
As it is with countrys so it is with men, there was never yet any

one man that had all excellences, let his parts, naturall and
acquired, spirituall and morall, be never so large, yet he stands
in need of something which another man hath, (perhaps meaner than
himself,) which shows us perfection is not below, as also, that
God will have us beholden one to another.

CHAPTER XV.

THE PURITAN REIGN OF TERROR.

The ten years which followed the death of Governor Winthrop
early in 1649, were years of steady outward prosperity, yet causes
were at work, which gradually complicated the political situation
and prepared the necessity for the explanation which the mother
country at last peremptorily demanded, Simon Bradstreet being
selected as one of the men most capable of suitable reply. So long
as Winthrop lived, his even and sagacious course hindered many
complications which every circumstance fostered. Even in the
fierce dissensions over Anne Hutchinson and her theories, he had
still been able to retain the personal friendship of those whom as
a magistrate he had most severely judged. Wheelwright and
Coddington, who had suffered many losses; Sir Harry Vane, who had
returned to England sore and deeply indignant at the colonial
action; Clark and Williams, bitter as they might be against
Massachusetts principles, had only affection for the gracious and
humane governor, who gave himself as freely as he gave his
fortune, and whose theories, however impracticable they may at
times have seemed, have all justified themselves in later years.
Through the early privations and the attempts of some to escape
the obligations laid upon them, by the mere fact of having come
together to the unknown country, he set his face steadily against
all division, and there is no more characteristic passage in his
Journal than that in which he gives the reasons which should bind
them to common and united action. Various disaffected and uneasy
souls had wandered off to other points, and Winthrop gives the
results, at first quietly and judicially, but rising at the close
to a noble indignation.

"Others who went to other places, upon like grounds, succeeded no
better. They fled for fear of want, and many of them fell into it,
even to extremity, as if they had hastened into the misery which
they feared and fled from, besides the depriving themselves of the
ordinances and church fellowship, and those civil liberties which
they enjoyed here; whereas, such as staid in their places kept
their peace and ease, and enjoyed still the blessing of the
ordinances, and never tasted of those troubles and miseries, which
they heard to have befallen those who departed. Much disputation
there was about liberty of removing for outward advantages, and
all ways were sought for an open door to get out at; but it is to be
feared many crept out at a broken wall. For such as come together
into a wilderness, where are nothing but wild beasts and beast-like
men, and there confederate together in civil and church estate,
whereby they do, implicitly at least, bind themselves to support
each other, and all of them that society, whether civil or sacred,
whereof they are members, how they can break from this

without free consent, is hard to find, so as may satisfy a tender or good conscience in time of trial. Ask thy conscience, if thou wouldst have plucked up thy stakes, and brought thy family 3000 miles, if thou hadst expected that all, or most, would have forsaken thee there. Ask again, what liberty thou hast towards others, which thou likest not to allow others towards thyself; for if one may go, another may, and so the greater part, and so church and commonwealth may be left destitute in a wilderness, exposed to misery and reproach, and all for thy ease and pleasure, whereas these all, being now thy brethren, as near to thee as the Israelites were to Moses, it were much safer for thee after his example, to choose rather to suffer affliction with thy brethren than to enlarge thy ease and pleasure by furthering the occasion of their ruin."

What he demanded of others he gave freely himself, and no long time was required to prove to all, that union was their only salvation.

He had lived to see the spirit of co-operation active in many ways. Churches were quietly doing their work with as little wrangling over small doctrinal differences as could be expected from an age in which wrangling was the chief symptom of vitality. Education had settled upon a basis it has always retained, that of "universal knowledge at the public cost"; the College was doing
its work so effectually that students came from England itself to share in her privileges, and justice gave as impartial and even-handed results as conscientious magistrates knew how to furnish. The strenuous needs and sacrifices of the early days were over. A generation had arisen, knowing them only by hearsay, and for even the humblest, substantial prosperity was the rule. Johnson, in his "Wonder-Working Providence," wrote words that held no exaggeration in their description of the comfort which has, from that day to
this, been the characteristic of New England homes. "The Lord hath been pleased to turn all the wigwams, huts, and hovels the English dwelt in at their first coming, into orderly, fair, and well-built houses, well furnished many of them, together with orchards, filled with goodly fruit-trees, and gardens with variety of flowers.... There are many hundreds of laboring men, who had not enough to bring them over, yet now, worth scores, and some, hundreds of pounds. The Lord whose promises are large to His Sion, hath blessed his people's provision, and satisfied her poor with bread, in a very little space. Everything in the country proved a staple commodity. And those who were formerly forced to fetch most of the bread they eat, and the beer they drink, a thousand leagues by sea, are, through the blessing of the Lord, so increased, that they have not only fed their elder sisters, Virginia, Barbadoes and many of the Summer Islands, that were preferred before her for fruitfulness, but also the grandmother of us all, even the fertile isle of Great Britain."

With such conditions the colonists were happy, and as the work of their hands prospered, one might have thought that gentler modes of judgment would have grown with it, and toleration if not welcome have been given to the few dissenting minds that appeared among them. Had Winthrop lived, this might have been possible, but the new generation, fast replacing the early rulers, had their prejudices but not their experience, and were as fierce opponents of any new _ism_ as their fathers had been before them, while their rash action often complicated the slower and more considerate movements of the elders that remained.

For England the ten years in which the Colony had made itself a power, had been filled with more and more agitation and distress. There was little time for attention to anything but their own difficulties and perplexities, the only glances across seas being those of distrust and jealousy. Winthrop happily died before the news of the beheadal of Charles I. had reached New England, and for a time, Cromwell was too busy with the reduction of Ireland and the problem of government suddenly thrust upon him, to do anything but ignore the active life so much after his own heart, in the new venture of which he had once so nearly become a part. It is possible that the attitude of New England for a time based itself on the supposition, that life with them was so thoroughly in harmony with the Protector's own theories that interference was impossible. There were men among them, however, who watched his course warily, and who were not indisposed to follow the example he had set by revolt against hated institutions, but for the most part they went their way, quietly reticent and content to wait for time to demonstrate the truth or error of their convictions. But for the most there was entire content with the present.

Evidently no hint of a possible and coming Restoration found slightest credence with them, and thus they laid up a store of offences for which they were suddenly to be called to account. When at last the Restoration had been accomplished and Charles II, whose laughing eyes had held less mockery for William Penn than any among the representatives of sects he so heartily despised, turned to question how Quakers had fared in this objectionable and presumptuous Colony of New England, the answer was not one to propitiate, or to incline to any favor. The story is not one that any New Englander will care to dwell upon, even to-day, when indifference is the rule toward all theological dissension, past or present. It is certain that had Winthrop lived, matters could never have reached the extremity they did. It is equally certain that the non-combatants conquered, though the victory was a bloody one. Two sides are still taken to-day, even among New England authorities. For Quakers, there is of course but one, yet in all their statements there seems to be infinitely less bitterness than they might reasonably have shown. That one or two wild fanatics committed actions, which could have no other foundation than unsettled minds, cannot be denied by even the most uncompromising advocate of the Quaker side. But they were so evidently the result of distempered and excited brains, that only a community who held every inexplicable action to result from the direct influence of Satan, could have done anything but pass them by in silent forbearance.

Had John Cotton been alive in the year in which the Quakers chose Boston as their working ground, his gentle and conciliating nature, shown so fully in the trial of Anne Hutchinson, would have found some means of reconciling their theories with such phases of the Puritan creed as were in sympathy with them. But a far different mind held his place, and had become the leading minister in the Colony. John Norton, who had taken Nathaniel Ward's place at Ipswich, was called after twenty years of service, to the Boston church, and his melancholy temperament and argumentative, not to say pragmatical turn of mind, made him ready to seize upon the first cause of offence.

News of the doings of the obnoxious sect in England had been fully
discussed in the Colony, and the law passed as a means of
protection against the heresies of Anne Hutchinson and her school,
and which had simply waited new opportunity for its execution,
came into exercise sooner than they had expected.

It is difficult to re-create for our own minds, the state of
outraged susceptibility--of conviction that Jehovah in person had
received the extremity of insult from every one who dared to go
outside the fine points for a system of belief, which filled the
churches in 1656. The "Inward Light" struck every minister upon
whose ears the horrid words fell, as only less shocking than
witchcraft or any other light amusement of Satan, and a day of
public humiliation had already been appointed by the General
Court, "to seek the face of God in behalf of our native country,
in reference to the abounding of errors, especially those of the
Ranters and Quakers."

The discussion of their offences was in full height, when in July,
1656, there sailed into Boston harbor a ship from the Barbadoes,
in which were two Quaker women, Mary Fisher and Anne Austin.

Never were unwelcome visitors met by a more formidable delegation.
Down to the wharf posted Governor and Deputy-Governor, four
principal Magistrates, with a train of yeoman supplemented by half
the population of Boston, who faced the astonished master of the
vessel with orders which forced him to give bonds to carry the
women back to the point from whence they came. This might have
seemed sufficient, but was by no means considered so. The unhappy
women were ordered to goal till the return of the vessel; a few
books brought with them were burned by the executioner, and from
every pulpit in the Colony came fierce denunciations of the
intruders.

They left, and the excitement was subsiding a little when a
stronger occasion for terror presented itself in another vessel,
this time from England, bearing eight more of the firebrands, four
men and four women, besides a zealous convert made on the way from
Long Island, where the vessel had stopped for a short time. Eleven
weeks of imprisonment did not silence the voices of these self-
elected missionaries, and the uncompromising character of their
utterances ought to have commended them to a people who had been
driven out of England for the identical cause. A people who had
fallen to such depths of frenzied fanaticism as to drive cattle
and swine into churches and cathedrals and baptize them with mock
solemnity, who had destroyed or mutilated beyond repair organs,
fonts, stained glass and every article of priestly use or
adornment, might naturally have looked with understanding and
sympathetic eyes on the women who, made desperate by suffering,
turned upon them and pronounced their own preachers, "hirelings,
Baals, and seed of the serpent."

The Quakers frowned upon Church music, but not before the Puritan
Prynne had written of choirs: "Choirsters bellow the tenor as it
were oxen; bark a counterpart, as it were a kennel of dogs; roar
out a treble, as it were a sort of bulls; and grunt a bass, as it
were a number of hogs." They arraigned bishops, but in words less

full of bitterness, than those in which one of the noblest among Puritan leaders of thought, recorded his conviction. Milton, writing of all bishops: "They shall be thrown down eternally, into the darkest and deepest gulf of hell the trample and spurn of all the other damned ... and shall exercise a raving and bestial tyranny over them ... they shall remain in that plight forever, the basest, the lowermost, the most dejected and down-trodden vassels of perdition."

No word from the most fanatical Quaker who ever appeared before tribunal of man, exceeded this, or thousands of similar declarations, from men as ready for martyrdom as those they judged, and as obstinately bent upon proving their creed the only one that reasonable human beings should hold. The wildest alarm seized upon not only Massachusetts but each one of the confederated colonies. The General Court passed a series of laws against them, by which ship-masters were fined a hundred pounds if a Quaker was brought over by them, as well as forced to give security for the return of all to the point from whence they came. They enacted, also, that all Quakers who entered the Colony from any point should "be forthwith committed to the House of Correction, and at their entrance to be severely whipped, and by the master thereof to be kept constantly to work, and none suffered to converse or speak with them during the time of their imprisonment."

No Quaker book could be imported, circulated or concealed, save on penalty of a fine of five pounds, and whoever should venture to defend the new opinions, paid for the first offence a fine of two pounds; for the second, double that amount and for the third, imprisonment in the House of Correction till there should "be convenient passage for them to be sent out of the land."

Through the streets of Boston went the crier with his drum, publishing the law which was instantly violated by an indignant citizen, one Nicholas Upsall, who, for "reproaching the honored Magistrates, and speaking against the law made and published against Quakers," not only once but with a continuous and confounding energy, was sentenced to pay a fine of twenty pounds, and "to depart the jurisdiction within one month, not to return, under the penalty of imprisonment."

Then came a period in which fines, imprisonments, whippings and now and then a cropping of ears, failed to lessen the numbers who came, with full knowledge of what the consequences must be, and who behaved themselves with the aggressiveness of those bent upon martyrdom. More and more excited by daily defiance, penalties were doubled, the fine for harboring a Quaker being increased to forty shillings an hour, and the excitement rising to higher and higher point. Could they but have looked upon the insane freaks of some of their visitors with the same feeling which rose in the Mohammedan mind, there would have been a different story for both sides. Dr. Palfrey describes the Turk's method, which only a Turk, however, could have carried out: "Prompted by that superstitious reverence which he (the Turk) was educated to pay to lunatics, as persons inspired, he received these visitors with deferential and ceremonious observance, and with a prodigious activity of genuflections and salams, bowed them out of his country. They could make nothing of it, and in that quarter gave up their enterprise in despair."

The General Court was the despairing body at this time. Months had passed, and severity had simply multiplied the numbers to be dealt with. But one remedy remained to be tried, a remedy against which Simon Bradstreet's voice is said to have been the only one raised, and the General Court, following the advice of Endicott and Norton, passed the vote which is still one of the darkest blots on the old records--

"Whereas, there is an accursed and pernicious sect of heretics lately risen up in the world who are commonly called Quakers, who take upon them to be immediately sent of God and infallibly assisted; who do speak and write blasphemous things, despising government and the order of God in church and commonwealth, speaking evil of dignities, reproaching and reviling magistrates and the ministers of the Gospel, seeking to turn the people from the faith, and to gain proselytes to their pernicious ways; and whereas the several jurisdictions have made divers laws to prohibit and restrain the aforesaid cursed heretics from coming amongst them, yet notwithstanding they are not deterred thereby, but arrogantly and presumptuously do press into several of the jurisdictions, and there vent their pernicious and devilish opinions, which being permitted, tends manifestly to the disturbance of our peace, the withdrawing of the hearts of the people from their subjection to government, and so in issue to cause division and ruin if not timely prevented; it is therefore propounded and seriously commended to the several General Courts, upon the considerations aforesaid, to make a law that all such Quakers formerly convicted and punished as such, shall (if they return again) be imprisoned, and forthwith banished or expelled out of the said jurisdiction, under pain of death; and if afterwards they presume to come again into that jurisdiction, then to be put to death as presumptuously incorrigible, unless they shall plainly and publicly renounce their cursed opinions; and for such Quakers as shall come into any jurisdiction from any foreign parts, or such as shall arise within the same, after due conviction that either he or she is of that cursed sect of heretics, they be banished under pain of severe corporal punishment; and if they return again, then to be punished accordingly, and banished under pain of death; and if afterwards they shall yet presume to come again, then to be put to death as aforesaid, except they do then and there plainly and publicly renounce their said cursed opinions and devilish tenets."

This was not the first time that death had been named as the penalty against any who returned after banishment, and it had proved effectual in keeping away many malcontents. But the Quakers were of different stuff, the same determined temper which had made the Puritan submit to any penalty rather than give up his faith, being the common possession of both.

In an address made to the King, partly aggressive partly apologetic in tone, the wretched story sums itself up in a single paragraph: "Twenty-two have been banished upon pain of death. Three have been martyred, and three have had their right ears cut. One hath been burned in the hand with the letter H. Thirty-one persons have received six hundred and fifty stripes. One was beat while his body was like a jelly. Several were beat with pitched ropes. Five appeals made to England were denied by the rulers of Boston. One thousand, forty-four pounds' worth of goods hath been taken from them (being poor men) for meeting together in the fear of the Lord, and for keeping the commands of Christ. One now lieth in iron fetters condemned to die."

That Massachusetts felt herself responsible for not only her own safety but that of her allies, and that this safety appeared to be menaced by a people who recognized few outward laws, was the only palliation of a course which in time showed itself as folly, even to the most embittered. The political consequences were of a nature, of which in their first access of zeal, they had taken no account. The complaints and appeals of the Quakers had at last produced some effect, and there was well-grounded apprehension that the sense of power which had brought the Colony to act with the freedom of an independent state, might result in the loss of some of their most dearly-prized privileges. The Quakers had conquered, and the magistrates suddenly became conscious that such strength as theirs need never have dreaded the power of this feeble folk, and that their institutions could never fall before an attack from any hands save those of the King himself, toward whom they now turned with an alarmed deprecation. The Puritan reign of terror for New England was over, its story to this generation seeming as incredible as it is shameful. Brutality is not quite dead even to-day, but there is cause for rejoicing that, for America at least, freedom of conscience can never again mean whipping, branding and torturing of unnamable sorts for tender women and even children. Puritan and Quaker have sunk old differences, but it is the Quaker who, while ignoring some phases of a past in which neither present as calm an expression to the world as should be the portion of the infallibility claimed tacitly by both sides, is still able to write:

"The mission of the Puritans was almost a complete failure. Their plan of government was repudiated, and was succeeded by more humane laws and wiser political arrangements. Their religion, though it long retained its hold in theory, was replaced by one less bigoted and superstitious. It is now a thing of the past, a mere tradition, an antiquated curiosity. The early Quakers, or some of them, in common with the Puritans, may illustrate some of the least attractive characteristics of their times; but they were abreast, if not in advance, of the foremost advocates of religious and civil freedom. They were more than advocates--they were the pioneers, who, by their heroic fortitude, patient suffering and persistent devotion, rescued the old Bay Colony from the jaws of the certain death to which the narrow and mistaken policy of the bigoted and sometimes insincere founders had doomed it. They forced them to abandon pretentious claims, to admit strangers without insulting them, to tolerate religious differences, and to incorporate into their legislation the spirit of liberty which is now the life-blood of our institutions. The religion of the Society of Friends is still an active force, having its full share of influence upon our civilization. The vital principle--'The Inward Light'--scoffed at and denounced by the Puritans as a delusion, is recognized as a profound spiritual truth by sages and philosophers."

Through it all, though Simon Bradstreet's name occurs often in the records of the Court, it is usually as asking some question intended to divert attention if possible from the more aggressive phases of the examination, and sooth the excited feelings of either side. But naturally his sympathies were chiefly with his own party, and his wife would share his convictions. There is no surprise, therefore, in finding him numbered by the Quakers as among those most bitterly against them.

It is certain that Simon Bradstreet plead for moderation, but some of the Quaker offences were such as would most deeply wound his sense of decorum, and from the Quaker standpoint he is numbered among the worst persecutors.

In "New England Judged by the Spirit of the Lord," a prominent Quaker wrote: "Your high-priest, John Norton, and Simon Bradstreet, one of your magistrates, ... were deeply concerned in the Blood of the Innocents and their cruel sufferings, the one as advising, the other as acting," and he writes at another: point "Simon Bradstreet, a man hardened in Blood and a cruel persecutor."

There is a curious suggestiveness in another count of the same indictment. "Simon Bradstreet and William Hathorn aforesaid were Assistant to Denison in these executions, whose Names I Record to Rot and Stink as of you all to all Generations, unto whom this shall be left as a perpetual Record of your Everlasting Shame."

William Hathorn had an unwholesome interest in all sorrow and catastrophe, the shadow of these evil days descending to the representative Nathanael Hawthorne, whose pen has touched Puritan weaknesses and Puritan strength, with a power no other has ever held, but the association was hardly more happy for Bradstreet then, than at a later day when an economical Hathorn bundled him out of his tomb to make room for his own bones.

CHAPTER XVI.

HOME AND ABROAD.

In the midst of all this agitation and confusion Anne Bradstreet pursued her quiet way, more disposed to comment on the misdoings of the Persians or Romans than on anything nearer home, though some lines in her "Dialogue between Old England and New," indicate that she followed the course of every event with an anxious and intelligent interest. In 1657, her oldest son had left for England, where he remained until 1661, and she wrote then some verses more to be commended for their motherly feeling than for any charm of expression:

UPON MY SON SAMUEL HIS GOEING FOR
ENGLAND, NOVEM. 6, 1657.

Thou mighty God of Sea and Land,
I here resigne into thy hand
The Son of prayers, of vowes, of teares,

The child I stayed for many yeares.
Thou heard'st me then and gave'st him me;
Hear me again, I give him Thee.
He's mine, but more, O Lord thine own,
For sure thy Grace is on him shown.
No friend I have like Thee to trust,
For mortall helps are brittle Dust.
Preserve O Lord, from stormes and wrack,
Protect him there and bring him back;
And if thou shall spare me a space,
That I again may see his face,
Then shall I celebrate thy Praise,
And Blesse thee for't even all my Dayes.
If otherwise I goe to Rest,
Thy Will bee done, for that is best;
Perswade my heart I shall him see
Forever happefy'd with Thee.

There were others of much the same order on his return, in 1661,
but her feelings centered then on the anxieties and dangers of the
course which had been resolved upon. The enemies of the Colony
were busy in London, and the King was strongly inclined to take
very decisive measures for its humiliation. Explanations must be
made by some one who had had personal experience in every case now
used against them, and after long and troubled consultation the
Colonial Government reluctantly decided to send two Commissioners
to England, selecting John Norton and Simon Bradstreet as best
capable of meeting the emergency.

There was personal peril as well as political anxiety. The King
constitutionally listened to the first comer rather than the
second, and had already sided with the Quakers. To Norton it
seemed a willful putting of his head into the lion's jaws, and he
hesitated, and debated, and at last, from pure nervousness fell
violently ill. The ship which was to carry them waited, and
finally as it seemed impossible for him to rally his forces, began
unlading the provisions sent on board. The disgusted Government
officers prepared explanatory letters, and were on the point of
sending them when Mr. Norton came to his senses, and announced
that the Lord had "encouraged and strengthened his heart," and he
went decorously on board.

The mission, though pronounced by some Quaker historians a
failure, was in reality after many delays and more hard words a
tolerable success. The King was still too uncertain of his own
position to quarrel with as powerful a set of friends as the
Massachusetts Colony were now disposed to prove themselves, and
the Commissioners returned home, bearing a renewal of the charter,
though the letters held other matters less satisfactory to the
Puritan temper. The King required an oath of allegiance from all,
and that "all laws and ordinances ... contrary or derogative to
his authority and government should be annulled and repealed."

Toleration was made obligatory, and one clause outraged every
Puritan susceptibility; that in which it was ordered that, "in the
election of the Governor or Assistants, there should be only
consideration of the wisdom and integrity of the persons to be
chosen, and not of any faction with reference to their opinion or
profession."

Governor Dudley's shade must have looked with amazed dismay and wrath upon this egg, which could hardly fail to "a Toleration hatch," filled with every evil his verses had prophesied, and there were many of the same mind. But popular dissatisfaction in time died away, as no ill results came from the new methods, which were ignored as often as possible, and the working of which could not be very effectually watched in England. Simon Bradstreet, though censured by many, pursued his quiet way, thankful to be safely at home again with his head in its proper place, and his wife rejoiced over him in various poems which celebrated the letters he wrote, and every detail of his coming and going.

The summer of 1666 brought one of the sharpest trials her life had ever known, the destruction of her house by fire taking place in July. Each change of location to one of her tenacious affections and deep love of home, had been a sharp wrench, and she required long familiarity to reconcile her to new conditions. Though the first and greatest change from England to America would seem to have rendered all others trivial and not to be regarded, she had shrank from each as it came, submitting by force of will, but unreconciled till years had past. In Andover she had allowed herself to take firm root, certain that from this point she would never be dislodged, and the house had gradually become filled not only with treasured articles of furniture and adornments, but with the associations to which she always clung. There were family portraits and heirlooms brought from the old home in Lincolnshire; a library of nearly eight hundred volumes, many of them rare editions difficult to replace, as well as her own special books and papers.

For these last there was no hope of renewal. Many of them were the work of her early womanhood; others held the continuation of her Roman Monarchy; small loss to the world at large, but the destruction of a work which had beguiled many hours of the bodily suffering from which she was seldom free. The second edition of her poems, published after her death, held an apology found among her papers, for the uncompleted state of this monarchy, in which she wrote:

To finish what's begun was my intent,
My thoughts and my endeavors thereto bent;
Essays I many made but still gave out,
The more I mus'd, the more I was in doubt:
The subject large my mind and body weak,
With many more discouragements did speak.
All thoughts of further progress laid aside,
Though oft persuaded, I as oft deny'd,
At length resolv'd when many years had past,
To prosecute my story to the last;
And for the same, I, hours not few did spend,
And weary lines (though lanke) I many pen'd:
But 'fore I could accomplish my desire
My papers fell a prey to th' raging fire.
And thus my pains with better things I lost,
Which none had cause to wail, nor I to boast.
No more I'le do, sith I have suffer'd wrack,
Although my Monarchies their legs do lack:
No matter is't this last, the world now sees

Hath many Ages been upon his knees.

The disaster finds record in the Rev. Simon Bradstreet's diary:

"July 12, 1666. Whilst I was at N. London my father's house at
Andover was burnt, where I lost my Books and many of my clothes,
to the valieu of 50 or 60 pounds at least; The Lord gave, and the
Lord hath taken, blessed bee the name of the Lord. Tho: my own
losse of books (and papers espec.) was great and my fathers far
more being about 800, yet ye Lord was pleased gratiously many
wayes to make up ye same to us. It is therefore good to trust in
the Lord"

The "newe house" built at once and furnished with the utmost
elegance of the time, Simon Bradstreet's prosperity admitting the
free expenditure he always loved, could by no means fill the place
of the old. She looked about each room with a half-expectation
that the familiar articles with which so much of her outward life
had been associated, must be in the old places, and patiently as she
bore the loss, their absence fretted and saddened her. One of her
latest poems holds her sorrow and the resignation she came at last
to feel:

"In silent night when rest I
took, For sorrow neer I did not
look,
I waken'd was with thundring nois
And Piteous shreiks of dreadfull voice;
That fearfull sound of fire and fire,
Let no man know is my desire.

I, starting up the light did spye,
And to my God my heart did cry
To strengthen me in my Distress
And not to leave me succourlesse,
When coming out, beheld a space,
The flame consume my dwelling place.

And, when I could no longer look,
I blest his name that gave and took,
That layd my goods now in the dust;
Yea so it was, and so 'twas just.
It was his own; it was not mine
ffar be it that I should repine.

He might of All justly bereft
But yet sufficient for us left.
When by the Ruines oft I past,
My sorrowing eyes aside did cast,
And here and there the places spye
Where oft I sate, and long did lye.

Here stood that Trunk and there that chest;
There lay that store I counted best;
My pleasant things in ashes lye,
And them behold no more shall I.
Vnder thy roof no guest shall sitt,
Nor at thy Table eat a bitt.

No pleasant tale shall 'ere be told,

Nor things recounted done of old.
No Candle 'ere shall shine in Thee,
Nor bridegroom's voice ere heard shall bee.
In silence ever shalt thou lye;
Adieu, Adieu; All's vanity.

Then streight I 'gin my heart to chide,
And did thy wealth on earth abide?
Dids't fix thy hope on mouldering
dust, The arm of flesh dids't make thy
trust? Raise up thy thoughts above the
skye That dunghill mists away may
flie.

Thou hast a house on high erect,
Fram'd by that mighty Architect
With glory richly furnished,
Stands permanent tho: this be fled.
'Its purchased and paid for too
By him who hath enough to doe.

A prise so vast as is unknown
Yet by his gift is made thine own.
Ther's wealth enough, I need no more;
Farewell my Pelf, farewell my Store.
The world no longer let me Love,
My hope and Treasure lyes Above."

The fortunes of the new house were hardly happy ones. With the
death of his wife Governor Bradstreet left it in possession of a
younger son, Captain Dudley Bradstreet, who was one of the most
important citizens of Andover, having been "selectman, colonel of
militia, and magistrate," while still a young man. His father's
broad yet moderate views and his mother's gentle and devoted
spirit seem to have united in him, for when the witchcraft
delusion was at its height, and even the most honored men and
women in the little community were in danger of their lives, he
suddenly resolved to grant no more warrants for either apprehension
or imprisonment. This was shocking enough to the excited
popular mind, but when he added to such offence a plea, which
he himself drew up for some of the victims, who, as they admitted,
had made confession of witchcraft "by reason of sudden surprisal,
when exceedingly astonished and amazed and consternated and
affrighted even out of reason," there was no room left for any
conviction save that he was under the same spell. Loved as he had
been by all the people whom he had served unselfishly for twenty
years, the craze which possessed them all, wiped out any memory of
the past or any power of common sense in the present, and he fled
in the night and for a long time remained in hiding. The delusion
ended as suddenly as it had begun, a reaction setting in, and the
people doing all in their power to atone for the suspicion and
outrage that had caused his flight. Placable and friendly, the old
relations were resumed as far as possible, though the shadow had
been too heavy an one ever to pass entirely.

Another terror even greater had come before the century ended: An
act of treachery had been commited by a citizen of Andover, a
Captain Chubb, who had in 1693 been in command of Fort Pemaquid,
and having first plied a delegation of Penobscot Indians with
liquor, gave orders for their massacre while still in their

drunken sleep. In an after attack by French and Indians upon the fort, he surrendered on promise of personal safety, and in time, returned to Andover, disgraced, but abundantly satisfied to have saved his scalp.

The rest of the story is given by Cotton Mather in the Magnalia:

"The winter, (1693) was the severest that ever was in the memory of Man. And yet February must not pass without a stroke upon Pemquid Chub, whom the Government had mercifully permitted after his examination to retire unto his habitation in Andover. As much out of the way as to Andover there came above thirty Indians about the middle of February as if their errand had been for vengeance upon Chub, whom, with his wife they now massacred there." Hutchinson comments gravely: "It is not probable they had any knowledge of the place of his abode, but it caused them greater joy than the taking of many towns. Rapin would have pronounced such an event the immediate judgement of Heaven. Voltaire, that in the place of supposed safety, the man could not avoid his destiny."

The towns mustered hastily, but not before the flames of the burning buildings had arisen at many points, and terrified women and children had been dragged from their beds and in one or two cases murdered at once, though most were reserved as captives. Dudley Bradstreet and his family were of this latter number. The house was broken into and plundered; his kinsman who attempted defence, cut down on the spot, and the same fate might have overtaken all, had not an Indian who had received some special kindness from the colonel, interfered and prevented the butchery. The family were carried some fifty rods from the house and then released and allowed to return, and by this time the soldiers were armed and the party routed. No sense of safety could be felt then, or for many years thereafter, and from terror and other causes, the house was in time forsaken by its natural owners and passed into other hands, though no tenant, even of sixty years standing has had power to secure to it any other title than that which it still holds--"the Bradstreet house."

*   *   *   *   *

For its first occupants possession was nearly over. The vitality which had carried Anne Bradstreet through longer life than could have been imagined possible, was nearly exhausted.

Constant weakness and pain and occasional attacks of severe illness marked all the later years of her life, which for the last three, was a weariness to herself, and a source of suffering to all who saw her suffer. Certain that it could not last long, she began at one time the little autobiographical diary, found among her papers after death, and containing the only personal details that remained, even these being mere suggestions. All her life she had been subject to sudden attacks of faintness, and even as early as 1656, lay for hours unconscious, remaining in a state of pitiful weakness many days thereafter. One of these attacks found record on a loose paper, added by one of her sons to the manuscript book of "Religious Reflections," and showing with what patience she met the ills for the overcoming of which any physician of the time was powerless, and against which she made a

life-long resistance. It was the beginning of a battle which has
ever since held its ground in New England, to "enjoy poor health,"
yet be ready for every emergency, being a state of things on which
the average woman rather prides herself, medicine, quack or home-
brewed, ranking in importance with the "means of grace."

SUBMISSION AND RELIANCE.

"July 8th, 1656. I had a sore fitt of fainting, which lasted 2 or
3 days, but not in that extremity which at first it took me, and
so moch the sorer it was to me, because my dear husband was from
home (who is my chiefest comforter on Earth); but my God, who
never failed me, was not absent, but helped me, and gratiously
manifested his Love to me, which I darc not passe by without
Remembrance, that it may bee a support to me when I shall have
occasion to read this hereafter, and to others that shall read it
when I shall possesse that I now hope for, that so they may bee
encourage'd to trust in him who is the only Portion of his
Servants. O Lord, let me never forgett thy Goodness, nor question
thy faithfullness to me, for thou art my God: Thou hast said, and
shall not I believe it? Thou hast given me a pledge of that
Inheritance thou hast promised to bestow upon me. O, never let
Satan prevail against me, but strengthen my faith in Thee, 'till I
shall attain the end of my hopes, even the Salvation of my Soul.
Come, Lord Jesus; come quickly."

DELIVERANCE FROM A FITT OF

FAINTING. Worthy art Thou O Lord of

praise!
But ah! it's not in me;
My sinking heart I pray thee raise,
So shall I give it Thee.

My life as Spider's webb's cut off,
Thos fainting have I said,
And liveing man no more shall see,
But bee in Silence layd.

My feblee Spirit Thou didst
revive, My Doubting Thou didst
chide, And tho: as dead mad'st me
alive, I here a while might 'bide.

Why should I live but to thy Praise?
My life is hid with Thee;
O Lord no longer bee my Dayes,
Then I may froitfull bee.

"August 28, 1656. After much weaknes and sicknes when my spirits
were worn out, and many times my faith weak likewise, the Lord was
pleased to uphold my drooping heart, and to manifest his Love to
me; and this is that which stayes my Soul that this condition that
I am in is the best for me, for God doth not afflict willingly,
nor take delight in grieving the children of men: he hath no
benefitt by my adversity, nor is he the better for my prosperity;
but he doth it for my Advantage, and that I may be a Gainer by it.
And if he knowes that weaknes and a frail body is the best to make
mee a vessell fitt for his use, why should I not bare it, not only
willingly but joyfully? The Lord knowes I dare not desire that

health that sometimes I have had, least my heart should bee drawn from him, and sett upon the world.

"Now I can wait, looking every day when my Saviour shall call for me. Lord, grant that while I live I may doe that service I am able
in this frail Body, and bee in continual expectation of my change, and let me never forget thy great Love to my soul so lately expressed, when I could lye down and bequeath my Soul to thee, and Death seem'd no terrible Thing. O, let mee ever see thee, that Art invisible, and I shall not bee unwilling to come, tho: by so rough a messenger."

Through all the long sickness the family life went on unchanged, save in the contracting circle, from which one child and another passed. There was still strength to direct the daily round of household duties, and to listen with quick sympathy to the many who came to her trouble. There was not only the village life with its petty interests, but the larger official one of her husband, in which she shared so far as full knowledge of its details allowed, Simon Bradstreet, like Governor Winthrop, believing strongly in that "inward sight" which made women often clearer judges than men of perplexed and knotty points. Two bits of family life are given in a document still in existence and copied by the New England Historical and Genalogical Register for 1859. To it is appended the full signature of Anne Bradstreet, in a clear, upright hand, of singular distinctness and beauty when compared with much of the penmanship of that period. But one other autograph is in existence. It is evident from the nature of the document, that village life had its infelicities in 1670, quite as fully as to-day, and that a poem might have grown out of it, had daily life been thought worthy of a poem.

"This witnesseth, that wee heard good(tm) Sutton say, there was noe horses in his yard that night in wch Mr Bradstreetes mare was killed, & afterwards that there was none that he knew of; but being told by Mr Bradstreete that hee thought hee could p've hee drave out some, then hee sd, yes, now I remembr there was 3 or 4.

"Further, wee testifie the sd. Sutton sd. att yt tyme there was noe dogg there, but his wch was a puppy, & Mr Danes that would not byte.

        ANNE BRADSTREET
        MERCY BRADSTREET
        DUDLEY BRADSTREET
        JOHN BRADSTREET
        EDWARD
        WHITTINGTON
        ALEXANDER
         SESSIONS
         [his marke]
        ROBTE. RB BUSELY."

Law was resorted to in even small disagreements with a haste and frequency excellent for the profession employed, but going far to intensify the litigious spirit of the day, and tolerant as Simon Bradstreet was in all large matters, his name occurs with unpleasant frequency in these petty village suits. This suit with goodman Sutton was but one of many, almost all of which arose from the trespasses of animals. Fences were few, and though they were viewed at intervals by the "perambulators," and decided to be "very sufficient against all orderly cattle," the swine declined to come under this head, and rooted their way into desirable garden patches to the wrath and confusion of their owners, all persons at last, save innholders, being forbidden to keep more than ten of the obnoxious animals. Horses, also, broke loose at times, and Mr. Bradstreet was not the only one who suffered loss, one of the first tragedies in the little town, being a hand to hand fight, ending in a stabbing of one of the parties, both of whom belonged to good families and were but lightly judged in the trial which followed. They were by no means a peaceful community, and if the full truth be told, a week of colonial life would prove to hold almost as large a proportion of squabbles as any town record of to-day.

The second one gives some difficulties connected with the marriage of Governor Bradstreet's daughter Mercy, which took place Oct. 31, 1672, but not till various high words had passed, and sufficient hard feeling been engendered to compel the preparing of the affidavit, which probably, whatever its effect may have been on the parents, did not touch the happiness of the young pair for whose respective rights they had debated.

"When Mr. Johnathan Wade of Ipswich came first to my house att Andover in the yeare 72, to make a motion of marriage betwixt his son Nathaniel and my daughter Mercy hee freely of himself told mee what he would give to his son vz. one halfe of his Farme att Mistick and one third p't of his land in England when hee dyed, and that hee should have liberty to make use of p't of the imp'ved and broken upp ground upon the sd Farme, till hee could gett some broken upp for himselfe upon his owne p't and likewis | that hee should live in and have the use of halfe the house, and untill he had one | of his owne built upon his p't of the farme. I was willing to accept of his | offer, or at least sd. nothing against it; but p'p'ounded that hee would make | his sd soil a deede of guift of that third p't of his land in England to enjoy to | him and his heires after his death. This hee was not free to doe, but sd. it was | as sure, for he had soe putt it into his will, that his 3 sons should have | that in England equally devyded betwixt them, vz. each a 3 p't. I objected | he marry | againe and have other children, wich hee thought a vaine obieccon. Much | othr discourse there was about the stocke on the Farme, &c., but remayneing unwilling | to give a deede for that in England, saying he might live to spend it, and often | repeating hee had soe ordered it in his will, as aforesd., wch hee should never altr without | great necessity, or words to that purpose. Soe wee p'ted for that tyme leaveing | that mattr to further consideracon. After hee came home hee told sev'all of my | Friends and others as they informed me, that hee had p'ffered to give his son Nathaniel bettr then 1000 lb | and I would not accept of it. The next tyme hee came to my house, after some | discourse about the premises and p'esining his resolucon as form'ly ingaged, and left it to him to add wt he pleased | towards the building of him a house &c., and soe agreed that the young p'sons might | p'ceede in marriage with both or Consents, wch accordingly they did. S. BRADSTREET."

"The Honble Simon Bradstreet Esqr | made Oath to the truth of the above written Sept. 21th, 1683, before Samuell Nowell, Assistant.

"The interlines [as aforesaid], line 19th, and [as they informed me] line 22th, were before the Oath was made."

The brackets are in the original and were used as quotations marks. Governor Bradstreet's name and all above it are in his handwriting; all below it is in Mr. Nowell's.

Another Mercy Bradstreet, niece of the Mercy whose name figures in the foregoing statement, and the daughter of the oldest son, married Dr. James Oliver, from whom are descended Dr. Oliver Wendell Holmes and Wendell Phillips, while Lucy, the daughter of Simon, the second son, became the ancestress of Dr. Channing and of Richard N. Dana, the poet and his distinguished son. Many of the grandchildren died in infancy, and the pages of the second edition of their grandmother's poems are sprinkled with elegies long and short, upon the babies almost as well loved as her own, though none of them have any poetical merit. But her thoughts dwelt chiefly in the world for which she longed, and there are constant reminders of what careless hold she kept upon the life which had come to be simply a burden to be borne with such patience as might be given her.

CHAPTER

XVII. THE

END.

Through all these later years Anne Bradstreet had made occasional records, in which her many sicknesses find mention, though never in any complaining fashion.

Now and then, as in the following meditation, she wrote a page full of gratitude at the peace which became more and more assured, her doubting and self-distrustful spirit retaining more and more the quietness often in early life denied her:

MEDITATIONS WHEN MY SOUL HATH BEEN REFRESHED WITH THE CONSOLATIONS WHICH THE WORLD KNOWES NOT.

Lord, why should I doubt any more when thou hast given me such assured Pledges of thy Love? First, thou art my Creator, I thy creature; thou my master, I thy servant. But hence arises not my comfort: Thou art my ffather, I thy child. Yee shall [be] my Sons and Daughters, saith the Lord Almighty. Christ is my brother; I ascend unto my ffather and your ffather, unto my God and your God. But least this should not be enough, thy maker is thy husband. Nay, more, I am a member of his Body; he, my head. Such Priviledges, had not the Word of Truth made them known, who or where is the man that durst in his heart have presumed to have thought it? So wonderfull are these thoughts that my spirit failes in me at the consideration thereof; and I am confounded to think that God, who hath done so much for me should have so little from me. But this is my comfort, when I come into Heaven, I shall understand perfectly what he hath done for me, and then shall I be able to praise him as I ought. Lord, haveing this hope, let me pruefie myoolf ao thou art Pure, and let me bee no more affraid of

Death, but even desire to be dissolved, and bee with thee, which is best of all.

Of the same nature are the fragments of diary which follow:

July 8th, 1656. I had a sore fitt of fainting which lasted 2 or

3
days, but not in that extremity which at first it took me, and so much the sorer it was to me because my dear husband was from home (who is my chiefest comforter on Earth); but my God, who never failed me, was not absent, but helped me, and gratiously manifested his Love to me, which I dare not passe by without Remembrance, that it may be a support to me when I shall have occasion to read this hereafter, and to others that shall read it when I shall posesse that I now hope for, that so they may bee encourag'd to trust in him who is the only Portion of his Servants.

O Lord, let me never forget thy Goodness, nor question thy faithfulness to me, for thou art my God: Thou hast said and shall I not beleive it?

Thou hast given me a pledge of that Inheritance thou hast promised to bestow upon me. O, never let Satan prevail against me, but strengthen my faith in Thee 'till I shall attain the end of my hopes, even the Salvation of my Soul. Come, Lord Jesus; come quickly.

What God is like to him I
  serve, What Saviour like to
  mine?
O, never let me from thee swerve,
  For truly I am thine.

Sept. 30, 1657. It pleased God to viset me with my old Distemper of weakness and fainting, but not in that sore manner sometimes he hath. I desire not only willingly, but thankfully, to submitt to him, for I trust it is out of his abundant Love to my straying Soul which in prosperity is too much in love with the world. I have found by experience I can no more live without correction than without food. Lord, with thy correction give Instruction and
amendment, and then thy strokes shall bee welcome. I have not been refined in the furnace of affliction as some have been, but have rather been preserved with sugar then brine, yet will He preserve me to His heavenly kingdom.

Thus (dear children) have yee seen the many sicknesses and weaknesses that I have passed thro: to the end that, if you meet with the like, you may have recourse to the same God who hath heard and delivered me, and will doe the like for you if you trust in him: and, when he shall deliver you out of distresse, forget not to give him thankes, but to walk more closely with him then before. This is the desire of your Loving Mother,
                A. B.

With this record came a time of comparative health, and it is not till some years later that she finds it necessary to again write of sharp physical suffering, this being the last reference made in her papers to her own condition:

May 11, 1661. It hath pleased God to give me a long Time of

respite for these 4 years that I have had no great fitt of
sickness, but this year, from the middle of January 'till May,
I have been by fitts very ill and weak. The first of this month
I
had a feaver seat'd upon me which, indeed, was the longest and
sorest that ever I had, lasting 4 dayes, and the weather being very
hott made it the more tedious, but it pleased the Lord to
support my heart in his goodness, and to hear my Prayers, and to
deliver me out of adversity. But alas! I cannot render unto the
Lord according to all his loving kindnes, nor take the cup
salvation with Thanksgiving as I ought to doe. Lord, Thou that
knowest All things, know'st that I desire to testefye my
thankfulnes, not only in word, but in Deed, that my Conversation
may speak that thy vowes are upon me.

The diary of "Religious Reflections" was written at this period
and holds a portrait of the devout and tender mind, sensitive and
morbidly conscientious, but full of an aspiration that never left
her. The few hints as to her early life are all embodied here,
though the biographer is forced to work chiefly by inference:

TO MY DEAR CHILDREN:

This Book by Any yet unread,
I leave for you when I am dead,
That, being gone, here you may find
What was your living mother's
mind. Make use of what I leave in
Love
And God shall blesse you from above.
          A. B.

MY DEAR CHILDREN: Knowing by experience that the exhortations
of parents take most effect when the speakers leave to speak, and
those especially sink deepest which are spoke latest--and being
ignorant whether on my death-bed I shall have opportunity to speak
to any of you, much lesse to All--thought it the best, whilst I
was able to compose some short matters, (for what else to call
them I know not) and bequeath to you, that when I am no more with
you, yet I may bee dayly in your remembrance, (Although that is
the least in my aim in what I now doe) but that you may gain some
spiritual Advantage by my experience. I have not studied in this
you read to show my skill, but to declare the Truth---not to sett
forth myself, but the Glory of God. If I had minded the former,
it had been perhaps better pleasing to you,--but seing the last is
the best, let it bee best pleasing to you. The method I will
observe shall bee this--I will begin with God's dealing with me
from my childhood to this Day. In my young years, about 6 or 7 as
I take it, I began to make conscience of my wayes, and what I knew
was sinful, as lying, disobedience to Parents, &c., I avoided it.
If at any time I was overtaken with the like evills, it was
a great Trouble. I could not be at rest 'till by prayer I had
confest it unto God. I was also troubled at the neglect of Private
Dutyes, tho: too often tardy that way. I also found much comfort
in reading the Scriptures, especially those places I thought most
concerned my Condition, and as I grew to have more understanding,
so the more solace I took in them.

In a long fitt of sicknes which I had on my bed I often communed
with my heart, and made my supplication to the most High who sett
me free from that affliction.

But as I grew up to bee about 14 or 15 I found my heart more carnall, and sitting loose from God, vanity and the follyes of youth take hold of me. About 16, the Lord layed his hand sore upon me and Smott mee with the small pox. When I was in my affliction, I besought the Lord, and confessed my Pride and Vanity and he was entreated of me, and again restored me. But I rendered not to him according to the benefitt received.

After a short time I changed my condition and was maryed, and came into this Contry, where I fond a new world and new manners, at which my heart rose. But after I was convinced it was the way of God, I submitted to it and joined to the church at Boston.

After some time I fell into a lingering sicknes like a consumption, together with a lamenesse, which correction I saw the Lord sent to humble and try me and doe mee Good: and it was not altogether ineffectual.

It pleased God to keep me a long time without a child, which was a great grief to me, and cost mee many prayers and tears before I obtained one, and after him gave mee many more, of whom I now take the care, that as I have broght you into the world, and with great paines, weaknes, cares, and feares, brought you to this, I now travail in birth again of you till Christ bee formed in you.

Among all my experiences of God's gratious Dealings with me I have constantly observed this, that he hath never suffered me long to sitt loose from him, but by one affliction or other hath made me look home, and search what was amisse so usually thos it hath been with me that I have no sooner felt my heart out of order, but I have expected correction for it, which most commonly hath been upon my own person, in sicknesse, weaknes, paines, sometimes on my soul, in Doubts and feares of God's displeasure, and my sincerity towards him, sometimes he hath smott a child with sicknes, sometimes chastened by losses in estate,--and these Times (thro: his great mercy) have been the times of my greatest Getting and Advantage, yea I have found them the Times when the Lord hath manifested the most love to me. Then have I gone to searching, and have said with David, Lord search me and try me, see what wayes of wickednes are in me, and lead me in the way everlasting; and seldom or never, but I have found either some sin I lay under which God would have reformed, or some duty neglected which he would have performed. And by his help I have layed Vowes and Bonds upon my Soul to perform his righteous commands.

If at any time you are chastened of God, take it as thankfully and Joyfully as in greatest mercyes, for if yee bee his yee shall reap the greatest benefit by it. It hath been no small support to me in times of Darkness when the Almighty hath hid his face from me, that yet I have had abundance of sweetness and refreshment after affliction, and more circumspection in my walking after I have been afflicted. I have been with God like an untoward child, that no longer than the rod has been on my back (or at least in sight) but I have been apt to forgett him and myself too. Before I was afflicted I went astray, but now I keep thy statutes.

I have had great experience of God's hearing my Prayers, and returning comfortable Answers to me, either in granting the thing

I prayed for, or else in satisfying my mind without it; and I have
been confident it hath been from him, because I have found my
heart through his goodnes enlarged in thankfullnes to him.

I have often been perplexed that I have not found that constant
Joy in my Pilgrim age and refreshing which I supposed most of the
servants of God have; although he hath not left me altogether
without the wittnes of his holy spirit, who hath oft given mee his
word and sett to his Seal that it shall bee well with me. I have
sometimes tasted of that hidden manna that the world knowes not,
and have sett up my Ebenezer, and have resolved with myself that
against such a promise such taste of sweetnes, the Gates of Hell
shall never prevail. Yet have I many times sinkings and droopings,
and not enjoyed that felicity that sometimes I have done. But when
I have been in darknes and seen no light, yet have I desired to
stay myself upon the Lord. And, when I have been in sickness and
pain, I have thought if the Lord would but lift up the light of
his Countenance upon me, altho he ground me to powder, it would
bee but light to me; yea, oft have I thought were if hell itself,
and could there find the Love of God toward me, it would bee a
Heaven. And, could I have been in Heaven without the Love of God
it would have been a Hell to me; for in Truth, it is the absence
and presence of God that makes Heaven or Hell.

Many times hath Satan troubled me concerning the verity of the
Scriptures, many times by Atheisme how could I know whether there
was a God; I never saw any miracles to confirm me, and those which
I read of how did I know but they were feigned. That there is a God
my Reason would soon tell me by the wondrous workes that I see, the
vast frame of the Heaven and the Earth, the order of all things, night
and day, Summer and Winter, Spring and Autumne, the dayly
providing for this great houshold upon the Earth, the preserving
and directing of All to its proper end. The consideration of
these things would with amazement certainly resolve me that
there is an Eternall Being.

But how should I know he is such a God as I worship in
Trinity, and such a Savior as I rely upon? tho: this hath
thousands of
times been suggested to mee, yet God hath helped me ever. I have
argued this with myself. That there is a God I see. If ever this
God hath revealed himself, it must bee in his word, and this must
be it or none. Have I not found that operation by it that no
humane Invention can work upon the Soul? Hath not Judgments
befallen Diverse who have scorned and contemd it? Hath it not been
preserved thro: all Ages mangre all the heathen Tyrants and all of
the enemies who have opposed it? Is there any story but that which
shows the beginnings of Times, and how the world came to bee as
wee see? Doe wee not know the prophecyes in it fullfilled which
could not have been so long foretold by any but God himself? When
I have gott over this Block, then have I another pott in my way,
That admitt this bee the true God whom we worship, and that be his
word, yet why may not the Popish Religion bee the right? They have
the same God, the same Christ, the same word; they only interprett
it one way, wee another. This hath sometimes stuck with me, and
more it would, but the vain fooleries that are in their Religion,
together with their lying miracles and cruell persecutions of the
Saints, which admitt were they as they terme them, yet not so to
be dealt with all. The consideration of these things and many the
like would soon turn me to my own Religion again. But some
new

Troubles I have had since the world has been filled with Blasphemy, and Sectaries, and some who have been accounted sincere Christians have been carryed away with them, that sometimes I have said, Is there ffaith upon the earth? and I have not known what to think. But then I have remembered the words of Christ that so it must bee, and that, if it were possible, the very elect should bee deceived. Behold, faith our Savior, I have told you before. That hath stayed my heart, and I can now say, Return, O my Soul, to thy Rest, upon this Rock Christ Jesus will I build my faith; and if I perish, I perish. But I know all the Powers of Hell shall never prevail against it. I know whom I have trusted, and whom I have believed, and that he is able to keep that I have committed to his charge. Now to the King, Immortall, Eternall, and invisible, the only wise God, bee Honor and Glory forever and ever! Amen. This was written in much sicknesse and weakness, and is very weakly and imperfectly done; but, if you can pick any Benefitt out of it, it is the marke which I aimed at.

For a few of the years that remained there were the alternations to which she had long been accustomed, but with 1669 she had become a hopeless and almost helpless invalid, longing to die, yet still held by the intense vitality which must have been her characteristic, and which required three years more of wasting pain before the struggle could end. In August, of 1669, she had written one of the most pathetic of her poems:

Aug: 31, 69.

As weary pilgrim now at rest,
Hugs with delight his silent nest
His wasted limbes now lye full
soft That myrie steps have trodden
oft. Blesses himself to think upon
his dangers past, and travails done.
The burning sun no more shall heat
Nor stormy raines on him shall beat.
The bryars and thornes no more shall scratch,
nor hungry wolves at him shall catch
He erring pathes no more shall tread
nor wilde fruits eate, instead of bread
for waters cold he doth not long
for thirst no more shall parch his tongue.
No rugged stones his feet shall gaule,
nor stumps nor rocks cause him to fall.
All cares and feares, he bids farewell
and meanes in safity now to dwell.
A pilgrim I, on earth, perplext,
Wth sinns wth cares and sorrovys vext
By age and paines brought to decay.
And my Clay house mouldring away
Oh how I long to be at rest
and soare on high among the blesst.
This body shall in silence sleep
Mine eyes no more shall ever weep
No fainting fits shall me assaile nor
grinding paines my body fraile Wth
cares and fears n'er cumbred be Nor
losses know, nor sorrows see
What tho my flesh shall there consume

it is the bed Christ did perfume
And when a few yeares shall be gone
this mortall shall be cloth'd upon
A corrupt Carcasse ddwne it lyes
A glorious body it shall rise
In weakness and dishonour sowne
in power 'tis rais'd by Christ alone
When soule and body shall unite
and of their maker have the sight
Such lasting joyes shall there behold
as care ne'r heard nor tongue e'er told
Lord make me ready for that day
then Come dear bridegrome, Come away.

The long waiting ended at last, and her son, Simon Bradstreet, wrote in his diary:

"Sept. 16, 1672. My ever honoured & most clear Mother was translated to Heaven. Her death was occasioned by a consumption being wasted to skin & bone & she had an issue made in her arm bee: she was much troubled with rheum, & one of ye women yt tended herr dressing her arm, s'd shee never saw such an arm in her Life, I, s'd my most dear Mother but yt shall bee a Glorious Arm.

"I being absent fro her lost the opportunity of committing to memory her pious & memorable xpressions uttered in her sicknesse. O yt the good Lord would give unto me and mine a heart to walk in her steps, considering what the end of her Conversation was, yt so wee might one day have a happy & glorious greeting."

Dorothy, the wife of Seaborn Cotton and the namesake of her grandmother, had died in February of the same year, making the first break in the family circle, which had been a singularly united one, the remainder all living to advanced years. Grief at the loss had been softened by the certainty that separation could not last long, and in spite of the terror with which her creed filled even the thought of death, suffering had made at last a welcome one. No other touch could bring healing or rest to the racked and weary body, and deeply as Simon Bradstreet mourned her loss, a weight rolled away, when the long suffering had ended.

That the country-side thronged to the funeral of the woman whose name was honored in every New England settlement, we may know, but no record remains of ceremony, or sermon, or even of burial place. The old graveyard at Andover holds no stone that may perhaps have been hers, and it is believed that her father's tomb at Roxbury may have received the remains, that possibly she herself desired should lie by those of her mother. Sermons were preached in all the principal churches, and funeral elegies, that dearest form of the Puritan muse, poured in, that by John Norton being the best illustration of manner and method.

A FUNERAL ELOGY,

Upon that Pattern and Patron of Virtue, the truely pious, peerless matchless Gentlewoman

MRS. ANNE BRADSTREET,

right Panaretes,

_Mirror of her Age, Glory of her Sex, whose
Heaven-born-Soul its earthly Shrine, chose its native
home, and was taken to its Rest upon 16th
Sept. 1672._

Ask not why hearts turn Magazines of passions,
And why that grief is clad in several fashions;
Why she on progress goes, and doth not borrow
The small'st respite from the extreams of sorrow,
Her misery is got to such an height,
As makes the earth groan to support its weight,
Such storms of woe, so strongly have beset her,
She hath no place for worse, nor hope for better
Her comfort is, if any for her be,
That none can shew more cause of grief then she.
Ask not why some in mournfull black are clad;
The sun is set, there needs must be a shade.
Ask not why every face a sadness shrowdes;
The setting Sun ore-cast us hath with Clouds.
Ask not why the great glory of the Skye
That gilds the stars with heavenly Alchamy,
Which all the world doth lighten with his
Rayes, The _Persian_ God, the Monarch of the
dayes; Ask not the reason of his extasie,
Paleness of late, in midnoon Majesty,
Why that the pale fac'd Empress of the night
Disrob'd her brother of his glorious
light. Did not the language of the stars
foretel
A mournfull Scoene when they with tears did Swell?
Did not the glorious people of the Skye
Seem sensible of future misery?
Did not the low'ring heavens seem to express
The worlds great lose and their unhappiness?
Behold how tears flow from the learned hill,
How the bereaved Nine do daily fill
The bosom of the fleeting Air with groans,
And wofull Accents, which witness their Moanes.
How doe the Goddesses of verse, the learned quire
Lament their rival Quill, which all admire?
Could _Maro's_ Muse but hear her lively strain,
He would condemn his works to fire again,
Methinks I hear the Patron of the Spring,
The unshorn Deity abruptly sing.
Some doe for anguish weep, for anger I
That Ignorance should live, and Art should die.
Black, fatal, dismal, inauspicious day,
Unblest forever by Sol's precious Ray,
Be it the first of Miseries to all;
Or last of Life, defam'd for Funeral.
When this day yearly comes, let every one,
Cast in their urne, the black and dismal stone,
Succeeding years as they their circuit goe,
Leap o'er this day, as a sad time of woe.
Farewell my Muse, since thou hast left thy shrine,
I am unblest in one, but blest in nine.
Fair Thespian Ladyes, light your torches all,
Attend your glory to its Funeral,

To court her ashes with a learned tear,
A briny sacrifice, let not a smile appear.

Grave Matron, whoso seeks to blazon thee,
Needs not make use of witts false Heraldry;
Whoso should give thee all thy worth would
swell So high, as'twould turn the world infidel.
Had he great _Maro's_ Muse, or Tully's tongue,
Or raping numbers like the _Thracian_ Song,
In crowning of her merits he would be
Sumptuously poor, low in Hyperbole.
To write is easy; but to write on thee,
Truth would be thought to forfeit modesty.
He'l seem a Poet that shall speak but true;
Hyperbole's in others, are thy due.
Like a most servile flatterer he will show
Though he write truth, and make the Subject, You.
Virtue ne'er dies, time will a Poet raise
Born under better Stars, shall sing thy praise.
Praise her who list, yet he shall be a debtor
For Art ne're feigned, nor Nature fram'd a better.
Her virtues were so great, that they do raise
A work to trouble fame, astonish praise.
When as her Name doth but salute the ear,
Men think that they perfections abstract hear.
Her breast was a brave Pallace, a Broad-street,
Where all heroick ample thoughts did meet,
Where nature such a Tenement had tane,
That others Souls, to hers, dwelt in a lane.
Beneath her feet, pale envy bites her chain,
And poison Malice, whetts her sting in vain.
Let every Laurel, every Myrtel bough
Be stript for leaves t'adorn and load her brow.
Victorious wreaths, which 'cause they never fade
Wise elder times for Kings and Poets made
Let not her happy Memory e're lack
Its worth in Fame's eternal Almanack,
Which none shall read, but straight their lots deplore,
And blame their Fates they were not born before.
Do not old men rejoyce their Fates did last,
And infants too, that theirs did make such hast,
In such a welcome time to bring them forth,
That they might be a witness to her worth.
Who undertakes this subject to commend
Shall nothing find so hard as how to end.
        Finis & Non,
            JOHN NORTON.

Forty years of wedded life, and a devotion that remained unaltered
to the end, inclined Simon Bradstreet to a longer period of
mourning than most Puritan husbands seemed to have submitted to,
but four years after her death, the husband, at seventy-three,
still as hale and well-preserved as many a man of fifty, took to
himself another wife.

She was the widow of Captain Joseph Gardner of Salem, killed in
the attack on the Narragansett fort in December, 1675, and is
described by her step-son Simon, in his diary as "a Gentl. of very
good birth and education, and of great piety and prudence." Of her

prudence there could hardly be a doubt, for as daughter and sister of Emanuel and George Downing, she had had before her through all her early years, examples of shrewdness and farsightedness for all personal ends, that made the names of both, an offence then and in later days. But no suspicion of the tendencies strong in both father and son, ever rested on Mistress Gardner, who was both proud and fond of her elderly husband, and who found him as tender and thoughtful a friend as he had always been to the wife of his youth. For twenty-one years he passed from honor to honor in the Colony, living in much state, though personally always abstemious and restrained, and growing continually in the mildness and toleration, from which his contemporaries more and more diverged. Clear-sighted, and far in advance of his time, his moderation hindered any chafing or discontent, and his days, even when most absorbed in public interests, held a rare severity and calm. No act of all Bradstreet's life brought him more public honors than his action against Andros, whose tyranny had roused every man in New England to protest and revolt. Almost ninety years old, he met the deputation who came to consult him, and set his hand to a letter, which held the same possibilities and was in many senses, the first Declaration of Independence. From the Town House in Boston went out the handbill, printed in black letter and signed by fifteen names, the old patriarch heading the list. Bancroft, who is seldom enthusiastic, tells the story of the demand upon Andros of immediate surrender of the government and fortifications, and the determination of the passionate and grasping soldier to resist.

"Just then the Governor of the Colony, in office when the charter was abrogated, Simon Bradstreet, glorious with the dignity of four-score years and seven, one of the early emigrants, a magistrate in 1630, whose experience connected the oldest generation with the new, drew near the town-house, and was received with a great shout from the free men. The old magistrates were reinstated, as a council of safety; the whole town rose in arms, with the most unanimous resolution that ever inspired a people; and a declaration read from the balcony, defending the insurrection as a duty to God and the country. 'We commit our enterprise,' it is added, 'to Him who hears the cry of the oppressed, and advise all our neighbors, for whom we have thus ventured ourselves, to joyn with us in prayers and all just actions for the defence of the land.' On Charlestown side, a thousand soldiers crowded together; and the multitude would have been longer if needed. The governor vainly attempting to escape to the frigate was, with his creatures, compelled to seek protection by submission; through the streets where he had first displayed his scarlet coat and arbitrary commission, he and his fellows were marched to the town-house and thence to prison. All the cry was against Andros and Randolph. The castle was taken; the frigate was mastered; the fortifications occupied."

Once more Massachusetts assembled in general court, and the old man, whose blood could still tingle at wrong, was called again to the chair of state, filling it till the end of all work came suddenly, and he passed on, leaving a memory almost as tenderly preserved as that of "the beloved governor," John Winthrop.

In the ancient burial place at Salem may still be seen the tomb of the old man who had known over sixty years of public service.

SIMON BRADSTREET.

Armiger, exordine Senatoris, in colonia Massachusettensi
ab anno 1630, usque ad anum 1673. Deinde ad anum 1679,
Vice-Gubernator. Denique ad anum 1686, ejusdem coloniae,
communi et constanti populi suffragio, Gubernator. Vis,
judicio Lynceario preditus; guem nec numma, nec honos
allexit. Regis authoritatem, et populi libertatem, aequa
lance libravit. Religione cerdatus, vita innocuus, mundum
et vicit, et deseriut, 27 die, Martii, A. D. 1697.
Annog, Guliel, 3t ix, et Aet, 94.

Few epitaphs hold as simple truth. "He was a man," says Felt, "of
deep discernment, whom neither wealth nor honor could allure from
duty. He poised with an equal balance the authority of the King,
and the liberty of the people. Sincere in Religion and pure in his
life, he overcame and left the world."

The Assembly was in session on the day of his death and, "in
consideration of the long and extraordinary service of Simon
Bradstreet, late Governor, voted L100, toward defraying the
charges of his interment."

They buried him in Salem where his tomb may still be seen in the
old Charter Street burying-ground, though there is grave doubt if
even the dust of its occupant could be found therein. His memory
had passed, and his services meant little to the generation which
a hundred years later, saw one of the most curious transactions of
the year 1794. That an ancestor of Nathanael Hawthorne should have
been a party to it, holds a suggestion of the tendencies which in
the novelist's case, gave him that interest in the sombre side of
life, and the relish for the somewhat ghoul-like details, on
which he lingered with a fascination his readers are compelled to
share. On an old paper still owned by a gentleman of Salem, one
may read this catastrophe which has, in spite of court orderings
and stately municipal burial, forced Simon Bradstreet's remains
into the same obscurity which hides those of his wife.

"Ben, son of Col B. Pickman, sold ye tomb, being claimed by
him for a small expence his father was at in repairing it aft ye yr
1793 Or 1794 to one Daniel Hathorne, who now holds it." Having
taken possession, Daniel Hawthorne, with no further scruples
cleaned out the tomb, throwing the remains of the old Governor and
his family into a hole not far off. The New England of Simon
Bradstreet's day is as utterly lost as his own dust. Yet many of
the outward forms still remain, while its spirit is even
more evident and powerful.

Wherever the New England element is found--and where is it not
found?--its presence means thrift, thoroughness, precision and
prudence. Every circumstance of life from the beginning has taught
the people how to extract the utmost value from every resource.
Dollars have come slowly and painfully, and have thus, in one
sense, a fictitious worth; but penuriousness is almost unknown,
and the hardest working man or woman gives freely where a need is
really felt. The ideal is still for the many, more powerful than
the real. The conscientiousness and painful self-consciousness of
the early days still represses the joyful or peaceful side of

life, and makes angles more to be desired than curves. Reticence is the New England habit. Affection, intense as it may be, gives and demands small expression. Good-will must be taken for granted, and little courtesies and ameliorations in daily life are treated with disdain. "Duty" is the watchword for most, and no matter how strange the path, if this word be lined above it, it is trodden unquestioned.

As in the beginning, the corner-stone still "rests upon a book." The eagerness for knowledge shown in every act of the early colonial years has intensified, till "to know" has become a demon driving one to destruction. Eternity would seem to have been abolished, so eager are the learners to use every second of time. Overwork, mental and physical, has been the portion of the New England woman from the beginning. Climate and all natural conditions fostered an alertness unknown to the moist and equable air of the old home. While for the South there was a long perpetuation of the ease of English life, and the adjective which a Southern woman most desires to hear before her name is "sweet"; the New England woman chooses "bright," and the highest mark of approval is found in that rather aggressive word. Tin pans, scoured to that point of polish which meets the New England necessity for thoroughness, are "bright," and the near observer blinks as he suddenly comes upon them in the sun. A bit of looking-glass handled judiciously by the small boy, has the same quality, and is warranted to disconcert the most placid temperament; and so the New England woman is apt to have jagged edges and a sense of too much light for the situation. "Sweetness and light" is the desirable combination, and may come in the new union of North and South. The wise woman is she who best unites the two. Yet, arraign New England as we may--and there are many unmentioned counts in the indictment--it is certain that to her we owe the best elements in our national life. "The Decadence of New England" is a popular topic at present. It is the fashion to sneer at her limitations. Our best novelists delight in giving her barrenness, her unloveliness in all individual life--her provincialism and conceit, and strenuous money-getting.

"It is a good place to be born in," they say, "provided you emigrate early," and then they proceed to analyze her very prominent weaknesses, and to suppress as carefully as possible just judgment, either of past or present. Her scenery they cannot dispense with. Her very inadequacies and absurdities of climate involve a beauty which unites Northern sharpness of outline with Southern grace of form and color. The short and fervid summer owns charms denied a longer one. Spring comes uncertainly and lingeringly, but it holds in many of its days an exquisite and brooding tenderness no words can render, as elusive as that half-defined outline on budding twigs against the sky--not leaves, but the shadow and promise of leaves to be. The turf of the high pasture-lands springing under the foot; the smell of sweet fern and brake; the tinkle of cow-bells among the rocks, or the soft patter of feet as the sheep run toward the open bars--what New England boy or girl does not remember and love, till loving and remembering are over for the life we live here? Yet in all the ferment of old and new beliefs--the strange departures from a beaten track--the attitude always, not of those who have found, but of those who seek, there has ever been the promise of a better day. The pathos which underlies all record of human life is made plain, and a tender sadness is in the happiest lines. And this is the real story of New England. Her best has passed on. What the future holds for her it is impossible to say, or what strange development may come from this sudden and overmastering Celtic element, pervading even the remotest hill-towns. But one possession remains intact: the old graveyards where the worthies of an elder day sleep quietly under stones decaying and crumbling faster than their memories. It all comes to dust in the end, but even dust holds promise. Growth is in every particle, and whatever time may bring--for the past it is a flower that "smells sweet and blossoms in the dust"--for present and future, a steady march toward the better day, whose twilight is our sunshine.

INDEX.

End of Project Gutenberg's Anne Bradstreet and Her Time, by Helen Campbell

Made in the USA
Las Vegas, NV
08 December 2021

36538002R00115